ANDEAN ADVENTURES
An Unexpected Search for Meaning, Purpose and Discovery

Revised and Updated Second Edition

By
Allan J. "Alonzo" Wind

ISBN: 979-8-9907983-6-6
Imprint: Independently published

Second Edition

COMMENTS ABOUT
"ANDEAN ADVENTURES FIRST EDITION"

"I have known Allan aka 'Alonzo' since our Peace Corps days together in Ecuador. His adventures bring me back to my days of youthful optimism and the desire to be a true humanitarian. This lovely, amusing and very entertaining story of Allan's Andean Adventures shows the reader the power of compassion, kindness, open mindedness and the importance of being true to oneself and those around us. Allan uses anecdotes and humor to remind us of the importance of understanding, respecting and accepting our cultural differences."
— *Rachel Zelon, CEO Hunger Relief International*

"I had no idea, when Allan was driving me around in his Brown Bomber apparently trying to kill us all, that he would find genuine and faith-inspired ways of improving the world for ordinary people. His transformation into Alonzo, an international development activist, stirs the imagination for us, young and old."
- *Kris Organ, Service Employees International Union Organizer, retired.*

"I had the opportunity to meet Alonzo Wind in action in South Africa and appreciated what USAID under his lead was doing to address HIV AIDS there. This narrative from the beginning of his career is a fun window into his early experiences on another continent. I find inspiring his message about encouraging national service in arenas like the Peace Corps, once it is re-established again. As someone who encourages people to do all they can to promote the social good, this is a rewarding and positive read."
- *Todd Krim aka "Mr. Charity"*
*President & CEO **TKG** |THE KRIM GROUP*
Instagram: @ToddKrim Website: www.TheKrimGroup.com
***Where Influence Meets Social Good*™**

STAY IN TOUCH

As a thank you for purchasing this book, I may provide exclusive free content in my private email newsletter distribution list. Click here to join the email newsletter distribution list for free:

https://enableennoble.net/subscribe/

Or email me at:

Andean Adventures Partner

DEDICATION

This book is dedicated to my wife and daughter Kathia Mabel and Katrina Rose, who joined these adventures in progress, have been loyal, patient and accepting, enduring far more than ever could have been expected of them. It is also dedicated to my deceased parents, Mel and Peggy Wind, who encouraged my curiosity and inquisitiveness, and to my sister Yvonne who has been always supportive of my writing and travels over the years.

TABLE OF CONTENTS

INTRODUCTION REVISED EDITION

Over the last eight years, finding much inspiration and motivation in public life has been hard. As some have built walls, both real and imagined, we have become isolated from the other side of these walls. The intense political polarization filters what news there is from here or the outside world. We only see a particular set of frames from the horror showreel that is unspooling.

We're adrift as a nation threatened again by an authoritarian dictator wannabe and a deranged confederacy of dunces as if drunkenly aiming to see how close they can make it to the precipice. The long-feared yet poorly anticipated global pandemic placed us into a contaminated and chaotic coronavirus where international discourse and exchanges were suspended. While much as returned, the chaos of the supply chain interruptions and consequent damage to global trade are still affecting us.

Even Peace Corps was almost completely uprooted globally for the first time in its nearly 60-year history. There are few venues and fewer means to consider the needs of the poor and developing nations of the world. Churches and preachers when they are heard from seem to be focused more on how they can rush to re-open physical spaces without regard for the public health.

I offered this book four years ago to recall simpler times. I wanted to remind us when service in Peace Corps and nongovernmental organizations (NGOs) abroad offered a chance to help. When service abroad offered greater meaning and purpose. This book is for the younger generations who have seen their opportunities and futures seized from them by the viral pandemic, the virus of racism and the virus of authoritarian Trumpism. It is also for those with children or grandchildren derailed by the disruption and the deformed public discourse.

Words have power. I have some stories to share. My life took a direction I had never anticipated from the start. I served in Peace Corps a full two years thinking that I would return home afterwards. That proved not to be the case.

I saw the most abject poverty and struggled to find ways to grasp how to fight it and how to understand it. I saw plenty of action in decades of service overseas. I was shot at, arrested, threatened with expulsion. I also encountered the most unexpected surprises along the way.

I lived and worked almost four decades in Latin America, Africa and the Middle East. Although I have also seen crushing disappointments, I remain relentlessly and stubbornly optimistic. The rich and enlightening experiences I faced at the first steps of my career helped me shape all that came after.

I want to share these with you, dear reader, in a spirit of fellowship and sincerity. There are lessons and experiences that are informative and instructive. This book represents one important slice of my life story and that of many wonderful people.

Are you considering life options overseas? Are you interested in finding opportunities for greater meaning and purpose? Are you interested in a story of failure, redemption, challenges, faith and perseverance?

The Andean Adventures here are the first which really determined my life. Though I would go on to others, these were formative and decisive.

The Andean countries of Ecuador, Bolivia and Peru are not that far from the United States. But they also were and remain a different and unfamiliar world to most. Far less known than our immediate southern neighbors that have been targeted by those more interested in a Wall than a Bridge.

Feel free to let me know what you think. And since the story of Andean Adventures is one that begs a context it seems best to start from the beginning. How I ended up going to the Andes is an important part of the story.

CHAPTER 1

⬛ ◆ ⬛

EARLY IDEALISM OFFERS
THE KINDLING

I grew up before age 10 in the Vandeveer Project, a mix of Jewish and other ethnic groups living in three-story apartment buildings in central Brooklyn. We lived not far from the famous "Junction," the intersection of Flatbush and Nostrand Avenues. My sister, my parents, and I lived in a two-bedroom apartment. We didn't think of ourselves as poor those days, but our family was working-class Jewish, and we didn't have a lot of money.

Neither my father nor mother had much of an education beyond high school, a year of college, if that. My father had been in the Coast Guard during World War II and then the Merchant Marine. He shunned the business of his father. Ultimately, he was a bartender, working at the Friars Club in midtown Manhattan for most of my childhood and then at the Blue Note Club. He served show business clients mostly. From them, he caught flashes of something better for himself and his family. Those flashes remained as weak embers, never to catch fire.

My sister and I knew little of our mother. She had supposedly been an orphan, but the story was patchy. My mother worked at a department store cosmetics counter and then was a telephone operator for a time before marrying. She left work then, only to return to the workforce as a clerk for a department store when we were older. When you look at the few photos from the late 1950s or early 1960s, she seems to have been glamorous, dark, and exotic. She was relatively tall and slender and looked a bit like Elizabeth Taylor in those days.

The Vandeveer had historically been ethnically mixed, with a large number of Jews heading up Nostrand Avenue. In photos of my elementary school 3rd and 4th grade classes there was one Black boy, Philip, who I happened to be friends with. My parents liked Philip but worried that there were more Blacks coming after him. It was about to become, as they called it then, a 'changing' neighborhood. This meant in the language of my parents and neighbors that the 'schvartzes' were moving into the neighborhood more and more. That was the Yiddish term they used as a non-intentional slur. But it was also a goad for instigating 'white flight'.

My best friend in elementary school was Charles Small. I remember him particularly because his father had a bakery on Nostrand Avenue where, from time to time, we would go to get free black and white cookies. Those cookies are such a New York thing. I think Seinfeld had a whole episode about them. What was it that made them so addictive? Nothing good, I am sure, in hindsight, but the memory remains from so long ago.

I have a strong memory from when, at age 7 or 8, I got my first bicycle upgraded to a banana seat and wheelie bike with high-rise handlebars. I think some called them ape-hanger handlebars. The bike was cool because you could do wheelies with it and it looked like a chopper bike if you squinted enough. I remember one time doing something I probably shouldn't have been doing and careening down a flight of cement stairs to the basement of a neighboring apartment building. I think I was knocked out and all scratched up, to the point of being pretty covered in blood, as I made my way back to our building and apartment on the third floor. My mother screamed when she saw me at the door, "Oh my God, you look like you came back from the Vietnam War!" Luckily despite the blood, nothing was broken.

Another memory that has never faded is when a classmate at school, a tough Italian kid called Joey, who fought with everybody, got killed. He had climbed on top of one of those old Good Humor Ice Cream trucks on Foster Avenue. Somehow he fell and, I think, cracked his head or was run over. I don't remember all the details, but it is one of those child traumas that never quite fade away. It was mentioned as a lesson and warning to other kids for a long time, "Remember Joey!"

Our upstairs neighbors, the Finkelsteins, were post-war refugees from the Holocaust Nazi concentration camps in Europe. They had saved and scrimped their cash, including reparations money from post-war Germany. They had enough to do better. They ended up buying a house in another growing and prosperous newly developed area of Brooklyn called Georgetown. This new neighborhood was diverse enough for them, with a mix of only Jewish and Italian.

The Finkelsteins had two sons who were one year older and three years older than me. They reached out to my parents to invite us to join them and rent the top-floor apartment of their new corner house. While my father had big dreams and aspired to be better, with this, we would still be renters. But we would be living in a larger three-bedroom apartment of a private family house rather than an old prewar apartment building. The house would have a shared washing machine and a dryer, which my parents and the Finkelsteins partnered on. They were in the basement beyond their garage.

We moved out of the Vandeveer to Georgetown in May 1969. Almost everyone in the area was new to it. One of the most established had been an immigrant Italian family a few houses down. The entrepreneurial Frank Griseta, who I think had been a chef, bought two semidetached houses that shared a yard space in between, which he filled with luscious tomato vines, grapes, and other vegetables. We were friends with their two kids, Joey and Antoinette.

Moving there was how I got to enroll at age 10 in the 5th grade of PS 312, in the Bergen Beach area of Brooklyn. I still remember our 5th grade teacher Mrs. Alexander. The school catchment area was next to Paedegat Bay, an inlet of Jamaica Bay, which separated us from Canarsie. It actually fronted as well across the street from our new house. These were abandoned wetlands and dumping grounds for the new construction in this area of Brooklyn. With the tumult of the 1969-1970 school year, the class had an innovative ecology-minded curriculum.

One of the first projects that came up in the autumn of that year was a cleanup campaign for part of Paedegat Bay. I ended up being one of the main student ringleaders promoting the cleanup of the marshlands and wetlands. With the help of our teacher we contacted the Con Edison utility and contractors and complained about the dumping that had gone on. We organized over 25 kids and their parents for the cleanup effort for several days. We got Con Ed or the Sanitation Dept to send over huge dump trucks to lug away the heavy items, dumped furniture, tires, and the garbage we pulled out.

The father of one of my Italian classmates and friends, Anthony Vaccaro, was a City Councilman of some influence. Mr. Vaccaro liked me since he saw me as a good Jewish influence on his son. He got reporters of the press interested in the effort, and I ended up interviewed by a New York Post reporter. The paper did a write up about what we were doing and my motivations as representative of the kids. I became infamous in school with the article. The reporter quoted only me by name and used some quotes from me about how I found my inspiration. I was identified as a principal ringleader among the kids in school.

We got caught up in Earth Day preparations in the spring of 1970. A bunch of us raised money through sponsorships for the planned first Earth Day walk in April. We raised nearly a thousand dollars or so. Part of that was used to pay for overtime for a school bus to take a dozen of us to Union Square in Manhattan for the Earth Day marches and rally. I still remember some speakers that day. In particular, the Democratic Senator from Wisconsin, Gaylord Nelson. I wrote to him back and forth after the rally about the importance of pushing President Nixon on more environmental legislation.

So began my political awakening and inspiration at ten years old. I was already somewhat precocious and stood out from the kids in my neighborhood. Meanwhile, I had a growing passion for reading, particularly science fiction. I helped out in a new neighborhood bookstore a few hours a week. My 'pay' for this illegal child labor consisted of science fiction paperbacks.

My tendency to stand out increased at Roy Mann Junior High School in the next couple of years. I was identified early as an IGC kid ('intellectually gifted') and fast-tracked into the SP (special progress) program. This meant I skipped 7th grade and went directly into 8th grade following 6th. In 8th grade, I took the standardized tests for the academically specialized New York City public high schools. I ended up with the choices of Stuyvesant High School and Dewey beyond my neighborhood high school of South Shore HS (where my sister would attend).

Stuyvesant was one of the city's top science and math schools together with Bronx Science. It was consistently a top-ranked school across the country. It had been a boys-only school until 1969. Luckily, Stuyvesant became 'co-ed' three years before I entered its ninth-grade freshman class.

Going to Stuyvesant immediately cut me off from the mainstream of our neighborhood and many friends I had among the neighbors. My sister, who attended the neighborhood high school, remained a part of the neighborhood environment.

For me, going to high school usually meant a trip of over an hour each way. I would walk at least fifteen minutes for a city bus. This would take me to the end of the line of either the IRT Lexington trains or the "LL", which ended at Rockaway Parkway in Canarsie. I had a train ride of nearly 45 minutes if there were no delays. This was common for anyone attending Stuyvesant from one of the outer boroughs. If I was staying later for after-school activities, it wasn't unusual that I had close to a twelve-hour day away from home. It could be longer if I went to a friend's house somewhere in the city.

At the storied and famous Stuyvesant High School, at the old building on 15th Street and First Avenue in Manhattan, my politics became at first a bit contrarian. I was the only kid in my

7

freshman class homeroom in the fall of 1972 to state support for Nixon's re-election over George McGovern. Why I took that stance when my instincts were liberal is a puzzle to me to this day; I suppose I was playing with being a contrarian since I reveled in the horror this evoked in my classmates.

"Genius" had been my nickname throughout junior high, a sobriquet sneered by bullies and repeated by friends alike. But at Stuyvesant, most of the school fell into the nerdy category of students, who were even more academically accomplished in many cases than I was.

I had a class in comparative civilizations during ninth grade at Stuyvesant. I remember we were each assigned a country to "follow" and specialize in. I ended up assigned to Kenya. I collected what I could in the library and read up on Kenya, but then I also reached out to the Kenyan Mission of the United Nations up First Avenue.

I ended up being a bit adopted by them and given a wealth of material about Kenya, its leaders, its culture, etc. I became quite enamored with decolonialism, Kenya, and Africa. This reinforced my ambition and dream of going to the Peace Corps to serve and help after college.

I took Spanish for three years at Stuyvesant for the foreign language requirement. I took conversational Hebrew for one year for the rumored automatic "A". I had no idea then that the Spanish would do me in good stead. I did well enough in the sciences, including earth science, biology, chemistry, and physics. I enjoyed history and social studies. Math, particularly calculus, not so much.

I did well in English, particularly composition. Thus, I had the great fortune of being selected for Frank McCourt's class in creative writing for two years. I got Frank's class thanks to my sophomore English teacher, Connie Miller, and the English Department Chairman, William Ince. They were impressed with the science fiction stories I had begun to write.

The celebrated late author of Angela's Ashes, T'is, and Teacher Man was a free-spirited English teacher and storyteller in the Stuyvesant High School English department. Frank shared many of the same stories that would go into his books. He encouraged me and the entire class to tell our stories and to be authentic.

I'm not sure how authentic my stories were. But I even managed to sell some short stories to publishers outside, notably to the Perry Rhodan science fiction series, published by Ace Books. One of my stories was even re-published 25 years later in an anthology of Forrest J. Ackerman, subtitled "50 of the Best Short Science Fiction Stories by Unknown Authors." An amusing classification!

Science fiction was an undeniable passion of mine. It led me to organize, with a bunch of friends, a science fiction magazine at Stuyvesant that we called 'ANTARES', after the red star. Bob Kleiman and I were co-editors in chief. I found myself with the self-applied nickname 'Galactic Emperor', shortened by others to just 'Galactic'. This, of course, was pre-Star Wars.

As an official student publication/club, our faculty advisor at ANTARES was our own Frank McCourt. I do no know how we got him to agree to do it, as science fiction was hardly one of his favorites. He would make fun of us at times in a good-natured way. We were in his English class, and it was like we couldn't get enough of him. His humor and humanity still managed to infuse our magazine. And his avatar was there through the comic artwork of the brilliant James W. Fry.

I cherish our first issues of ANTARES, particularly from James Fry's and others' artwork. James did a splendid satire of the life of Frank McCourt that makes me laugh to this day. He also did a number of cartoons about our key ANTARES crew of writers and artists, called SPACE ROT, a satirical take on Star Trek. If you want to have a laugh, check it online here: Space Rot ANTARES

I was drawn into science fiction's creative mysteries and idealism, reading and going to science fiction bookstores and conventions in Manhattan. Despite my nerdiness, I found myself in the clutches of a buxom blonde science fiction groupie called Phoebe. She had been next to me on the line at a "Star Trek Lives!" Convention in midtown Manhattan in February 1974, a visitor from Montauk Long Island in the city.

I guess I was a charmer who had 'game' without realizing it; almost before I knew what was happening, Phoebe had her hands on me. She also used the moniker of "Andromeda" for better stage effect. She was ten years older than me and must have assumed I was at least older than statutory rape age, thanks to a trace of facial stubble. While Phoebe initially panicked when she found out my real age, we still had a memorable fling for the next months. I think she actually joined the army sometime later, and I lost touch.

My class at Stuyvesant included some formidable overachievers. Among them, Tim Robbins, the actor and producer, was in my grade; Paul Reiser, the actor, was in the grade ahead of us. Gail Strickler, who came from my junior high school and would become a textile industry maven and an Obama Administration trade official, was also in my grade. Jonathan Greenberg, who would become a noted writer, journalist, publisher, and social activist, was in my class with Frank McCourt. He was a fellow witness and audience member of Frank's humor and storytelling. Naomi Oreskes, a highly respected Harvard professor and science historian, was a year ahead. Many celebrities and brilliant and famous leaders in their field were graduates, in fact.

Science fiction wasn't my only passion of course. I was also distracted by girls, flirting and fumbling with several in the first years of high school before going almost 'steady' with one, Karen. Karen was, for me, quite the standout temptation compared to other girls I'd flirted with in junior high school and the first two years at Stuyvesant. She was a smart, witty, blond, Teutonic-looking "shiksa" compared to the Jewish brunettes I had previously pursued. I enjoyed her self-deprecating sense of humor. She was also a great artist, leaning toward the fantasy elves and unicorn side of things. I suppose she also reminded me of the forbidden love with Andromeda!

I am sure I looked swarthy and exotic to her mother, with my Jewfro. I always got the sense that her mother viewed me very skeptically. I was sure that in her eyes she imagined some uber Jew ravishing her pure Teutonic daughter. But she was always very nice and very flexible when hanging out with Karen and me. More than flexible – she did nothing to discourage us. I would join them on summer and other holiday trips at times to Delhi in upstate New York and once to Provincetown on Cape Cod, and Karen and I were essentially left to our own devices.

I applied to about ten universities in my senior year, including, of course, CUNY and SUNY. My SAT scores were good generally, although not particularly stellar for the scene at Stuyvesant. Perhaps I had been overly distracted between girls and science fiction. I think I scored initially a 1330, maybe a bit around 1440 the second time, on the scale of 1600.

I applied to ten top-drawer schools, but really, the only private school that offered me entry and a partial scholarship was the University of Chicago. I picked Chicago because I found it appealing to be in a city that is distinct and a distance away from New York. Having a partial scholarship was important because it was clear that my father would be able to put forward little for college. I would have to be mostly self-sufficient.

Thanks to my friend Gerry Seidman, I got a great off-book summer job at 'Amy's', then a fast-casual Mediterranean food place. They had three locales, but I worked at the restaurant near Lincoln Center. I was the only American working there. The place was filled with undocumented Greek immigrant workers, so-called illegals. I came to really appreciate how hard they worked. I was taught to make falafel and babaganoush, grilling the eggplants just-so in the kitchen, cleaning the tables, filling the special Amy's sauce shakers, and helping at the register. When I got ready to leave for Chicago at the end of the summer with some hefty savings, the Greeks insisted I have a sendoff party with them in Astoria, where there was fantastic Greek food, lots of ouzo and dancing on the tables.

My high school girlfriend Karen went to Michigan State University, which was relatively nearby to Chicago, or so I thought. MSU was in East Lansing, still a five-hour bus ride away. Though we would each make the trip once or twice at the beginning of freshman year, our relationship did not survive the distance and other distractions.

CHAPTER 2

⬤ ◆ ⬤

POLITICS STRIKES A SPARK OR TWO

I didn't have the easiest of times as a freshman at the University of Chicago, at least at first. I was assigned my freshman year to Thompson House in Pierce Tower, an all-male house that had not been my choice at all. I wanted one of the co-ed dorms. Pierce was kind of funky as it was an eight-story apartment tower. Four of the floors were all male dorms and four were co-ed. My first roommate was this really fussy jock type called Howard, and we did not get along at all. When Karen came to visit one weekend before we broke up, he even tried coming on to her.

Eventually he moved out to a single room and I got as a new roommate a huge Cuban guy from Miami, Nelson Sanchez. Nelson had a great stereo hookup for the room. He also had an unexpected and unusual love for not only the Miami Sound Machine but Neil Diamond, Barry Manilow and a host of other romantic crooners. He was quite the character; I still remember to this day a prank exploit he pulled on me when I came home to the room from some late-night party. I found the darkened room on Nelson's side quite normal and undisturbed, with Nelson "asleep" in his bed, and my side of the room VANISHED. My furniture and belongings, including the bed, desk, and chair, were removed, dismantled, and disappeared. Yet for all that, Nelson was a great guy, tolerant and tolerable, easygoing, quick to forgive and forget.

Pranks were all too common as a freshman. I remember getting drunk with a bunch of friends one evening. We had been somehow talking about and making fun of Idi Amin Dada and other tinpot dictators in Africa. At some point after midnight, someone got the bright idea of calling the police with a bogus threat. I picked up the phone to general hysterical merriment in a phony East African accent. I said, "This is Idi Amin, I have an atomic bomb and I am not afraid to use it at the UN. I am from Uganda… and Ugandaaaaa is in East Africaaaaaaa." Ending with a long stretch of the last vowels. Surprise, surprise, about an hour or two later, when I was in my bed and the others scattered, I found myself woken up by a banging on the dorm door.

The Chicago Police had come for me, unsmiling and unsympathetic to my half-drunk half-terrified protestations. I was dragged out and taken to the Cook County lockup.

It was not an easy night there, and the next morning, a court-appointed attorney told me that an "I" bond would be filed to allow me to leave on bail. If I kept my nose clean and mouth shut, then this would eventually go away. Charges were dismissed, despite a no-tolerance policy on prank calls and the like. I don't remember the full run-in with the university authorities. They had played some role in helping me out after I learned my lesson downtown in the lock-up. Luckily, there were somehow no long-term consequences. I certainly learned to abandon pranks!

I got actively interested in music. I'd sometimes hit the near-northside of Chicago with some friends and classmates to hear the Kingston Trio. With others, I would sometimes go to the Checkboard Lounge on Cottage Grove Avenue, one of only two white guys in a wholly Black frequented club. I felt at home anywhere. Southern rock was big with different friends. We'd play incessantly groups like the Charlie Daniels Band, Allman Brothers, and Lynyrd Skynyrd.

I enjoyed Skynyrd, especially with one of my best friends, Kris. He was a Yankee transplant to Birmingham Alabama's upmarket suburbs in Vestavia Hills. Though Kris wasn't really a Southerner, he seemed pretty close to one to me. There was endless drinking and music at parties. We had plenty of half-drunken escapades, including one up to Stevens Point, Wisconsin, with Kris and his roommate Andrew. Andrew was from the Florida Panhandle. I think we originally joined a school

With my Regents Park apartment as a base, Gerry and I formed the group 'Student Union,' which went on to co-sponsor a bunch of parties for students. We had one memorable party at the top-

floor penthouse recreation party room of Regents Park. I can still remember a Chicago Maroon headline referring to our creation of the Student Union as "Wind's Latest Political Abortion." Ouch!

The U of C had a demanding academic program. But it also had a heady brew of politics, sex, drugs, rock and roll. I assumed I would be on a pre-med track, majoring initially in biology when I enrolled. Mrs. Wind wanted her son to be a doctor, which seemed the most natural thing to me. Unfortunately, I stumbled and tripped over organic chemistry during the Common Core program, which taught me the folly of my ways. My advisor, who seemed to view me as a hopeless case for medicine, pushed me to switch majors. I switched to political science\social policy with more of a minor in biology.

I dabbled in politics in different directions throughout my school career. One girlfriend, Kat, a sensible, politically active Quaker, spoke urgently about social injustice and the corporate state. She nudged my social conscience and connected me to the Democratic Socialist Organizing Committee. She also turned me on to acid, and everyone drank and did pot. I remember a skinny-dipping adventure into Lake Michigan's brisk waters once with her and other friends.

I raised funds and organized for DSOC and lots of other causes. I bought a 1968 brown Chevy Impala while at school. It made plenty of trips back and forth to New York and elsewhere. One stormy weekend, I drove Kat, Kris, and other friends to a No Nukes rally in Washington. Unfortunately, the car did not make it. We got hit with a near-fatal sudden black ice freeze coming off Lake Erie in Ohio. My car and others spun out of control and smashed into a highway median in the rear. We were lucky not to be killed or injured. I remember the gas tank had been damaged and burst. There was a fifty-car pile-up.

With the lax safety rules at the time, I took it to a cheap mechanic shop. In the end they did little about the huge dents in the trunk (filled with no nukes political pamphlets) and bumper. They strapped on a replacement gas tank of sorts. The car was a continuing death trap, no doubt. I managed to hold on to it and keep driving it for the rest of my time in Chicago, nicknaming the Impala "the Brown Bomber". I am amazed I didn't kill myself or others in that car, but it was sturdy and reliable.

I got involved with different local good government causes as part of my extracurricular education. Particularly Common Cause Illinois, where I volunteered for over a year in various areas. These included fundraising, membership, and political lobbying. I lobbied for approval by the Illinois State Senate of "sunset" legislation to set a time limit on the plethora of do-nothing commissions and bodies. They wasted needless tax dollars long after their political purpose had ceased to exist. Sunset rules were a good government reform then.

At Common Cause, I got to know Rahm Emanuel, another volunteer and a fascinating observer of Chicago Machine dynamics. Rahm and I went to the lobby in the state capital, Springfield, and even briefly met with Governor "Big Jim" Thompson thanks to Rahm's connections. Rahm would later go on to a meteoric rise in Illinois and national Democratic party politics. Rahm's family was connected with the Democratic Machine. His father was a pediatrician for the kids of Mayor Richard J. Daley, and later on for his son Richard M. Daley, who would eventually succeed him as Mayor. Rahm himself had just finished 2020 two terms as Mayor in conflict-ridden Chicago and would go on to be appointed U.S. Ambassador to Japan by President Biden.

Volunteering for Common Cause exposed me for the first time to some of the then-unusual intricacies of Illinois politics. At the time, the Illinois State House had about 150 members, who were elected from 50 multi-member constituencies. I learned how these multi-member constituencies had the uncommon and strange characteristic of essentially forcing the election from each district of two majority party members and one minority party member.

While multi-member districting was clearly a connivance developed in part for the care and feeding of the Democratic party machine and the Republican leadership, it meant that in Chicagoland the voter threshold to elect one Republican state assemblyman was much lower than the two Democratic safe seats. Similarly, in downstate Illinois, it was the exact opposite. This multi-member structure preserved a status quo between the two parties. It also meant that, as an unintended result, among the minority members elected on both sides, you had some pretty unusual members. A few were total nutcases. But many were strong reformers and good government types electable thanks to the lower voter thresholds.

This got me thinking of options at the start of my senior year. I examined the 21st ward where my apartment was located. The Republican minority member in the ward or district was an old Jewish guy named Bernie Epton. He was a graduate of the U of C but seemed out of touch and non-responsive to many people. I fantasized about going after Bernie in 1980 and challenging him on the minority seat side? He didn't seem to have much energy left; could I mobilize students and others in Hyde Park who might be excited by fresh blood?

I began to explore options and fundraising schemes. I thought I could manage it. Hubris perhaps, but it seemed very doable given the number of people voting for the minority (Republican) candidate in the 21st ward—only about 5000 or less, compared to four or five times that on the Democratic side. I figured that a well-organized campaign in the university community and nearby could help get the vote out.

Bernie went on to run a quixotic mayoral campaign in Chicago in 1982. He was the Republican candidate against Black Congressman Harold Washington, an icon on the southside. His state assembly career ended then. The U.S. Supreme Court would decide in 1982 that Illinois' quaint multi-member districts were unconstitutional. From then on, I am sure it was the death knell for any Republican representatives in Chicago and probably many Democrats in much of Downstate.

But as it turned out I met one day in the winter of 1979-80 Congressman John Anderson and his wife Keke in a Chicago Loop station. Anderson was mounting at the time a quixotic campaign of his own for the Republican presidential nomination. He had not yet picked up that much steam and attention, but college kids were definitely attracted. I was mesmerized myself. I found him so rational and compassionate.

After meeting Anderson, I volunteered for his campaign and stayed on board for five months. I stayed until the disappointing results of the Illinois and Wisconsin primaries. Anderson was the Bernie Sanders of his time, and yet a Republican. He drew huge crowds of college students, but few came out to vote in a critical campaign against Reagan and Bush.

I was so caught up in the idealism and brilliance of the Anderson message, which offered such an attractive mélange of the best of both parties then. I was unimpressed by Carter then and uninspired by the later Teddy Kennedy challenge. John Anderson seemed to offer a desperately needed breeze of fresh air in American politics.

But, when it was clear that Reagan or Bush would take every Republican primary, he made the choice in April 1980 to run as an independent. This was fine; I supported him actively up to that point. But then he fatefully brought on Machine Democrat Pat Lucey from Wisconsin as his running mate. Much of his appeal on campuses melted away from the different message, and I drifted away also.

I gave up on the Anderson campaign in some frustration. I still was inattentive to my college studies in that fateful final quarter of the school year. It's hard to know where my head was at that time. I really screwed up. I had dabbled a bit in pot but didn't smoke that much because I was a bit afraid of smoking generally. I saw the effect of cigarette smoke on my parents, particularly my father. I flirted with acid with friends who were Deadheads but avoided becoming an acidhead myself. I drank heavily with friends at some of the local bars and watering holes in Hyde Park. I somehow avoided becoming an alcoholic or druggie.

However, I was distractible, procrastinated, and read only part of what I had to do for assignments. I was also unproductive on papers and class schedules, so that whole quarter proved to be a wash. I think I had almost all the incompletes from my classes.

This proved fatal since, in late May, I got word from my student advisor that I had too many incompletes to fully graduate. I had no idea I did not have enough credits to graduate, and so would be on the sidelines while the rest of my class graduated in June. I was embarrassed and depressed by this. My mother and sister flew out to Chicago for my graduation and I didn't have the heart to stop them and tell them, until they arrived.

What a student advisor I had. Thank you very much, Mr. Arlen Larsen. I still remember his name and his cavalier and inattentive attitude toward me. Could he not have been a little more proactive and drilled home the impending danger to me? He was an idiot, but I was, of course, a bigger idiot for not doing the needful. I felt paralyzed and embarrassed.

I had choices – go forward full steam ahead or lick my wounds and try to fix things? I took on a bit of an attitude like Senator John Blutarsky in the movie 'Animal House' on being expelled from school. "Seven years of college down the drain, nothing left to do but join the fucking Peace Corps!" At least I rationalized it so.

I still had plans in place for post-graduation. I interned with the Illinois Bureau of the Budget, researching issues on HMO alternatives for public aid recipients. This would be in the state capital. I then planned to join my Peace Corps service training in late August 1980. I decided to go forward with it, ignore the screw-up with my degree, and deal with it later somehow.

CHAPTER 3

PEACE CORPS IGNITABLES

Joining the Peace Corps right after school was something I always expected and wanted to do. I had the dream dating back at least to freshman year in high school. There was something deeply appealing to me about the idealism and commitment it represented and the connection to JFK.

I had applied to Peace Corps early in my senior year at the ACTION office in Chicago and was accepted conditionally for Peace Corps in late 1979. I went to the offices to see the Trainee Assignment Criteria sheets. I met this large Black Returned Peace Corps Volunteer (RPCV) in a dashiki and with lots of African memorabilia in his office. He gave me the Peace Corps pep talk, which I didn't need, and then pulled out possible assignment options.

The first option was for the Gilbert and Ellice Islands in the South Pacific. I frowned and said I was worried I'd end up isolated and just sitting in a hammock with coconuts and little to do.

The second option was Bangkok, an urban development program. I wrinkled my nose a little and pointed out that I grew up in a big city and had other ideas about what a Peace Corps experience should be like—villages and rural countryside, for one.

The third option was Mauritania, working with a maternal and child health program. Hmmm, I thought about it.

"Isn't Mauritania a Muslim country?" I asked. It is, the big RPCV assured me. So, does it make sense for a Jewish guy to be working in a female-oriented program in a Muslim country? He rolled his eyes from a little impatience but acknowledged my point. "Good catch," he said. "I will have to get back to Washington on that point."

The final choice that seemed to be in the cards was Ecuador, in South America. Working in the Rural Public Health program. I sighed in relief. Well, that makes more sense, no? I studied Spanish in high school, and I had been pre-med before and was now studying health policy among other things. And so Ecuador is where I would go. I would need to get medical clearance, which in practice would mean that I would need to get my four wisdom teeth prophylactically removed. This was to avoid problems in case something was to happen during Peace Corps service.

But first, I had an internship offered in the Illinois Bureau of the Budget in Springfield, Illinois. Given the abortive university graduation, I kept it quiet since I really wanted to do this seven-week internship. I had been studying health policy at the University of Chicago. I had an opportunity to join the state government and earn a modest stipend while working on a research project focused on a key priority. "How to improve the cost-effectiveness and efficiency of health services for the poor and indigent in Illinois." I expected I would work in this field after returning from the Peace Corps.

I studied the expenditures that the Illinois State Government made for Medicaid health services for public aid recipients, specifically those families receiving Aid to Families with Dependent Children (AFDC—basically welfare). A large number of resources were being used to reimburse hospitals for the use of hospital emergency rooms by welfare recipient families.

I studied the feasibility of federal reimbursement for the state to develop health maintenance organization (HMO) arrangements for welfare families. I conducted a document review and traveled to Washington, D.C., to meet with officials from the Health Care Financing Administration in the Department of Health and Human Services. I explored and drafted options I could recommend for the State of Illinois. It was cutting-edge work for its time.

For a bit over a month, I examined the state government's budget process and the funding of health benefits for welfare recipients from the Illinois Department of Public Aid. Under Governor Thompson's moderate Republican administration, I was tasked with how best to ensure federal co-funding of innovative programs. These pilots would shift some public aid recipients to high-quality, cost-effective HMOs.

This was among the first initial efforts to promote HMOs for public aid recipients and was widely seen as a good government initiative. It was not just pushing for cost savings and budget cuts on the poor. We wanted to see if health would measurably improve for the poor if they were signed up for the HMOs.

Living in Springfield was pretty crazy and a big change from big city Chicago. While I still had my car, I would often drive my bike around and watch the town roll up its streets at dark. I shared a three-bedroom ranch house rental with two other State Government interns. There wasn't much to do other than renting out whatever we could find at the nearby Blockbuster Video. Or we could go to the nearby roadhouse for some pretty basic rock and roll, pizza and beer.

Still, I had a good supervisor in the Bureau of the Budget, and it was an instructive internship, for what I thought would be my life after the necessary Peace Corps detour. I still imagined I would be returning from Peace Corps to take up work in health policy, after cleaning up the mess of my undergraduate incompletes.

I was invited to the August wedding of Tom, a university classmate. Tom lived in Portland, Oregon, and we had been pondering the logistics. Tom and I came up with the scheme that I would drive out to Portland from Springfield cross country after the internship. I would give Tom my brown bomber car as a wedding gift of sorts (since it was hardly legal to sell it with the huge improvised repair in the back). In return Tom was going to give me a one-way plane ticket from Portland back to New York City.

It was an incredible trip. I stopped at all these funky places along the way driving west from Chicago. I remember Wall South Dakota and the famous Wall Drug Store. The Sioux Black Hills

Badlands around Mt. Rushmore. I remember the change in the landscape in the big sky country of Montana before Missoula. It reminded me of Robert Pirsig's descriptions in "Zen and the Art of Motorcycle Maintenance."

Idaho passed quickly and I got to the dry country of eastern Oregon, stopping to see Dave, another classmate that I'd been good friends with. I eventually made it out to the very green and rainy Portland but with little time before the wedding and related receptions at Tom's house.

Both Tom and Teresa, his new wife, were profoundly Catholic; Teresa had just gotten pregnant some months before leading to this quick union. But they seemed incredibly happy with each other.

I enjoyed being there for Tom at the wedding. Time was short afterwards for me as well as I had to get back out to New York.

I flew to New York and spent a week or two saying goodbye to my parents and sister. Then I flew on Peace Corps' dime to Kingsville Texas where I joined Peace Corps training. My group would have four weeks of training in Harlingen County, Texas, and across the border near Monterrey, Mexico. We would then have a week of 'staging' in Miami where shaky volunteer candidates would be weeded out through a series of simulations. Then, finally, we would fly down to Quito at the end of September for language training. But first I'd have to make it through each of those hurdles.

Peace Corps Training was held over the late summer in a dorm of Texas A&I college in Kingsville TX. Not as big as its famous cousin Texas A&M, with which it later merged, it was in the hot and dusty area of Harlingen County, not far from the Mexico border. It was led by Professor Joe, a public health epidemiologist, and a group of Peace Corps training staff.

Classes of about eight hours a day subjected us to a wide range of technical material on public health, nutrition, sanitation and related topics. We also faced many exercises and simulations designed to gauge whether we were likely to succeed or not as volunteers. These would intensify over time.

There wasn't a lot to do in this town and certainly few distractions for us. I was sharing a dorm room with Ed, a likable, athletic Californian whose father was a city manager for Laguna Beach. Ed was a Christian but was very much caught up in the liberation theology ethos. He followed Paulo Freire from Brazil, who had written the dense but revolutionary "Pedagogy of the Oppressed". We came from opposite coasts and were opposites in so many ways, but we hit it off, each of us enjoying the odd humor and outlooks of the other.

As I recall, there were only five men in the group of trainees and about 30 women, so it was a great ratio for me. I found myself particularly drawn to a spunky ginger-haired nurse named Janet. Janet seemed, in many ways, a bit of a hippie from the Pacific Northwest. I hit the jackpot when I realized the attraction was mutual.

Janet was about ten years older than me, but limber and catlike in her movements. I enjoyed being with Janet. I wondered what she saw in me, an overweight Jew from New York with a big Jewfro and barely the stirrings of much facial hair. Perhaps it was a case of opposites attracting. Perhaps she saw me as sharing with her a bit of irreverence for authority with my 'Question Authority' t-shirt.

Ed found himself pairing off with Sabrina, a young Chicana activist from California. This made things fun and convenient at times if the four of us wanted to go off campus for some mischief.

The Texas training included an exercise for several days across the border in some Mexican villages near Monterey. It was meant to mirror the kind of life we might find in Ecuador. I don't remember much of the training details, but one thing I do remember was the painful ride back across the border to the USA. We traveled in a few vans that was hot and dusty, and we hadn't eaten too much on the Mexican side, given the types of communities we had been in. The line to cross the border on the highway was a long one.

Some folks in my van got the bright idea to buy some avocados that someone was selling outside along the roadside. They made guacamole from some supplies we had brought from what was essentially a camping adventure. I ate some of the guacamole, and I remember getting deathly ill from it a couple of hours later— food poisoning of some sort. Ever since that time, 40 years later, I still cannot eat avocados or guaca. It still just disgusts me, to the continuing annoyance and frustration of my wife.

There was a lot of bonding beyond the pairings Ed and I chose. Over the weeks of the health training, I became friends in a brotherly, protective way with many of the women in our volunteer candidate group. I remember in particular Ginny, a raucous irreverent nurse from western North Carolina. Ginny, who loved to be as vulgar as possible with a straight face, would crack me and anyone else up. Rachel was a fellow New Yorker, who intimidated me a bit since I felt she could see through any façade I might be putting up. But she was not hesitant to grab my hand on the dance floor for one of the group's impromptu parties. There were definite advantages to the sex ratio in the health group!

There were a few dropouts during the month of technical training. The sifting and sieve we would go through during the 'staging' would drop even more. We traveled as a group to Miami Beach and stayed in a hotel for a week. There, we were submerged in a series of exercises, simulations, and interview panels. Even forceful efforts questioned the motivation and staying power of the trainees. The logic of this process, as I understood it, was to try to get those mostly likely to drop out to do so before the travel to Ecuador.

At the Miami staging our group of 35 health volunteers merged with another 120 from different technical backstops. These included agriculture, forestry and fishing, education. We all would eventually make up what would come to be known as

Omnibus 34. That is, the 34th deployed group of volunteers to be placed in Ecuador since the start of Peace Corps in the early 1960s. The sex ratio evened out as we merged with groups with a much larger proportion of men.

Cost was clearly a concern for the Peace Corps. Losing prospective volunteers to early terminations and quitting was an expensive proposition. It was cheaper for the Peace Corps to cut losses early on and not have to write off a much larger cost later on. There were, in fact, a significant number who did quit during the staging, but the four of us from the health group – me, Janet, Sabrina, and Ed – stayed on. We eventually lost at least ten percent of our Omnibus 34 training group in Miami, from among those who wondered if Peace Corps was right for them. They backed out from traveling down to Quito.

Arrival in Quito was an eye-opener, albeit not a lung opener. I felt quite a bit of the difference in altitude with the dry air on arrival. Quito was almost 10,000 feet high compared to sea level. It tired you out quickly. I felt a headache in my forehead from the lack of oxygen. It was amazing though, coming off the plane exit stairs. I looked up to the overhanging green hillsides rising up to meet the volcano Pichincha, with clouds swirling around its broad crown. The hillsides showed a patchwork of different plots big and small rising up to the top, beyond the tree line.

Our arrival in Quito brought us to the ASDELA Peace Corps Training Center. ASDELA was the nonprofit organization that would run our Spanish language and cultural training. It would last about nine weeks. They would also manage our three-week practicums in our eventual assigned communities. This would take place before we were to be sworn in as official Peace Corps Volunteers mid-December.

We were then distributed out to many different initial Ecuadorian host families. My host family was a socially mobile middle-class family in a new northern suburban development of Quito. They lived a bit beyond the famous Estadio Nacional Atahualpa soccer stadium. They had household help in their apartment. I think it was the first time I saw that. I was surprised and put off by the casual nastiness of the treatment at times of the maid. It wasn't personal or physical. It was just a certain level of irritable meanness. They could never be pleased or satisfied.

It was complicated adapting to host family situations. Living with a host family meant adjustments. I held my tongue repeatedly.

But I loved the immersion in Quito. But I was utterly fascinated by the beautiful variety and diversity of cultural sites across Quito. The colonial center of Quito was like nothing I had ever seen. I never tired of looking at the green flanks of the Pichincha volcano. Or any of the beautiful snowcap volcanos to the south and north of the city.

My Spanish seemed to go swimmingly well in Quito, where I found the inflections and formalisms in the local dialect easy to follow. I resolved to keep a journal of my experiences when I went out to my assigned community, Buena Fe. I re-read the transcription of it as I prepared this memoir and I have to admit, it did leave my eyes rolling a bit. Still, wouldn't that be true of any of us, going back to read our diaries from age 21 or so?

I will include the diary portions here from my Peace Corps training. They show my thinking and experiences and the kinds of questions I was wrestling with.

PEACE CORPS DIARY: PRACTICUM IN BUENA FE ECUADOR

10-30 NOVEMBER

FIRST IMPRESSIONS: My tutors and my family are one and the same, Sr. and Sra. Rosario Betancourt de Montes. Rosario has done well for himself. He owns and manages the Farmacia San Martin below his apartment and the Centro Medico San Martin up the main street of town. He is a nurse, and I get the feeling the Centro Medico is a recent expansion of a Dispensary he used to have. I believe the expansion may have come with the hiring of a new doctor, Victor Lopez, from Ibarra, bringing the medical complement to two. Dr. Lopez sleeps with the family in the apartment above the Farmacia and both doctors take their meals there.

The president of the cabildo is Sr. Victor Zurita, a real politician who is running for the council on the MPD (leftist-Communist) ticket. After being introduced to Victor, Dr. Lopez, Rosario and I walked down the street. Rosario and the doctor began to laugh, and say together "I brought, I did, I want, I made, always I this or that."

I asked them, "Do you mean he always says "I" instead of "We"? Exactamente. Well, a common sickness of politicians everywhere.

Buena Fé (GOOD FAITH) was only recently made a parroquia – a parish center. It retains the cabildo (local council) system of organizing the Seguro Social Campesino dispensario – the Peasant Farmers Social Security Dispensary. This dispensary, a small clinic with a few hundred affiliated peasant farmer family members, is a quasi-governmental parallel system to that offered by the Ministry of Health.

Buena Fé is a rather large town, perhaps 20,000 people, and oddly enough it had both a Farmers Social Security Dispensary and a Ministry of Health sub-center (I would learn much more about all that later, especially since as a Health Peace Corps Volunteer I was supposed to be working with the Dispensary and somewhat surprisingly not the local health ministry sub-center).

Main Street is paved and runs with a lot of shops, restaurants and clinics about six or seven blocks. Electricity came to the town about four years ago. The main street has electric streetlights and the lit portion runs considerably further than the commercial area. Judging from the number of TV antennas I can see, there must be over 150 families with TVs in the center. There may be much more because my family has a TV but lacks an antenna.

My new host family: Señor and Señora Betancourt de Montes, a daughter Alexandra, and two boys, Martin and Alfonso. Rosario is probably around 35 or so, with a considerable paunch giving him a staggering roly-poly effect when he walks. I'm not sure whose belly was bigger, but he was far shorter than me. The fact that he is jolly to match his appearance is amusing. In costume he'd make a great –albeit short – Santa Claus.

His wife, Sra. Betancourt has greater Negroid features than Rosario, who looks like a light mestizo. Rosario's wife seems a few years older than Rosario and she keeps herself in good shape. Of the children, only Alfonso has definite Negroid features, looking quite a bit like his mother. The older boy, Martin and the daughter, Alejandra, 7 and 6 years old, have mestizo features, with Martin a bit lighter than his sister in complexion.

The town has something of a night life, which is probably only natural with streetlights. The main street is something of a major thoroughfare, a lot of trucks, bicycles and motorcycles constantly go up and down it.

There's a great variety in housing styles. On Main Street there are a few wooden houses, most buildings are concrete or cement, cinderblock and even some brick. Away from Main Street, the houses and building begin to get a bit shabbier as the road becomes gravel or dirt. Some are wood plank, a very few bamboos, and many seem to be in the process of improvement with a mixture of cement and cinderblock. On Main Street, some houses have glass for windows; away from it a very few do, in fact probably none really do.

I don't know if any space will be available, but I believe when I look for my place to live I'm going to look for it on the main thoroughfare despite the noise. There appear to be buses day and night going or coming from Quevedo, Santo Domingo and Esmeraldas.

This town is growing fast now, perhaps because being named a parroquia has meant a lot of government money. A lot of new housing, a playground area with basketball courts and a communal house for meetings and other city activities are being built. Quite stirring.

Much of the appearance of Buena Fé reminds me of the much larger city of Santo Domingo about an hour or so to the north, even the central park in the town. There is no telephone service yet in town and according to Rosario no telegraph, although I thought I saw a telegraph service sign up the road. I'll have to check out Quevedo, only 13-14 minutes away to the south. Apparently it has all of what Buena Fé may lack. That will be convenient when outfitting my quarters as a volunteer living here. I'll probably be able to get everything in either Buena Fé or Quevedo.

Weatherwise, the afternoon can be really hot, but the night and early morning have a refreshing pleasant crispness. There are several schools in the area, at least 3 or 4 judging from the types of uniforms I have seen on kids. The only house of worship I have seen so far is a Roman Catholic Church just off the main park in the center, complete with a bright neon cross on top.

One thing or two about the quarters of the Betancourt de Montes family. The apartment is a large one. I have space in the back room, which is perhaps 15' x 20'. It is also taken up by the family refrigerator, the shower stall, and the toilet stall – a water bassinet type with no seat (I'm re-learning how to squat). The odd touch is this box in one corner of the room with a quiet but quite alive chicken. I assume she is bound there, but she doesn't seem to resent it any. My bed is roughly queen size, with a soft foam mattress atop a steel spring frame. Quite comfortable, much better than my bed at my host family's house in Quito. In a strange and unexpected way, this poor family in various ways seems more comfortable than my middle-class Quito host family. But with a rural unsophisticated relaxed flair.

An interesting trap or test appears: the Señora just introduced me to two women who teach in the schools and are part of a church group. I gathered that these women were important to my ultimate acceptance here. I believe I somehow passed the test with flying colors.

Although there was one near-pitfall. The matter of religion inevitably came up, and they asked what religion I was. I said Jewish, and they said, "Yes, but do you believe in God, in Christ?" They clearly weren't really sure what Jewish meant. Then followed a discussion for five minutes in which I observed that Christ was Jewish. I said I believed in Christ as a wise teacher if not necessarily as the Messiah.

They seemed nevertheless satisfied with my answer – at least I guess it didn't raise any major red flags, but it had worried me for a bit. These women were obviously of the type who would have thought of me as some horrible American devil if I were to try to explain agnosticism to them. Or worse atheism. I guess I was lucky it didn't go much further than that. I would come to understand that Ecuadorian knowledge and familiarity with Jews and Judaism was quite limited. It was usually on a level with

Christ-killers and God-deniers, attitudes largely unmoved since the Inquisition five hundred years before.

After that encounter, I decided to walk around Buena Fe. I walked up and down the poorer streets, chatting with people along the way, and saw a boy that I recognized from a crowd when I first arrived in the town. He was so happy that I remembered him – clearly as an unusual visitor and new arrival I was the rock star and recognizable to all.

I asked where a good place to go for lunch was. He directed me to a place that served meals typical of Manabi, the dry coastal province directly to the west of Los Rios province. A lot of people in Buena Fé hailed from there. I ate a plate of rice with a chicken stew poured on top. When I finished I discovered that the boy had collected a huge crowd of other boys and men that were watching me with open fascination and curiosity. "Hola, Que dice?" I asked, walking up to him and tousling his hair in a friendly manner.

Everyone wanted to ask me a question, but there was an obvious pecking order in the interrogation on the street corner. I told stories of where I was from and my travels, and soon I had a crowd of nearly forty people around me. I explained to the kids and young men that I hoped to help teach in the schools in January after this short trip and a return to Quito for December. I asked if they would like that I teach health and nutrition and things like that. Never did I see such an enthusiastic bunch of young people. As I walked back to my 'host parents'' house, this crowd surged around me. I felt like a Pied Piper with an escort honor guard.

When I said goodbye to them all, and walked upstairs, my parents and Dr. Victor Lopez had been watching. Their look of incredulity and amazement helped my confidence in my credibility and acceptance here. A sound truck went by in the street outside, announcing a meeting at 2 PM of all the affiliated families of the clinic of the Farmers Social Security. I readied myself to deal with that next hurdle. The meeting had been called to present to the community the newly arrived public health volunteer from the Peace Corps, Señor 'Doctor' Alonzo. Me.

The results of the meeting were nothing short of incredible. My host "father" here Rosario Betancourt, Don Victor the president of the council, and the doctor of the dispensary clinic spoke. I then spoke in my somewhat mangled Spanish for five minutes on my reasons for coming to Ecuador, and what I hoped to do in collaboration with the people of Buena Fe. Despite my gringo accent and challenging grammar, I was strongly applauded. Three people followed giving speeches about how proud they were that I was in their community and how much it would no doubt help. This was my first introduction to the Latin predilection for speechifying which I would come to embrace – why use ten words when one hundred will do? Why allow one speech when five are better?

However, not all seemed happy. The shit hit the fan unexpectedly. A man stepped up who looked amazingly like an Adolf Hitler reborn. He spoke a rapid-fire Spanish in a voice that somehow evoked Adolf's German speeches from the 1930s. He shouted with great passion and emphasis that my arrival was a travesty, that I was not going where I was needed. He was certain my placement was to be among the rich people instead of the poor. This was somehow all the result of a shaky deal that the President of the Republic Jaime Roldós would hardly approve of.

I was shaken. What was Adolf doing in coastal Ecuador, and why was I the target of his polemical attack? Now what was I going to do after the machine gun speech of Spanish had chopped my body to bits? Luckily, I didn't have to respond. Both Don Victor and Rosario gave speeches contradicting Adolf and praised the blessings of my arrival and the abilities I would bring to bear for the people of Buena Fe. Adolf then spoke again. He had been tamed. He was somehow magically mollified that maybe I was a good person and acknowledged how wonderful and marvelous it was that I was there. He still insisted that my placement as a US Peace Corps volunteer was part of some inexplicable deal. A deal that meant that Buena Fé could only have potable water four hours a day.

I was at that point completely lost. After Rosario once again rose to defend me, in his guttural Manabitan coastal Spanish with few consonants under control, I decided to also interject. "Forgive me," I started. I then gave a halting but passionate speech on my role and the concept of Peace Corps. I was working without pay or personal gain and dedicated to the poor. With their help and with God as my guide we could together work out solutions to at least some of their problems.

Amazingly my fluency in Spanish improved with each passing moment. The emotion of my words somehow detonating any barriers to grammar and conjugations along the way. I promised to help not only the affiliated families of Farmers Social Security but all the families I could. I would visit all the neighborhood barrios of Buena Fe. In my mind it was an incredible barnstormer speech and when I was finished with "Gracias" the stomping and applauding was incredible. I probably could have been elected Mayor on the spot by acclamation.

People rushed up to me to shake my hand and slap my back. I was amazed by the unshakable enthusiasm and old Adolf himself threw his hands up in defeat and walked over to shake my hand. I was on a roll, and I had learned another lesson – there are few problems here that can't be managed by an impassioned and emotional speech.

With my throat hoarse and my stomach trembling with a threat of imminent diarrhea, I called for attention.

"Now", I said, "let's stop talking and start working. I can only help as much as you all can help me. I will set hours each day that I will be in the dispensary and post those hours on the door. If any and all of you want to talk with me about problems then you can find me in the dispensary during those hours."

Everyone seemed to like that idea – except perhaps the doctor and the nurses' aides. Since I was unconsciously setting up a new standard of service that they had never followed. Publicly they had applauded the revolutionary idea of posted hours.

A woman called out: "Can you also visit the poorer barrios if you are really serious about wanting to help the poorest of the poor?"

"Claro" I said, of course. Others spoke up. In ten minutes, I had scheduled three 'charlas' (public health talks or chats) on potable water, boiling water and eye infections in three different poor barrios of Buena Fe.

The next morning, I arose at 6 am. It was Wednesday, my second morning in Buena Fe, and I was scheduled to go to the neighborhood hamlet of Nueva Union for a health talk at 8 am. I wondered what I could prepare. With the oaktag and markers purchased the day before, I made a simple flipchart on preventing diarrhea and the use of boiled water. I finished it at 0730 AM and when my family got up in the morning they were incredulous, asking me how I had learned to make it. The reaction of the people who attended the talk was similar.

A simple educational aid, but people loved the colors and pictures I made of a happy child and an unhappy child. I think the health talk was effective at least with some of the people, and the questions were interesting ones. I was proud – I had managed to give my first health education talk and it was well received.

Later in the day, Rosario took me in his truck. We went to La Cooperativa in the north of Buena Fé and La Catorce, another small hamlet about 14 kms away from Buena Fé (thus the name – "The Fourteen"). There I spoke with the people and listened to their problems. They were variations on the need for potable clean water.

In addition, we went to the Quintemilla Sanchez primary school. There I spoke with the teachers and the school director to see if they were interested in me coming to give classes periodically. The response was – start immediately. The responsiveness and hunger for help from the people moved me enormously.

What did I really have to offer? Not much I thought. True, I had knowledge of basic principles of primary health care, of prevention and sanitation. Most of all it seemed that people loved the idea of a gringo there that they could talk to, exchange ideas, be a sounding board and talk about problems. They didn't seem to expect any great miracles from me being there as a Peace Corps Volunteer.

They realized I didn't have deep pockets of money, at least not with me. They seemed to have never had someone of authority that they could easily talk about problems with. I didn't have any authority or power to do much. But I came to realize that my willingness to listen, my ability to marshal empathy and compassion with the challenges they faced, was a valued asset. I recognized that it was a pastoral function that they hungered for. They needed to talk out problems with someone perceived to be non-judgmental and with good intentions.

That second day however brought me a new dollop of humility. When we stopped back at the house, Mrs. Betancourt asked me with an arched eyebrow, "Don Alonzo, can you tell me what my name is?" I was a little taken aback with her directness. In fact, I wasn't entirely sure. I stammered a little, "Well, I know Don Rosario's name, but I wasn't sure I really caught your first name,

Senora. I think it is "Charito"?" This led to a general level of hilarity and heavy laughter from all around in the house. I soon learned that I had completely misunderstood the introductions from the day before. I had confused myself terribly with the names.

For it turned out that my host father was actually named Don Guido Montes, and his wife's name was Rosario – not his. The use of the "o" at the end for the name had confused me, and I hadn't realized that Rosario was actually a woman's name. Guido was married to Rosario Betancourt. He generally used the affectionate diminutives of "Charito" or "Charo" which corresponded to the name Rosario. I had been going around thinking Guido's name was Rosario for a day and a half. Oh well, some humble pie.

This linguistic confusion had been abetted by the fact that since my arrival from Quito on my first field trip to coastal Ecuador, and the town of Buena Fé that would eventually become my Peace Corps site, I was working overtime to try to understand the local variant of Spanish. The Spanish in the area was very liquid and vowel heavy compared to the more labored and formal Spanish of Quito, Ecuador's mountain capital. It seemed like I rarely heard a hard consonant. My host father, Guido Montes, was from Manabí, and when he spoke it was usually at 78 RPM compared even to the Buena Fé locals. His wife Rosario came from the northern coastal area of Esmeraldas. This had a greater Black population, descended from former escaped slaves. It also had very particular language traits as I would come to know.

In any case, working with Guido Montes as my host and entrée into Buena Fé was its own magic, both good and bad. Guido Montes always seemed to be running at 220 volts even in a rest state. He was full of energy and full of ideas. I would come to understand that one needed a well-placed filter to handle the flood that would emanate from him. Some of the ideas were quite good, and others were more questionable.

Within my first 48 hours of a debut in Buena Fe, I realized that Don Guido was having a hard time thinking long-term. He thought my mission as a rural public health volunteer could bloom overnight. And indeed, the whole picture of developing options for rural public health improvement. He was abuzz with results, figures, specific goals to start from day one. Which was all well and good. But I figured that I needed time to understand what on earth was the reality I would face as a volunteer in Buena Fe, and what might really prove possible.

With only a few days on the job I needed to calm Don Guido down a bit. In fact, I was on my first practicum field trip during volunteer training. It would finish with my swearing in as a U.S. Peace Corps Volunteer in mid-December. Dr. Victor realized this, Rosario realized this, and eventually Don Guido came around. Still, listening to Guido fire off about a million ideas of what I could be doing and starting from the day before yesterday made me pause. I thought hard about what I was trying to do, what I really could do as a Peace Corps Volunteer in such a setting.

I wondered if the challenge given by the Peace Corps health program manager was more than I could handle. Almost all those in the Rural Public Health program were scattered in several dozen small hamlets and communities. The communities in almost all cases had fewer than 3000 inhabitants, and sometimes fewer than 1000. Here I was in what was really a small town on the edge of a medium size city, with 20,000 Ecuadorians. Could I really undertake some projects that might materially affect such a large population? Was this some sort of deranged hubris on my part? How could I make a dent, particularly in an environment where everybody wanted to talk to me about their problems?

The next day, Thursday, was an entirely different thing, and I spent the better part of the day getting even more overwhelmed. The day started innocuously enough. Rafael was a guy my age who lived across Main Street from Guido Montes' pharmacy and clinic. He was someone I had met the first day I arrived and was rapidly becoming a friend. I was helping him learn a bit of English. He took me to Quevedo, a medium size city only 15 kms south of Buena Fe. Quevedo is about the size of Santo Domingo de los Colorados with 80,000 people. It is more commercial, and also known as the "Chinatown" of Ecuador.

We strolled around and through the town and he pointed out different things and places to me. We went down to the Mercado, the central market, and he told me what different fruits, vegetables and fish were and how they might be best prepared. It was informative and useful to me. Then who should I notice walking down the street ahead but another Peace Corps volunteer trainee from my group, Cindy and an Ecuadorian man.

Cindy, in her gurgling voluble surprise to see me, introduced me to her "own" Rafael, in this case Don Rafael, president of the cabildo of El Progreso. We chatted and decided to eat lunch together at a nearby small Chinese restaurant, which the Ecuadorians call a 'chifa'. Don Rafael told me that there would be a meeting Sunday in the park of the larger village of La Mana. For the facilitators, tutors and volunteer trainers for Buena Fe, El Progreso II, La Libertad, Chipe-hamburgo and Guasaganda. Would I also come? Claro.

We said goodbye, and then my pal Rafael and I returned to Buena Fé because it was after 12 and I had posted hours in the afternoon at the Dispensary.

The ride between Buena Fé and Quevedo is less than 15 minutes. There is a steady stream of buses and every manner of conveyance almost every minute between the towns, running along Buena Fe's main street. There were colorful local open-air flatbed trucks with benches and covered awnings. That would go back and forth between Buena Fe and Quevedo. They charged only 5 sucres (about 10 cents). The main interprovincial buses also raced between the coastal cities of Guayaquil, Esmeraldas, Portoviejo, Santo Domingo and Quevedo. They would also stop for seconds in Buena Fe for passengers.

We got back in due time, and I picked up my health education material and went back to the dispensary. There I spent about 1 ½ hours talking to the patients who were waiting for their exams with the nurse. They awaited the doctor himself. His hours were still unclear and at best theoretical. When the doctor arrived, we talked shop for about 20 minutes. I was impressed with his interest and enthusiasm, which left me thinking that we'd be able to work effectively together in the future. We discussed the sorts of problems he saw from the patients from a medical point of view. Most complaints were over diarrheas, respiratory infections and skin ailments.

At 2:45 PM Don Guido arrived at the dispensary to fetch me. Together we went to pick up Doña Rosario. We continued to a pre-arranged visit to the Cooperativa Santa Rosa adult education school. The school taught women basic trades include sewing. There I gave another brief health class. I planned to return the following Thursday afternoon to give a more formal health talk and presentation.

From there we walked house to house in the barrio of Nuevo Progreso, and Don Guido and Dna Rosario introduced me to people. I made some preliminary exams of the kids, and I arranged to give a talk on nutrition there the following Monday night. We next went to the barrio of La Union, where we did the same series of house to house visits. I arranged to come back to give a health talk the following Tuesday night. My schedule was rapidly beginning to fill in.

By the time we returned to the Montes' home, it was about 6 pm, and I was sapped. Guido and Rosario were of course full of energy still, and sympathetically amused at my state. But of course, it required a lot of energy for me to concentrate in Spanish. I examined about 25 kids in the house to house visits. 20 of them had signs of either protein-calorie malnutrition, vitamin-mineral malnutrition, or worms.

Going house to house was a great way to meet people and see the reality of how they lived. It was almost impossible to walk twenty paces without being called and invited in from house to house. "Doctor Alonzo", they would call, "Come! Come". While I certainly wasn't a doctor, this was a name that would stick with me for a long time. Any person working in health was usually pegged with the honorific "Doctor". Every person greeted on the street inevitably meant stopping to chat and talk, even if I'd just seen them fifteen minutes ago and had nothing new to say. No matter – every passing greeting was an opportunity to stop and chat. I had an endless stream of friendly exchanges. It seemed there was endless novelty in this gringo walking through the streets of Buena Fe. I wondered if the novelty would ever wear off over the course of the next two years.

At 3 AM someone was pounding on the door downstairs. It was a woman whose husband had horrible cramps in his abdomen. Don Guido and I looked him over and sure enough it looked likely to be appendicitis. With no ambulances in Buena Fe, we rushed him to the main regional Ministry of Health (MOH) hospital in Quevedo in Guido's truck.

I went back to Buena Fé after we dropped him at the emergency room. Then a few hours later in the morning after a bit more sleep and showering, I went back to Quevedo to get to know the doctors at the MOH Hospital. I wanted to let them know that I and other rural public health Peace Corps Volunteers were deployed in surrounding communities. I greeted the Ministry's cantonal (county) Inspector General of Public Health, sort of the local health commissioner. I also met the Ministry of Health Hospital Director, and the Chief of Surgery.

These contacts with local officials were important. Ultimately in a country like Ecuador, the MOH provides oversight and supervision to health activities. That includes curative, prevention or public health. The Chief of Surgery seemed particularly enthused with having Americans in the area. His name was Dr. Jorge Suarez, and he spoke passable English and enjoyed the language practice.

Dr. Suarez explained to me that surgery and medicine were different in Ecuador compared to a country like the USA. No surprise there. He said that the responses to certain drugs and medicines were not textbook. He invited me to join him and observe in some surgical procedures sometime if I wanted. I wasn't sure I was ready for that, but I appreciated the offer.

When we returned to Buena Fe, it was just in time for my meeting with the Director of one of the major schools in the town. That went very well, and he seemed delighted to meet me. We cemented an arrangement for me to start teaching in the school with the start of the new school year in May 1981.

We also set up a General Assembly meeting of parents, students and teachers for the following Friday morning, November 21. It was to officially welcome me and let people know of my new involvement with the school.

Don Guido had suggested several times that I make up some signs explaining what the Peace Corps was, and my job would be. He insisted that this would help ease my full acceptance. I had to smile a bit at the idea. It smacked a bit of an advertising and marketing campaign in the middle of a rural Ecuador town. I spent the rest of the day searching ways to get my message across to the people and mulled over what could be discussed at the Sunday meeting in La Mana.

Don Guido, his mind always running and plotting to carry him as far as his legs could manage, had led me to Nuevo Progreso. It was a poor barrio of Buena Fe, where a small and humble chapel stood that the people had built themselves. It fit perhaps fifty people, with a modest table ringed by candles serving as the altar.

That night there was a visiting padre from Argentina. He spoke a quite different variety of Castilian with the dipthong "th" of Iberian Spanish. There were readings from the New Testament and the padre's own brief sermonettes, comingled for punctuation with some religious folkloric songs which the people joined in on with gusto. There were even mimeo sheets of the words for those of us who didn't know them. The songs were wonderful statements of liberation of the poor from the tyranny of the rich, and release from all sorts of oppression. "God is on our side" sort of stuff, which seemed to flow out from a well of deep piety in the people.

One real surprise for me was when one of the songs turned out to have the same melody as 'Hava Nagila', the Israeli folksong. What the history of the wanderings of that song is I can only guess at. I was moved by the service. Don Guido introduced me glowingly. I said a few words of greetings to the congregants and the padre. To my surprise he offered a "Holy Blessing of Our Lord Jesus Christ" for my mission here.

Afterwards I stayed to chat with the padre a bit about "liberation theology." My fellow Peace Corps trainee Ed had spoken to me of it. It was the movement of some members of the Church toward securing the needs of the poorer classes here on earth as well as heaven. It took a while for us to be talking about the same topic in my struggling Castilian.

Discussing abstract concepts is hard enough when the two people are talking a common native language. It's almost impossible when you are trying like I was to pick my way through potential minefields. I chose words delicately to avoid potential offense. At the same time, I was not completely sure I understood fully what he was saying!

The Argentine priest warmed to the topic and spoke well of the social consciousness of most priests in Ecuador and Latin America. The conservative element in the Church was still lodged at the level of the bishops. Only one bishop in Ecuador stood out otherwise, the one in Riobamba being a socially enlightened type. The padre offered the hope that will perhaps change with time. Indeed, the Pope's visit to Brazil, the padre observed, was something to be very encouraged about.

After leaving the small chapel, I went back to the house and sat outside with Don Guido and a next-door neighbor, Victor. He was a young man of 20 working as a mechanic and going to night school in his spare time. I commented about my experiences in the service and with the priest and was fascinated by Don Guido's next words.

"I am not a Catholic myself, I follow the Mission of the Rosicrucians from California," he said. "I am enchanted with the mystical aspects of the mind, the powers of the mind. I have found that a thorough understanding of parapsychology is important in patient care."

I was incredulous. "Parapsychology? Don't you mean psychology, Don Guido?"

Victor observed, "No, parapsychology. Don Guido and I have some books on the ways of the mind, spiritual forces on the astral plane, as well as yoga."

"And meditation." added Guido.

Incredible. Unexpected surprises. Here I was, sitting outside the house in the darkness thanks to one of Buena Fe's frequent blackouts. In the middle of the western coastal Ecuadorian jungle, with two gentlemen whose educations were a little better than average. We were sitting and talking of some of the most arcane topics possible.

It was not the sort of conversation I expected to have when I joined Peace Corps. I mentioned that to Don Guido and Victor.

Don Guido laughed easily, and Victor pursed his lips thoughtfully.

"Perhaps there are many surprises awaiting you here in Buena Fe," Victor mused.

Perhaps indeed, I thought to myself, if the past were any clue to the future.

The next day, Saturday, was in theory my day off. I slept late until the ungodly hour of 8:45, two hours later than usual. I lingered around in the morning, chatting with Doña Rosario and then driving back and forth with her brother Otton to the market in Quevedo. Guido came back from the medical clinic in mid-morning and he proceeded to open his bookcase and encourage me to peruse through it. Many were medical and health books in Spanish, and they would be helpful for me as references also. Quite a few looked like those silly books various "twitch groups" in the States hand out in shopping centers and subway stations. Fascinating.

What Guido really was could be described as an entrepreneurial *curandero*, a respected but largely untrained popular healer, with a lot of practical experience. He relied a lot on a full array of techniques including faith healing and folklore remedies. He had managed to pool his resources enough to open up his own health clinic and pharmacy. He hired a real physician to work some hours and provide credibility, coverage and in theory professional oversight.

I learned from Doña Rosario that health dispensaries asked for regular monthly pre-payments from affiliated families. This seemed to be an unusual and somewhat innovative primary health care cost recovery program for a quasi-governmental system. It was structured almost like a modest health insurance system.

Most of these community clinics for peasant farmers asked for 100 sucres in advance for three months of payments. Buena Fe's dispensary demanded 300 sucres besides the regular monthly payment.

I asked Rosario what the extra charge was for. She gave me a very general and non-specific response, which boiled down to that it was whatever the cabildo, the council, thought best. Was the payment a good thing she agreed with? Was it justified?

"No," she commented, "It was terrible, because it blocked some poorer members of the barrios from signing up as affiliates. They can't get health services from the Farmers Social Security."

I imagined this was the likely reason there were only 236 affiliated families in a town of close to 20,000 people.

"Whose idea was the 300 sucre service charge?"

"Oh, it was the nurse in the clinic."

"And you, Doña Rosario, as Vice president, don't agree with it?"

"Many people have problems with this nurse, because of her manner, her inability to organize things, and her unwillingness to go out house to house."

Now, this got me thinking hard on several different levels. I drew on my experiences in the States on studying health care finance in practice just before Peace Corps. Here I was in rural Ecuador and facing again the question of how primary health care services were administered and financed.

Common to almost every country in Latin America, the Ministry of Health was the provider of first resort for much of the population. The MOH operated major reference hospitals and health centers in major cities and provincial capitals. In a town like Buena Fé it had a medium size Health Sub-Center which had referral and counter-referral privileges with the MOH hospital in Quevedo, which provided some level of oversight.

However, Ecuador had another parallel system as well, which had developed during left-of-center governments in the 1960s and which had survived military rule in Ecuador which had ended last year. It was the Social Security system, and it was a separate nationwide network in the major cities of major specialized hospitals, general hospitals and health clinics. It was financed in part from general revenues and in part from the payroll contributions from employers and enrolled workers or employees.

This network was viewed as better financed, supplied and equipped than the MOH network, and doctors were seen as better trained and paid. Yet a network for salaried employees working in industry by definition was a largely urban system, where factories, businesses and government employees were concentrated.

If there was an extra 300 sucre charge being applied by this nurse, there was a good chance she was pocketing the money. I understood that any extra charges of this nature would be illegal under the IESS rules. It was also counter-productive. It was serving as a disincentive for other poor peasant families to join up as affiliates for the SSC dispensary.

We made a stop in the truck on the way back to Buena Fé which topped everything else in my experience so far, blowing my mind. Don Guido guided Otton to this huge house set back from the road, where a good friend of his happened to be who was reportedly a "brujo" – a male witchdoctor. Guido commented, "As everyone knows, the best witchdoctors are always men."

Don Guido's friend (I never did learn his name) was a giant of a man, especially here in Ecuador. He has a huge barrel chest that made him look like an outsized Buddha, especially when he laughed. Like other "Manabitas", coastal Ecuadorians from

Manabí province, his skin was a mix of yellowish and ruddiness. His eyes had a slightly oriental cast.

Don Guido introduced me to him, and his friend's face lit up and crinkled with delight. He asked what tribe I was part of. Surprised, I answered that I was part of the tribe of the Levites, with the original Hebrew name of Abraham ben Melech. He nodded with familiarity to that news.

The witchdoctor sat me down at a table, upon which lay a shiny polished black rock, weighing perhaps 2 or 3 kilos. He poured alcohol over it and instructed me to place it against my forehead, moving it around in continuous circles. The rock, he explained, was a true healing stone. It acted directly upon the magnetism of the body and the head to relieve anxieties, promote confidence and encourage honesty. A potent mix it seemed.

He gave me an old Tarot card deck, with the names for the ancient symbols in Spanish and English, and Guido motioned to me to shuffle the deck. I did a bit clumsily, shuffling it twice, and returned the deck to the brujo. He began laying the cards out in front of me, chanting some unrecognizable words that didn't sound Spanish. After he finished placing the cards, he waived around my head a twisted root that smelled of cinnamon but wasn't. This was all, I was made to understand, to remove me from the influence of "bad airs" and ghosts. Then he did my reading.

"You cast a presence of considerable and unusual strength. This makes a reading difficult because it is as if you stand aside a node, a fork between the very good and the very bad."

That didn't sound promising.

"The Hangman is upside down and the Wheel of Fortune is on the left. I believe you will be either exceptionally good for Ecuador and for your country, or very bad, very dangerous. At any rate you will be very strong."

That sounded very melodramatic; Christ, I thought, wonderful news also for my introduction in Buena Fe. That this wasn't the first time I had heard such an odd reading didn't put me in a better mood.

Rosario said, "Let's assume the best." Always the optimist!

"Claro," agreed the brujo.

He brought out a variety of herbs and told me which were to be used in infusions and which included in different concoctions, and for which disorders. I had confessed to Guido earlier a strong interest in folk medicine, and Guido had no doubt relayed this to his friend.

He brought out a jar of alcohol in which were immersed three dead and poisonous looking snakes, which he claimed to have been drowned in the fluid. They certainly didn't look happy. I thought I understood how the alcohol might draw out an anti-venom, as the solution was of course meant as a topical for snake bite. No idea how effective it might or might not be.

"The Colorado Indians are very renowned for their medicine men?", I asked. The Colorados were a close-knit tribe who lived about an hour north of Buena Fe and wore a very distinctive traditional dress.

"Oh yes," he answered. "But they need to go into a lot of trances using hallucinatory drugs, like marijuana and ayahuasca. Sometimes then they give their medicines to their patients, their patients may feel much better, but aren't healthier."

Then the brujo want into a nearby closet and brought out the remains of some pottery. He claimed they were pre-colonial, pre-Incan artifacts, the remains of a cup and vase with a peculiar symbol on them. He gave them to me as a gift and told me the symbol was a "Chan".

"What's a Chan?", I asked.

He straightened up from his stool, walked out to an anteroom of sorts I hadn't noticed before. I was surprised to see seven or eight people waiting patiently, apparently for readings or treatments of some kind.

He told them, "Ya mismo, ya mismo." Soon, soon. He then turned back to me and said, "Now I will have to tell you briefly the history of Ecuador and South America."

The story he then proceeded to tell me was an incredible one, especially for its inventiveness and creativity. Was it full of whoppers? I wasn't judgmental.

As the witchdoctor told it, the Chinese were the oldest civilization on Earth. Many, many thousands of years old, perhaps seven or eight thousand years old. The Chinese learned early how to master the earth and nature gods, and thus made travel across the sea a safe and practical matter.

Before then, the gods would frequently destroy the boats of those that had the temerity to challenge their domain. Eventually the Chinese learned to construct ocean-going vessels with balsawood. They reached the western shore of South America around or near the modern Ecuadorian province of Guayas. This land west of the Guayas river, southwest of modern Guayaquil, was the first to be settled.

The Chinese came as immigrants or chose to remain as such. They navigated down south to the area near the Peruvian border. There they clashed, made peace with and eventually intermarried with the Cañari tribes. The Cañari were fairly advanced themselves, as they were in fact the last remnants of the Ten Lost Tribes of Israel. They had been physically transported as a people in one of the great Miracles of all time. Part in Ireland in the Atlantic and part to southern Ecuador, to become, when merged with the Chinese, the first Ecuadorians.

In the first place I couldn't resist smiling, but I didn't say what I was really thinking. Instead, I said, "Oh incredible I never thought I could learn so much in seven weeks in Ecuador!" with my most sincere voice and gaze.

Anyway, the discussions of herbal medicines were valuable, and he had given me a seemingly old artifact as a gift. I thanked him deeply and he laughed, saying something very fast to Guido and Rosario, and invited me to come back and visit another time. I thanked him again and told him I certainly would come visit again. I certainly planned to as the conversation with him was positively the weirdest I had had so far in Ecuador.

When we finally returned to Buena Fé Sunday afternoon, I discovered that the boy we had treated for constipation had died on the operating table in Quevedo. He had died of intestinal obstruction because of an advanced case of worms, that in the end probably wasn't that extraordinary for the coastal jungle of Ecuador. He literally developed so many parasites that his insides had exploded from the pressure. Only seven years old. I felt terrible and responsible somehow.

I knew that I had nothing to do with his death, but I felt that if only I had examined the boy more closely... if only I had been able to convince the mother to take him to a real doctor sooner than the sham of Don Guido. If only, if only. Don Guido and others were typically stoic and philosophical about the loss and did not seem as troubled as I felt.

Are you cringing a bit from my descriptions? I guess I do as I re-read some of these diary entries decades later. I was quite a bit full of myself back then. Being trusted to help with a delivery was one thing – it actually wasn't the first time I had the opportunity to do so. As a high school student thinking about pre-med as a likely career direction, a friendly neighbor who was an obstetrician resident invited me to spend a 36-hour period with him for his rounds at Kings County Hospital, and had me masking and gloving up to assist even in some caesarians – an impossible occurrence today no doubt!

The witch doctor visit was mind-blowing to me then and still fascinates me. Nowadays, the use of psilocybin and magic mushrooms is making a bit of a comeback in the cultural zeitgeist, as is the idea of micro dosing. Shamanic experiences have always fascinated me a bit, and I've always welcomed the idea of learning more from them to the degree possible.

I understood in an intellectual sense that it was not my responsibility as a Peace Corps Volunteer to upend and try to actively change society mores and culture in the host country I was serving in. That very behavior could get me or anyone else kicked out if we weren't careful. It's sort of a 'Star Trek-Federation Prime Directive' thing at that point – at least, that's how I rationalized it. But that didn't stop me from being offended by a social order where things were clearly wrong and exploitative. Over time, it would raise for me the question of the purpose and direction my life would or should take.

That next Monday was an extraordinarily busy day. November 17 was exactly one week after my arrival in Buena Fé for my volunteer practicum and we were organizing like gangbusters. In addition to the birth and the meeting with Rosita, I had a scheduled meeting with an official from IESS from Quevedo. It was to discuss thoughts for my work and volunteer service here. That meeting included Rosita, representing Peace Corps headquarters in Quito, the Senora Presidente de la comunidad, and from the cabildo of the community, Don Victor and Dona Rosario. That meeting went well.

I listened to the IESS representative who shared his high-minded hopes and expectations for a Peace Corps volunteer. The Buena Fé leadership repeated their general and well-intentioned support. So far I seemed to be on the right track. I offered my most earnest hope to do all I could humanly do as a Volunteer over the next two years. I reminded everybody that I came free of charge but also without any real resources of my own. I had plenty of good will and ideas but would count on the leadership and the communities to help pitch in on any projects. I also asked for peoples' expectations to remain realistic in terms of what we might and might not do over the next two years. It seemed to be the right tone, and everyone seemed agreeable.

I also met with the officials of the Santa Rosa Cooperative. I planned to teach in their school and help the cooperative and its 490 member families in other general and unspecified ways. I viewed any help provided to Santa Rosa as part of my overall Volunteer services for Buena Fe. Don Guido, Dna Rosario and the residents of Santa Rosa wanted some sort of specific agreement of expectations laid out for their community.

As Santa Rosa seemed to be in many ways the poorest part of the town, this made sense to me. I'm sure the folks of Santa Rosa had plenty of experience with promises of help coming to Buena Fé from different quarters. Much was captured or fixed to the center main part of town, with less attention to the town's periphery. Really, the concerns of residents and neighbors was not too far from the reality of local politics and concerns in many towns back in the States.

I learned more that day of the underlying resentment the townspeople bore against the Seguro Social nurse and the doctor at the SSC Dispensary, Dr. Sevilla. I have to confess that the resentment is not something I completely understood at first, but it did seem almost universal. There were political ramifications to it on the Cabildo, so I treaded very cautiously. I needed to be careful to avoid an over-identification with whatever aspect of the SSC dispensary is the fuel of the resentment. I also needed to steer clear of any connection with local politics, which often seems to be everywhere.

Anyway, that same Monday I gave a charla, a health talk, on boiling water to prevent worms, a common problem and issue here. The charla was in Nuevo Progreso, a nearby neighborhood, and about 40 or 50 people showed up. I spoke for about a half hour with the help of some visual aids I had made for that very purpose. Dr. Victor Lopez, a friend in this town who works in Don Guido's little clinic behind the pharmacy, then got up. He spoke for about 20 more minutes, augmenting and reinforcing what I had said into terms the people could appreciate better.

I learned from his contribution. I liked his examples and admonitions in practical terms.

He said, "You have enough money for 15 sucres of beer time after time, but you don't have enough for 15 sucres of greens or fruit? Believe me, people will tell you that the opposite of sickness is health, when you are not sick you must be healthy, right? Lie! Because although you may not feel sick, you may be getting sick in your insides because of your living habits. Good health is not just for rich people – it's especially for poor people because you need your health above all to work. And many rich people think they are healthy when they are not.

"If your child gets a bad case of worms, how much will it cost you to cure? About 200 sucres, maybe more, and I'll bet three fourths of the little children in this room have works right now. How much does one pound of decent meat cost? About 20 sucres, no mas. What makes more sense, 20 sucres or 200 sucres?"

I was really impressed with his style and with his passion, which was much more appealing to the local people. He communicated more on an emotional level, where I tended to be more fact oriented. I would try to take some pages from his book in talking more simply and directly with people.

Dr. Lopez was also pleased with himself. Afterwards he promised to help organize a health club to meet every Thursday night as a forum for knowledge transfer and adult education. He saw the need to provide the kids and their parents some practical life skills such as how to brush your teeth, how to wash your hands properly, etc.

All this was marvelous to me. Dr. Lopez had not really taken on these extracurricular activities before. I could see that the most important part of my job as a future volunteer might be to help him and others like him take on these tasks and challenges. They were not at all difficult for him, so it was just a motivational thing that I could ideally help cultivate. At least I hoped I'd be able to do that.

Some volunteers labor two years to try and find a counterpart, an Ecuadorean local who may be able to carry on the work of the Peace Corps Volunteers after the Volunteer has left. And here, maybe, I had developed a good candidate after only one week of practicum training. At least a start!

Tuesday was a repeat of Monday's pace, with a charla to offer and the fiesta of the Patron Virgin of Monserrati, which I attended and participated in. The children seemed to love it when I joined in the singing of the songs with them – it boosted their own enthusiasm and confidence. And this from a nice Jewish boy.

The town president complained about the lack of facilities in Buena Fé and commented that she hoped I would be an enormous help. I had been asking for signs of collaboration and cooperation, and she showed me maps and blueprints of Buena Fe. She promised me large wall-sized copies of the maps for me to use in planning a house-to-house health campaign.

In addition, she took me to a large meeting hall and promised me access to use the room. She would organize a Grand General Assembly to be called when I returned as a Volunteer in

December. She also offered the use of sound truck and personnel and transportation for my efforts to reach outlying precincts. This was immensely helpful, matched by other local people I had been able to line up to help with a lot of tasks. As well, she offered her authority and prestige for requests for aid from the government, all with little suggestion from me.

I felt pretty content and pleased with the way things were going. Everything seemed to be falling into place to enable me to start a multi-pronged public health campaign in Buena Fé starting in December. I felt that this would allow me to start off not only on the right foot, but with a bang. There was a risk of course in creating too high expectations.

Looking back, I thought at the time this was manageable. I was trying to avoid promising anything beyond what I thought I really could do. I was keen to start things from the beginning as a partnership with the local Buena Fé leaders and concerned citizens. This seemed to my post-Chicago consciousness to be the essence of successful local politics. Local politics and support would be key to whether I could be fully successful and effective as a U.S. Peace Corps Volunteer in a town the size of Buena Fe.

Of course, in many ways, I was so naïve. Whether I admitted it or not, I was fully caught in the "white savior" moment, in what Bill Easterly from the World Bank would refer to as the vision of the "white man's burden." I was sure I could swoop down with limited life experience and very limited training and save the day. I could overcome entrenched injustice with some grit and determination. I also realize now that this was probably an inevitable phase of learning I had to go through. I was, of course, a product of my time and circumstances.

As I wrote in my journal, I realized I had to explain myself and the context better. No one back home understood anything at all about a little country like Ecuador or even Latin American mores. I took it upon myself to offer some digressions in this regard, writing about the food, the politics, and other aspects of life there. I was doing it for the folks back home, but also for myself.

It was a way to think through and analyze some of the different socio-economic and cultural characteristics of the country I was living in. It helped me to better consider the meaning.

After two weeks of my Peace Corps field practicum, I was to get a chance to see a little bit more of the neighboring area. Particularly the dry and impoverished province of Manabí where my host family had largely originated from.

But after a week or two in the field, I also began to learn of the dropouts and resignations of many Peace Corps volunteer candidates. I was saddened to learn about these departures. I was going to miss the company and association with some of the friends I had made during and subsequently during Peace Corps training in Texas.

It served as a reminder for me about what I was about, what I was trying to accomplish as a Peace Corps Volunteer. I would be reminded how important to me that purpose was, despite whatever hardships I might endure. It was as if I had to lift a mirror to myself and wonder was I in fact still committed to moving forward, to the purpose of this commitment of service?

Friday afternoon I joined Guido on another of his frequent "great ideas." We were to go to Montecristi on a quick road trip for the fair. Every year the area near Montecristi in the dry neighboring coastal province of Manabí hosts an agricultural and farming fair. It's much like a U.S. state fair. It's held near where Guido's parents and family live. This gave him a perfect opportunity to show me off and show me his native province.

We went with Rosario's brother Otton who drove. Victor, a young man of 20 who was a neighbor, and Guido's son Martin also went. We left Buena Fé about 11 AM and stopped in Santo

Domingo de los Colorados for lunch. We then arrived in Portoviejo, Manabi province, about 4:30 in the afternoon.

I ran into an IETEL telephone company office to call the training center office in Quito. I wanted to find out the site locations of those volunteers in the Portoviejo area. Guido and I both wanted to stop by and visit while we were in the area. It was then that I got the bad news about the others.

"Well, okay Allan, Barbara is in La Pila and Nancy is in Sosote."

"What about the others from my group?", I asked.

"There have been some problems. The following volunteers have terminated and resigned. Let me get the list."

List? I wondered.

"Wait a minute. Okay, Irene, Virginia, Mary, Sabrina and Ed have all resigned."

Wow, that was terrible news. Irene and Virginia were both much older women, and I could understand their difficult problems at learning a new language at their age. Virginia was 62, a great nurse but she also was a very heavy smoker, probably not a good thing for a PCV and their health out in the wild.

Irene was older still, 71, and would have become among the oldest PCVs in the world, comparable to Jimmy Carter's mother Miz Lillian. She was a superb nurse from the hill country of Montana, who had almost managed to visit every country in the world with her late husband.

The situation with Ed I did not really understand. Ed spoke particularly good Spanish already when we arrived in Quito. Curiously, his language score didn't change at all during the first six weeks of language training and immersion. Mine rose from much lower to match his. I'm not sure what that suggests other than that I worked hard at my Spanish, but it was curious.

Ed had gone off to his site for his practicum as I had gone to my community in Buena Fe. He had gotten frustrated with his site because the people weren't showing any cooperation and I heard rumors that 'campo' life didn't agree with him. Living in the rural countryside, the 'campo', is difficult, and I was in an unusual situation of being in a small town. Most volunteer trainees were in villages or hamlets. Still, the difficulty didn't sound like my contemplative friend Ed. Anyway, I was going to find out.

Silvana, the secretary at ASDELA Training Center, told me that Ed hadn't left Ecuador quite yet, nor had Sabrina. Rumors were that Ed would try to find his own sort of job through the Ecuadorian education ministry in Quito. He really liked life in the capital. I resolved to head up to Quito early Wednesday to pick up my mail, follow-up with Ecuadorian officials from the Social Security Institute (IESS) main offices and try to find out what was up with Ed and Sabrina. I also wanted to know how Janet was doing.

In the meantime, I was in Portoviejo with Don Guido, only an hour or so from the Pacific beaches. I explained the situation to Don Guido, and he said we would try to visit the volunteers who were in the area tomorrow morning, Saturday. During the rest of the afternoon, we went out to his family's small finca, or small farm, outside of Portoviejo, where I met all of Guido's relations. Then we had dinner at the farm, which I ate with some trepidation. I was worried that they hadn't washed the vegetables carefully, or boiled the water for ten minutes, despite Guido's rapid assurances. These were from my experience no small concerns. Afterwards we went out to Montecristi near the world-famous beach at Manta.

Montecristi, for your information, is where they make the world-famous Panama hats. Panama hats were never made in Panama, but in Ecuador. They were called that because the Ecuadorians sold them to the French and the Americans during the digging of the Panama Canal.

There is also a fabulously beautiful, ornate and huge church dedicated to the Virgin of Montserrat, near Montecristi. Montserrat was where about 100 years ago the Virgin Mary had been seen in a vision by several people. It had since become a shrine area, much like Lourdes in France or Our Lady of Fatima in Portugal, and maybe a half dozen other sites in Latin America. The Virgin of Montserrat complex is – I understand – one of the richest around.

Don Guido had been insisting since I met him that he wasn't Catholic like most Ecuadorians. He had teasingly described me a Catholic missionary because I had been so impressed with the poor peoples' mass in Nuevo Progreso. Now here he turned Catholic so fast it turned my head. He wanted to stay for the Catholic mass, and I wasn't that interested, so I went outside the church into the huge plaza with Otton and Victor. Perhaps he was doing it for his son Martin, or perhaps there was something about Montserrat that made Catholics of many people.

I gather that Montecristi has a usual market day on Friday, but the influx of people because of the Feast of the Virgin made things into a bit of a zoo. It was great. The market was a corridor fifty feet wide running around all sides of a square, around the central plaza park in the middle of the town. There were merchants of every possible thing imaginable. Loudspeakers, shouts and music brought sound from every direction. The place had a considerably rowdier appeal that that of your usual American flea market.

We wandered about there for an hour or so, until Guido's mass ended, and then all of us headed back to Portoviejo, where we spent the night. During the night I began to feel terrible, and had trouble sleeping because of an upset stomach. It was the first grim signs of what was to be my worst case of food poisoning up till then. This wasn't Montezuma's revenge – this was Eloy Alfaro's revenge, just as I had feared. Things got even worse when I ate breakfast with Don Guido at his insistence the next morning – not a smart idea.

In the morning I stopped by the sites of La Pila and Sosote where volunteers Barbara and Nancy were living. Both were happy to see me again. I introduced them to Don Guido, and we all exchanged gossip on what was going on. Unfortunately, I had to talk in English with Barbara because her Spanish was poor, and I hoped she would pull things together after a week or so. Peace Corps probably wouldn't let her be sworn in as a PC Volunteer unless her language skills were adequate. At the looks of it two weeks in her village had not helped much.

Later in the day we got to the Harvest Festival – the Fiesta de la Cosecha – a sort of state fair managed by the CRM – the big Manabí development agency. The area around Puerto Loro where the festival was held is the part of Manabí that is ridiculously hot and very dry. The dust was incredible, but I stuck it out as much as I could. The farm and animal husbandry exhibits were interesting and quite informative. They demonstrated a professional approach by CRM to farm extension activities. They had received ample support and technical assistance from Peace Corps and other US government agencies.

The band music was fairly good, but I was beginning to hurt a lot inside again, and there wasn't a single damn toilet anywhere nearby. I wasn't about to let loose a flood of diarrhea in the bushes; besides, I stupidly had no toilet paper with me. In addition, the others were nowhere to be found. Don Guido was in the crowd somewhere, and Victor and Otton had taken the truck to the beach at Manta when I had told them I was in no condition to go with them. At least I had my gear with me.

I left word with some of Guido's friends to explain that I had to leave early and couldn't wait until 7 PM to leave for Portoviejo. I had to leave **now**. Ugh – feeling miserable, I hitched a ride into Portoviejo where on impulse and in desperation I hopped aboard the first bus heading east to Quevedo. That was a big mistake. I should have waited. The nice comfortable seat I thought I had turned out to be 3 nice uncomfortable seats. The driver kept stopping outside to pick up passengers, bags of oranges, chickens and even a couple of sheep.

There are many kinds of buses in Ecuador, and one of the most uncomfortable are what we lovingly and pejoratively call, the "monkey-buses." We call them monkey-buses because they seem to have been designed to fit people the size of monkeys. It is essentially is a low-lying flatbed truck. Part of a bus frame is welded or attached to it. many rows of bench-like seats open on both ends of each row for "easy" entry and egress, and of course all the road dust as well. There is a platform on the back and a platform on the roof, with not much of a protective rail. No seat belts here of course.

Even so, it seems like hundreds of people packed themselves onto these things. They were hanging from the sides and balancing from the roof, along with bags of ever-present fruit and produce going to market. A bunch of chickens and somehow even a few fatalistic sheep, their legs tied, were thrown upon the roof to 'baa baa baa' the whole trip.

There are also minibuses which are not much better than vans. They pack in double the permissible passenger contingent. The ice cream truck 'rapidos' fly up the highways like quick express busses. The big interprovincial buses and the stately Pullman coaches that ply the roads between Quito and Guayaquil were the safest of all. Supposedly. Needless to say, with such a choice of service, prices vary, and the monkey buses are pretty cheap, almost as cheap as walking.

Anyway, there I was, with a horrible feeling like my insides were about to rupture soon. I was crowded onto this monkey bus, going up the dirty and rocky road five hours to Quevedo. I was sure I was going to die. And death is not that distant a fear, as accidents in these things are all too common and they can easily careen off the sides of embankments. After 2 ½ hours of this torture, I stumbled off the bus into this restaurant pit stop, in a town we had stopped in, gasping dramatically to the owner "I am an American doctor, please can I use your bathroom???"

Yes, I knew I wasn't a doctor or even close. In my defense everybody was calling me 'Doctor Alonzo' in the towns I worked in since I was some sort of health worker. I was living with the family of 'Doctor Guido' also, wasn't I? I figured this was the quickest and easiest way to make haste for any available toilet or latrine. I was right. I got to the bathroom, got my pants down and my rear end pointed in the right direction. My rear promptly did a rendition of the Hiroshima Bomb with little encouragement needed. God, I thought, it would never end. Horrible simply horrible.

Afterwards the stench was so overpowering, I promptly vomited my guts up as well. I spent nearly a half hour in the bathroom. I got myself cleaned up and presentable and stumbled out of the bathroom feeling somewhat better somehow. I offered to give the owner 20 sucres for his trouble and mine. He refused to take it, and instead took me to a small store down the street where I was able to buy an antispasmodic medicine to minimize the cramps.

The monkey bus had of course left long ago, and I was stranded in this small town on the dirt and gravel road to Quevedo. Happily, another bus rumbled into the small town ten minutes later. It was one of the more modern big inter provincial buses with real cushioned seats. I sank into the last one left and went to sleep immediately.

I woke up fifteen minutes outside Quevedo. I was able to watch with pleasure as our big cruiser passed the monkey bus I had gotten off of 45 minutes earlier. We left our dust in its path. The final nice thing on the bus ride was that somehow, silently, the driver understood my situation, and never asked for the fare. When I got off, I offered to pay, but he refused to accept the money, and wished me well in Ecuador. I guess a sick gringo is not too hard to distinguish.

I survived, somehow. Rosario, distraught over what had happened, prepared for me some anise tea. It was something very soothing for the intestines. In their pharmacy downstairs I found some Lomotil, a lifesaver of an antispasmodic. I slept ten hours and this morning felt much better. Guido and the rest it turned out didn't get back to Buena Fé until 4 am, because they had stayed at the Harvest Festival until 10:30 pm. It was probably a good thing I had escaped when I did – I don't think I could have survived the trip back in the truck 11 hours later.

Monday was a complete disaster, one of those days you simply want to forget. I had left the day after 10 AM free of responsibilities in Buena Fé so as to be able to go up and visit Janet yesterday. Her new site is in Puerto Limon, outside of Santo Domingo. I thought I would be able to see both her and Doug, an older volunteer already here for over a year, the same day on one trip.

Santo Domingo is a quick, speedy one-hour bus ride north, and there are all sorts of buses and transports that go by many times an hour. Puerto Limon is another matter. You have to then take an open-sided monkey bus from Santo Domingo and go up a rock and dirt road. It was much like the infamous one between Portoviejo and Quevedo I had had so much pleasure with on Saturday afternoon. It was an hour through that kidney smasher to her town. You feel like the wheels must really be chipped stone square 'yabba dabba do' wheels banging on each rock rather than inflated pneumatics. I got there to this sleepy dry little town only to find that she wasn't there – she in fact had gone for the day to Quevedo, near my own site!

It was 1 PM, the next bus would be leaving for Santo Domingo at 2 PM, and she wasn't due back until 3 PM. With the scheduling necessary to get to Doug's site at Julio Moreno village, I didn't think I could wait around. I had wanted to meet with Doug to get his advice and experience on some classes I would be carrying out soon. I took the 2 PM bus back, enjoyed the punishing terror for another hour. I bothered the bus driver to stop the other bus headed up to Puerto Limon at 3 so I could see if Janet were on it coming back from the other direction. She wasn't. When we got back to the bus terminal depot in Santo Domingo, I stumbled into the café for some tea, determined to wait a half hour to see if she would come. I had really hoped to catch up with Janet, who could always make me laugh and vice versa.

Santo Domingo was cold that afternoon, but that didn't explain the bad chills I was getting. It finally got so bad I raced into the clutches of the depot bathroom, where I dropped another H-bomb. Really staggering this time, I got myself on a bus back to Buena Fé and back to the house around 5 pm.

I simply couldn't make it on to Julio Moreno. Chills, hot flashes, a bad fever and cramps in my stomach. To the dismay of my hosts, who thought I looked like Death itself, I refused antibiotics, preferring to load up on aspirin and anise tea. Ecuadorans have a horrible fascination with antibiotics. While I probably needed something stronger, I didn't know what sort of infection I had, and which antibiotic would be best. I preferred sticking with aspirin for the pain, went to sleep about 6 PM and slept until 7:30 am, having had to get up at 1 AM to pee.

The next day was somewhat better but only in part. The fever broke rapidly during the night, but the cramps continued periodically. It fouls up my concentration and makes it difficult for me to understand spoken Spanish. Tropical diseases and infections are not fun.

I wasn't in fact the only one poisoned. Last night apparently Guido ran a temperature and didn't sleep well either, waking up with really nasty swollen throat glands. Perhaps it was just a coincidence or perhaps we picked up similar bugs in Portoviejo. Both of us had temperatures for a while at 40 C, or 104 F. Rather warm. I'm hoping I can get some decent medicine from the Peace Corps nurse in Quito tomorrow. Meanwhile tonight I have to give a class on worms to this impoverished family. I don't want to, but I have to because I promised.

I am left now feeling a bit rueful of the graphic description of the intestinal upset I was going through. It is a little comical now in part, but it also presaged what would, in fact, prove to be years and years of stomach and intestinal distress. I often went to doctors or nurses and got prescriptions for one treatment or another, or I would self-prescribe myself based on experience.

Things would often get better for a time but then would come back to afflict me in later years. Perhaps at that time, what I was often dealing with were cases of essentially 'travelers' diarrhea.' But in time things would grow more complicated. For now, I viewed this ailment as simply one more hurdle that I would simply have to make my way over in terms of being able to move forward.

DIARY 29 NOVEMBER – 7 DECEMBER 1980

Well, the report and diagnosis are in. The Peace Corps nurses told me, while tut-tutting, that it was clear I suffered from amoebic dysentery. It is a common enough affliction here on the equator, the statement of which did not relieve my pain and dizziness in the Quito offices. I did get medication though (three times daily for 20 days), more Lomotil, a stern admonition to not drink alcohol and orders to rest and take it easy.

With the Lomotil helping to keep me alive, I flipflopped over the question of whether or not to return to my site that night. If I left it would be so that I could stagger into Simon Bolivar high school and talk to the kids as promised. Or I could stay in Quito and rest. Like a good PCV, despite the temptation, I chose the former. After a hysterical roller coaster ride on an 'aerotaxi' small express bus, I got back to my site in record time – only three hours.

The aerotaxi is another element from the amazing variety of Ecuadorian buses and transport. It is not a Jetson air-car, although it might as well be. It is a van that fits about 15 people. The one I traveled on was a bit more comfortable since only 10 people were on it. The cruising speed is about 100 mph with at least one wheel on the road at any time. When the driver has to do things like pass a gasoline tanker truck going around a sharp blind curve, he will usually accelerate to 120 mph. Why not? The speedometer goes up that far and more.

They are called aerotaxis because they spend most of the time in the air. They offer a hair-raising experience. Most of the passengers alternate screams in terror with horrible retching. And the fare is so much less than a ride at Disney. All Ecuadorian buses supply for free small plastic barf bags. This is good as there is always an ample demand, especially on the mountain to lowlands runs. But they are fast, and I wanted fast, and I was going fine on my Lomotil for now. Anyway, I beat the odds once again and got into Buena Fé with ample time to gasp my greetings and make it to the high school. Duty duty duty.

I spent an hour or so talking with the kids in their classes and was enthusiastically well received. I was happy I had not given in to the temptation of staying on in Quito.

The attitude of kids and teachers after these classes is as if I was a wise and benevolent sorcerer. It's an odd position to be in. We normally assume that the underdeveloped countries associate age with wisdom. I was obviously young. One advantage I seemed to have is that most people assumed I was 28 or 29. No one suspects my real age of just 21.

The entire week I labored under considerable handicap because of my illness. The nurses in Quito had diagnosed my condition on Wednesday as a case of amoebic dysentery. The prescribed drug of Metronidazol by Thursday had helped chase away the periodic fever of 104 F complete with severe chills I had enjoyed. Unfortunately, the cramps remained until Sunday. Although with a lessening force. And after fasting for three days I was able to start eating again. My illness wasn't a total loss - I had dropped quite a bit of weight I could afford to lose. The nurses had prescribed serious rest, but I couldn't stay in bed. I would become awfully familiar with this and other gastrointestinal drugs in time.

Anyway, with rather less than desirable patience I tried to keep my commitments to the health class in Trece de Abril Tuesday nights. It was also a poor barrio of Buena Fé and a similar class to that I had given Saturday afternoon in San Felipe. Both places filled with some very poor people. Both meetings went very well, and despite having different tones to start with, ended up concluding in a similar way.

The Trece de Abril class got started due to house to house visits with Don Guido and Dna Rosario my first week. I was astonished by the prevalence of parasites and Protein-Energy Malnutrition among the kids. Guido knew well Don Romero Povea, a short dark man with 10 kids. They were all malnourished to some degree.

Guido and Rosario suggested that he might host a health talk on boiled water and parasites for the whole community. He was happy to do so.

Tentatively scheduled for the following Tuesday night, I had to delay it to the second Tuesday due to timing problems. I decided to go through with it this time since I didn't want to disappoint the people of Trece de Abril twice in a row. My passenger amoebas were themselves still on a wild rampage.

Doing my best to disguise my gritted teeth, we had our charla. We motivated participants to create a barrio-wide Health and Wellbeing Committee. It would coordinate future health talks and public health campaign, much like what had been set up in Nuevo Progreso a week earlier. The people were motivated, and I was optimistic. Community leaders in Trece de Abril promised to fan out to other communities to push participation and interaction.

I got back to Quito again on Saturday night, and stayed with my Ecuadorian host family there. Sunday became a rare day of rest, for some personal down time, for writing, reading, and listening to music. During the following days at the ASDELA Training Center, I was reunited with my friends from the Peace Corps volunteer training group.

We all traded stories about our sites and experiences during our three-week practicums. We said goodbye to those Trainees who had made the decision to drop out, to leave the program and Ecuador for various reasons. Some people had problems communicating and learning the language. Some people had personal problems; others had issues adapting to the rural lifestyle cut off from modern society.

I had had no such real problems or challenges. In fact, I was almost a little embarrassed because I thought I was thriving. My own experiences had seemed among the richest and most satisfying of the group. I felt I was adapting quite well. Very few volunteers had already chosen to initiate projects and campaigns during the Practicum. Among those few who had, my activities seemed to be the most ambitious.

Was I kidding myself? I didn't think so – I felt I had been well-placed to hit the ground running. Perhaps I would have faced more challenges had I been in a small and isolated hamlet, as in the case of many other Volunteers. But in a town like the size of Buena Fe, and close to the city of Quevedo, I thought I had an easy time with fitting in. Except for the intestinal turmoil.

This week for all is a time of serious reflection. Early next week we will take our official State Department Foreign Service Institute (FSI) language exams. We need to give presentations on our perceived roles as volunteers to Peace Corps Ecuador staff. It was a bit intimidating. D-Day would be Swearing-In Day, December 12, 1980. That would be the culmination of our several months of training, and the official start of service.

6 December 1980: It's a lazy Saturday afternoon in Quito, a pause between binges for most of the city. This weekend, actually the period starting from last Wednesday night through tonight is Big Party Time in Quito. It is the celebration of the 445th anniversary of the founding of Quito. The partying was wild and bizarre last night, running until the early morning. At least two-thirds of the city is sleeping it off this afternoon to be able to resume the orgy of drinking and partying in high gear this evening.

What happens is simple: a massive, truly massive consumption of alcohol is involved. The Ecuadorians in a wild frenzy dance in the streets with almost total abandon. It is really an incredible thing to see. Last night, at a hundred intersections in all the neighborhoods of this normally staid highlands city, traffic was blocked off. Bandstands set up for local groups and musical bands, and the people danced for hours.

Of course, in a spirit meant to promote friendship and mutual respect between the United States and Ecuador, the Embassy, Marine staff and guards made a good effort to share in the patriotic festivities. This was despite an unexpected, bitter, petty and vindictive Tuna War the USA is imposing on Ecuador. Inside the Hotel Chalet Suiza, the Marines constructed a stage platform. At 8 PM the Marine Corps Band mounted the stage to belt out some favorites in honor of the local bacchanal holiday. This was not so much a local crowd but heavily inflected by expats.

The songs performed as favorites were golden oldies but from the American Bandstand – not an Ecuadorian one for sure. Bottles of champagne were brought out, and people danced in the street in front of the hotel. The people dancing were almost all expats. They included Americans, Britons and Germans. There was a sprinkling of local co-opted folks, particularly young Ecuadorian women.

Just off from them, about 300 people gathered in clumps and groups in a stony silence watching the gringo circus in the street. Those 300 people were all Ecuadorians, who mostly respectfully applauded after each song from the Marine Band. Otherwise they stood and stared with incredulous eyes at this grotesque example of Americans showing the Ecuadorians how to celebrate their fiesta. They weren't hostile at all, but I think they did not know quite what to make of it. Very peculiar.

The music wasn't bad – one of the Marine vocalists even did a passable rendition of George Benson's snappy "On Broadway." But I had problems with some of the visuals in the tableau before me. Middle aged crewcut Marine sergeants and young corporals dancing away with wives that looked like they belonged on a military base. Embassy personnel and various eclectic elements of the local American and German expat communities did their thing in a bizarre parody of an American Saturday night dance.

I have several times said in letters to people back home that I think I am happier now than I ever was back in the States. This is true, and the primary reason is due to the people. I have explained my enjoyment of the Ecuadorian people in the past, but I can also comment on the natures of my fellow PCVs here. As a rule, I have never encountered a more wholesome, down to earth, amiable and dedicated group of people anywhere else. Naturally, people are people, and everyone has unique characteristics, tendencies, or quirks. PCVs, while certainly not angels, are at their core good people, and this fact has made me very proud to be part of Peace Corps.

I feel especially close to the group of people in the Rural Health Program of Omnibus 34. We have been together since August 25th, some 3 ½ months, and the bonds between us have been very tight. This is probably something that naturally occurs. A group of people from different backgrounds are placed together in intensive exercises in unfamiliar locales. South Texas, Mexico, Miami, Quito. When I was recruited in Chicago, they advised me that the friends I made in Peace Corps would be my friends for the rest of my life. I see now that this is absolutely true.

The Peace Corps network and grapevine is very tight in this country. It is possible to visit almost any part of the country and find a PCV who would be willing to put you up for a night or two. With the sense of warmth and contentment that comes from such mutual support networks, there is also a bit of sadness and regret now. That's because a number of friends have already left Ecuador. They decided that either personal or language problems prevented them from committing themselves to two years.

This week more people will choose to leave. One is my girlfriend Janet, the nurse from Oregon. Janet and I became an item in training. It was a rebound relationship for her. But now Janet is moving to re-connect with an old boyfriend she left back home. He now is joining Peace Corps too. She is trying to leave Thursday on a complicated arrangement. She will meet up with her old boyfriend and try to join him in the next Omnibus group which would come to do training here in March through May 1981.

Janet wants to marry him and return back with him to Ecuador if she can and Peace Corps/Washington give their ok. This is all up in the air and she will have to try to work it out in Washington first. I've mixed feelings. I knew our relationship from the start was going to be relatively short lived. We've made the adjustment back as friends after some final canoodling at the ASDELA training center. But I will miss her and her off the wall sense of humor.

Other friends are leaving perhaps to return. Ed left last week because he didn't think in the end Peace Corps was really for him. He hopes to come back to Quito under other auspices in a few months to teach English or something. Perhaps he will. Others may also leave in the next week if they fail Monday and Tuesday's FSI language exam, which is an important hurdle for some. I will miss all dearly.

Fundamentally, Peace Corps is an expression of deeply held optimism. It is a belief in the indefatigable ability of men and women to transcend obstacles and build better, more meaningful lives. It is a fellowship that spreads throughout the globe. We are change agents, missionaries of progress, caring people who respect one another and one another's culture. I believe in Peace Corps and I believe in my fellow PCVs and I believe in our Ecuadorian partners.

Peace Corps Ecuador has had such a rich history over the years. It has been memorialized in some outstanding ways by genuinely great writers. Moritz Thomsen, who has been described by Paul Theroux and the Washington Post as one of America's great writers, probably wrote the definitive memoir "Living Poor," followed up by several more books over the decades, including

"The Farm on the River of Emeralds." They are gems. I regret that most books are out of print or not available on the Kindle, which is a shame.

I first read Thomsen five years after my own Peace Corps service. It resonated with me as an honest and authentic tale of the people, the country, and volunteer service. Peace Corps has no doubt changed from the 1960s, as it changed in recent decades from the 1980s. I am sure when it comes back to this Coronaverse world, it will return with other major changes. But I hope it will survive and come to have even greater meaning.

I suppose the Peace Corps, in its first decade or so, had gotten something of a bad rap. Think of the 1985 Tom Hanks film *Volunteers*. It unfairly mocked and exaggerated aspects of the Peace Corps of the early 1960s. Sargent Shriver said the film was "like spitting on the American flag."

"*Volunteers*" made fun of Peace Corps in Thailand, a pretty safe locale. Ecuador was also seen as one of the less threatening and more easygoing places. It wasn't hard to enjoy yourself in a fairly relaxed lifestyle.

Still, Peace Corps Ecuador had its dangers. During my time there, we heard stories from time to time of female volunteers being sexually assaulted. I knew personally of several cases, including two rapes. Peace Corps senior management globally would not take seriously seriously the dangers for single Peace Corps women for far too many years.

Peace Corps country staff were not always as diligent or prepared in creating and supervising programs with clear objectives. I believe our Ecuador health program staff were more committed to professional program oversight than some of the other technical programs.

Our great Ecuadorian health program managers, Martha Desrosiers N.P. and then Dr. Miguel Artola, told us "Cuerpo de Paz no Cuerpo de Paseo." Cuerpo de Paz was Peace Corps in Spanish; Cuerpo de Paseo was a similar sounding derogatory name meaning more or less "Goofing-Off Corps". It was an admonition to take our volunteer assignments seriously. We were to dedicate ourselves to helping the communities we were serving while enjoying ourselves on the occasional breaks.

As a rural public health volunteer, much of my work was centered around persuasion, promotion, and promise. I was a health promoter, trying to find and promote different healthy behaviors. If adopted, these behaviors should help improve the nutrition, health, and well-being of the families I was living with.

I would promise people that if they did these things, and made the changes in their diets, practices and hygiene habits of handwashing, boiling water for drinking, they would see improvements in their daily lives. I would try to persuade them that better living didn't require the wealth of the 'patron.' It was within their reach through the changes they could introduce. In reality, nothing is harder than behavior change. For them, for you, for me.

I would persuade them that life was not a matter for fatalism or resignation. They could change the lives led by parents and grandparents. They were empowered to undertake change. I didn't call it that at the time, but I was all about being a change agent, pushing and promoting change across a host of different lifestyle choices.

Was I a plausible vehicle for this sort of promotion? Was I a convincing preacher for the promise of a better life? Hardly, in hindsight. Yet people still largely listened to me.

As I reflect back decades in perspective, I find it all rather remarkable that the people of Buena Fé and the different little precincts and hamlets I visited, rather uncomplaining, put up with this young pushy gringo. This guy had been plopped into their midst and was pushing for change in all sorts of ways. And of course, not only me but the 150 or more volunteers on average that were in Ecuador at any one time pushing to varying degrees similar sorts of messages.

My experiences as a Peace Corps Volunteer were amazingly rich, varied, and full of diversity and opportunity for growth and development. I worked hard and tried to look for ways to make a change and an impact in my interactions with Ecuadorians. If I add up my two years, I learned so much more than I managed to teach others. This is the truth of Peace Corps service distilled down – even if you are committed to give and serve you get and receive so much more back.

As a Volunteer I had "office hours" in the two local clinics of Social Security and the Ministry of Health in Buena Fe, where I might be reached. The medical and nursing staff seemed to initially expect me to try to stay in each clinic a certain number of hours each day. But within a number of weeks I realized that I was likely to be far more effective if I could actually work as a true extensionist. I had to go out and visit with people and finding them out in the community rather than waiting for them to come to the clinic. The reaction to this was mixed.

Some of the official government staff, who were often on rotation for a year or so in each of the clinics, went along with this idea in a positive way. Others, not so much. I enlisted the help of my Peace Corps program manager, on one or the other of Martha's initial monthly visits to the community. She helped promote this understanding of an extensionist role among my official counterparts. She encouraged me to offer or suggest that I invite the doctor or nurse to join me on these community and home visits. This worked for maybe a month. I soon came to realize that for many Ecuadorian government health counterparts, the theory of community outreach and extension was one thing. The practice was another.

Inevitably the pull of the four walls of the health post or clinic would assert itself. They would feel that they had to be found inside the building and be reachable in case of an emergency or need from patients. This was a contradiction I came to appreciate more and more over time. How do you balance health curative and clinical care (even to the degree they were able to address any of it) with the esoterism of health prevention? The government health ministry gave a lot of lip service to health promotion and extension. Sadly, there were plenty of practical reasons that undermine anyone doing it for a substantial amount of time.

Day to day, week to week, month to month, I would offer my "curriculum" of basic health "charlas" or talks. I would draw and add pictures and visuals to different rolls of oaktag or to newsprint sheets on a rudimentary flipchart. Once I got into my stride, my typical week might include anywhere from ten to twelve charlas in different schools or community meetings. I would try to conduct at least three or four home visits a day. Each visit might be quick. Or it might be a half hour to an hour long to see how a given family was doing and to get a sense of what sort of extra push they might need.

There were successes and there were failures in objective terms. From time to time I would be greeted with surprises during home or community visits. One family or another, proud to show off how they had adopted some ideas that I had suggested, perhaps made them their own, and had seen some benefit from it. There were also plenty of times when however polite they would treat me, change was too hard.

Once a month, all the health volunteers in the district would get together for a half-day. We would report on what we were doing and learn from each other how to handle problems that would come up. Martha would join us for those meetings every other month or so, driving down from Quito. We would then have lunch at some local "chifa" or other cheap restaurant.

Sometimes we would schedule visits to each other's sites, so we could help each other in one or another activity. We would schedule a day or two of some down time with other Americans. We would pick up on the latest gossip at that time, such as who had dropped out, or what was the news on someone's boyfriend or girlfriend. Twice a year, we got together in Quito or some other location for in-service training to learn new skills or improve in other ways. Again, each time it was a matter of finding out about more desertion and dropouts. It was surprising and hard to understand initially by me. But I soon realized that I really was a lucky one. So close to a small city like Quevedo, with larger restaurants, a movie theatre, and even an Olympic-size municipal swimming pool, I had easy access to the occasional distractions.

Many of my Peace Corps Volunteer peers lived in hamlets and villages that might or might not be near a serviceable road. In some cases, you had to walk in or ever ride a horse from the nearest gravel secondary road. In such circumstances, it was far easier to feel cut off from a social and cultural support system, to feel overly isolated and lonely.

To be sure, some people thrived in those environments and actively sought them out. They wanted to be cut off from their past lives and feel completely immersed in the new lives they adopted. But not everybody was up for that. Many, in fact, probably would have benefitted from some sort of system for closer contact from the Peace Corps office in Quito or their fellow volunteers. However, this was not usually possible.

I wrote a lot about the Montes family and remember them to this day. Dear Don Guido passed away suddenly from a heart attack a few years ago, sadly followed far too soon by his son Martin. Remarkably, in the last several years, first, other children from that family and then the parents reached out to me on Facebook. They re-established contact after decades, reflecting the long-lasting connections from my service.

There were also the Zambranos, Rafael, Eliecer, Patricio, Patricia, and others. A large family with lots of kids and cousins, they lived across the street from the Montes family, and had a small restaurant of sorts downstairs from their cinder block house.

Rafael was close to my age and was one of several points of entry to the youth and the community. He helped make my volunteer service easier, as a friend, buddy and advocate. He was a teacher to understand some of the challenges and drivers facing young Ecuadorians. With Rafael's help, I contacted folks in IEOS, the Ecuadorian Institute of Sanitary Works. This was to find ways to identify and encourage progress on water and latrine projects.

About a year into my service, Rafael got it into his head that he wanted to travel to New York and see something of that city and find work there. My old high school girlfriend, Karen, ended up helping to sponsor him. With her help back in New York as well as some distant cousins he had in Flushing Queens, he ended up travelling to New York and finding work. He bussed and waited tables and helped to wash dishes. I think he was able to eventually save close to $10,000 from his undocumented work forays. He returned to Ecuador with savings to invest in a business.

While Rafael was in New York, I got to know his crazy, comical but soulful younger brother Eliecer and the Zambrano cousins. I would go and pass time, usually checking in with them each day. Interactions with them and their friends were a great way for me to improve my Spanish. I learned more and more of the "jerga" or slang so typical of Ecuadorian youth.

Patricia flirted with me at times, and I lightly flirted back, but I was reluctant to get involved in a situation I might come to regret in that small town. Patricia was really lovely, but I was a bit turned off by her missing teeth and metal-repaired ones. This was something not uncommon from the local dental handiwork.

As I have mentioned, I was lucky as a volunteer to live in a small town that was so easily accessible to cities to the north and south. The main coastal highway between Quito and Guayaquil ran right through the town then. It provided transport literally every five minutes.

Santo Domingo de los Colorados was a large regional farm and market center about 60 kms north. There was a former Peace Corps office in Santo Domingo which had been closed by Peace Corps. But it was informally maintained by the many volunteers in the area as a useful resource

center and crash pad. A volunteer could spend the night in a sleeping bag and foam cushion rather than pay for a hotel room. Sometimes four or more shared a room.

Doug showed me the ropes there. He introduced me to fellow volunteers Neil and Lenny, who worked in different communities with the Ministry of Agriculture and Livestock. They provided me great contacts and resources for seed and other resources for about a dozen school vegetable gardens I eventually cajoled local Buena Fé teachers, parents and students to undertake. Sometimes admittedly those visits with other MAG volunteers would lead to all sorts of escapades, including the discovery of dynamite and rotten carcasses untended by local farmers.

The province of Esmeraldas, to the northwest of Quito, lay on the northern coast of the country. It was hot, humid and a bit sultry. It had some great beaches further up the coast. It also had a population with a high percentage of people of African descent. As mentioned earlier, the local belief was that many of the people were descended from runaway enslaved people. As well as those that had survived from shipwrecks carrying enslaved cargo.

Being near the road allowed for some extracurricular adventures and occasional flings in Esmeraldas. I got involved with Nancy, an agriculture volunteer from Chicago. She was a Black Volunteer who lived in Quininde, a regional center on the road between Santo Domingo and Esmeraldas. We dated in the latter half of my first year, and it gave us a fun outlet and release from loneliness. Yet it also contributed to an unexpected intercultural incident and put us briefly at risk of being kicked out as volunteers.

After about nine months on site, a group of us were invited to an in-service training outside of Quito. It was at a training center in a neighboring highlands valley. We were there for a week or so. Looking for some exercise and diversion, Nancy and I noticed there was a municipal pool with thermal baths up the street from the training center. Thermal baths were always a treat up in the highlands of the country. The air temperature was usually quite a bit cooler and with thinner air then the coastal part of the country.

One early morning Nancy and I and a few others snuck out before the classes to swim a bit in the pool. There were maybe three or four others in the pool, including one young light-skinned Ecuadorian couple. Nancy and I lounged for a bit in the pool in our bathing suits and hugged each other from time to time, exchanging some gentle kisses. We didn't realize that one Ecuadorian male in the pool suddenly left in a huff. He returned in short order with a ruddy, Indian-looking local police officer. The police officer came over to us and ordered us out of the pool.

We looked up surprised, not knowing what was happening. "Get out, get out, gringos!" The Ecuadorian guy in the pool yelled at us, in a very hostile way, difficult to assimilate in the early morning hours. We had no idea what we had done, nor why we were being chased out of the pool. We soon realized that the uniformed police officer was not yet done. "Get dressed, you are under arrest."

We were stunned. Arrested?

"What for? Under what charge and whose authority? We are Americans, we are Peace Corps Volunteers."

The police officer said, "Doesn't matter. The colonel told us to do it. You are under arrest."

What? We were shocked. We'd been flirty and hugged but nothing out of the ordinary.

Nancy, who was far more street-smart than me, came to her senses first. "It's racism pure and simple. It's because we kissed, Alonzo. The Colonel doesn't like to see that a White man and Black woman kiss; I am sure that is it."

We asked the other two volunteers who were with us to go get help and let the training center facilitators know what was happening. We tried to ask the colonel in the pool with his girlfriend or wife to stop the unjust act.

He ignored us, and said with his back turned, "Imperialistas Americanos, they think they can come here and do whatever they like."

Meanwhile, the police officer motioned us to get dressed. We complied, as police reinforcements were coming to the pool by that time. We asked to go back to the training center where the other volunteers were, but they didn't let us.

We were taken in a police car, first to the small district substation. Then the local lieutenant said, "Not here, to Quito, the headquarters there, orders of the colonel." We realized that this Ecuadorian in the pool must have been, indeed, someone high-ranking, high-status, and clearly with a strong current of anti-Americanism.

We were taken an hour or so away to the Quito lockup, and then things got even scarier. Nancy and I were separated, and she went off to the separate women's wing. I found myself wide-eyed in the main lockup in a large holding cell with about 20 or so arrested and detained people, the only foreigner in the group. I was dressed in green fatigue cargo pants and a pullover, with some military looking hiking boots.

After a few hours, I was befriended by Manuel, this skinny dark looking guy who told me he was from La Tola. La Tola was in the northern part of Esmeraldas province at the mouth of all these mangrove rivers and streams coming out to the Pacific Ocean. I told him my girlfriend lived in Esmeraldas Province, but in Quininde.

He asked, "Are you American?" I nodded.

"People don't like Americans. OK, I am going to let people know that you are really Colombian, one of the rebels there from across the border. Your pants and boots look military. You are big, and they are afraid of Colombians. You have to protect yourself. Stay alert."

It scared the shit out of me. The others in the cell didn't look particularly hostile but not particularly welcoming either.

Manuel continued, "You know everyone can tell you are a foreigner by the way you are dressed. But most people won't think American since you are not blond like a gringo, but you have an accent so they will guess you are Colombian. They are the foreigners most people first think of."

As the hours droned on, I was called out and asked to identify myself. I didn't have my passport or other ID on me, but I gave the Peace Corps phone number in Quito. I was sent back into the cell. More hours droned on. Soon it began to get dark.

The cell had a bunch of metal bunk beds with very thin foam cushions on them. No blankets, and I was cold. In the highlands of Quito, it gets chilly after the sun sets. They brought metal cups with some tea and bread. The food looked disgusting and I didn't eat it. Manuel had told me to take the upper bunk above his, and I did.

An eternity passed, and then the lights went out. After a bit I heard a noise of someone shaking the metal of the bunk beds, climbing up. Manuel beneath me grabbed the stranger and threw him to the ground, letting loose a bunch of curses in a liquid flow of Spanish I could barely follow. He then reached up and passed something to my hand. I felt the sharpness and realized it was a type of homemade shiv. I resolved to stay awake even though I had been drifting asleep. There were no more interruptions or attempts by strangers to get near me.

At sunrise, I saw Manuel with some fresh blood and bruises. I thanked him for helping me; he was a total stranger, but he had for some reason befriended me and protected me. "You're ok gringo, un pendejo but ok." I was lucky, and unhurt. In another half hour in the early morning light I was called outside the cell to meet someone.

It proved to be Michael Hirsh, the Peace Corps program and training officer and the office's number two.

"Well Mr. Wind, you have done it this time."

"Where's Nancy?" I asked. "Is she ok?"

He nodded. "She is already out in the car. We will get you out in a couple minutes."

Within a few more minutes, we were walking out of the Quito Jail, a bit up the slope of the volcano Pichincha. Michael and Silvana, a female Ecuadorian Peace Corps staff member, were driving us back to the Peace Corps offices.

Our belongings had already been recovered from the training center. I was worried we were going to be kicked out. I asked Nancy how she had been passing the day and night in the jail. Had she been cold or threatened?

Nancy was very relaxed and calm, "Oh no, the women were all very supportive, everyone helping each other, they gave me two blankets and a pillow. Everyone was very friendly." Quite a bit different from my experience!

Luckily, Mike was in an understanding mood. "Well you two, that is probably a first for Peace Corps in a long while here." We struggled to explain. He nodded, "Well you know this colonel doesn't like Americans and he is not alone. The idea of a white man and Black woman kissing was annoying to him. He used his pull to throw his weight around and embarrass us. I found out about it in the mid-afternoon, but I couldn't do anything about it until the next morning, today."

Mike looked at us.

"You know Quiteños can be quite conservative in their mores compared to Costeños. You can't do things in public here that you can on the Coast. We are not going to kick you out, but you can each head back to your sites and learn lessons from this experience."

It was a sobering reminder of some realities in Ecuador. My experience with Ecuadorians had almost always been positive and rewarding. But there was a certain segment that were anti-American in part because of the Tuna War between the US and Ecuador that had started in the Carter administration and worsened under Reagan.

The light-skinned, more European-looking colonel had easily manipulated and pushed around the lower caste, ruddy indigenous-looking police officers. It was an open expression of racism and white supremacy.

Luckily, Mike Hirsh, with the influence of the American Embassy, had been able to eventually bail us out. But only after we had been punished as symbolic examples for a certain extent. And certainly, my experience in the Quito lockup could have been even more ugly if not for the fortuitous help from Manuel.

Mike would prove to be a kind and generous mentor for many years later. I would see him again in other countries across Latin America, and we remain in touch even to this day.

My relationship with Nancy did not last that much longer, perhaps in part because of this mishap. We had fun together, but she was a long distance away. It was not easy for me to visit with any frequency or to coordinate any joint travel to Quito again. And as it turned out, a quite different relationship was about to appear from out of the blue.

I traveled to Santo Domingo a few weeks later to visit the site where Doug was. He had been dating Katie, another volunteer in his group, who worked in special education. Doug had arrived in Quito about eight months before me, so he was already looking to the end of his volunteer service in a few months. Doug had studied at Colgate. As it turned out, a former classmate and friend of his from Colgate, Katherine, was visiting him from the States and staying with Katie as well. Doug wanted to introduce me to his friend.

I got to Doug's house and walked in the door, and stopped in my tracks. It's hard to explain what happened. I locked eyes with this American woman with strawberry blonde hair in Doug's house and time stopped, apparently for both of us. She had a quick intake of breath and gasped. I inhaled quickly also and held my breath. Doug, who looked up and watched both of us, said it was like a lightning bolt flew between us. I caught myself and stammered hello. Katherine smiled and laughed to break the tension. It was like nothing I had experienced before.

Katherine and I fulfilled the niceties of saying hello and continuing the conversation with the folks in Doug's house. But in a few moments, we both stepped outside and spoke with each other. It had been like we were both reconnecting from some past life, although we had never met before.

Within moments, there was instant rapport and intimacy. We began to hold hands and talk with each other to learn who the other was and where they had come from this time around. I do not believe in physical reincarnation, but it was like we had met and known each other before. Within an hour or so, we both resolved we had to meet again.

Katherine was deeply spiritual and a Quaker, just as Kat in Chicago had been. She had studied ethnobotany and anthropology and was from outside San Diego California. She was profoundly brilliant yet modest and unassuming. She had even just received the Macarthur Prize – the so-called 'genius grant.'

She had a radiant face with plenty of freckles. I was entranced. Katherine planned to visit Doug and Ecuador for a couple of weeks. During November and December, she would then go south to visit other countries. Eventually, she planned to go to southern Chile.

She asked, "Are you planning to travel for the upcoming holidays? Could we meet up?"

I had thought I would take my three-week vacation at yearend and travel south to the other Andean countries of Peru and perhaps Bolivia. I definitely wanted to see her again.

We made notional arrangements to try to meet in Cusco, the old Inca imperial capital in the southern Peruvian highlands, in late December. She gave me approximate dates. We would try to send messages or local telegrams to the general post office to see how we could manage to meet up with each other.

This was not an easy proposition. In 1982, there were no cell phones or email. One of the fastest ways to send messages was by local telegram. It was not always reliable, particularly for someone without a fixed address or telephone. It would require some luck to cross paths and find each other, but we had confidence it would happen.

In December I took holiday, coordinating with the Peace Corps office in Quito. I had saved a bit of money from my monthly volunteer allowances. By travelling overland through the cheapest means possible, and staying at cheap hotels and pensions, I could make it last for quite a bit. I left Quevedo first for Guayaquil and then down to the border, crossing over to Peru. I stopped in a few towns along the way for a day or so then made it to Lima.

Lima in 1981 seemed grim, grey and even Stalinesque in its architecture. Some places retained deteriorated Colonial fixtures and structures. The sky was overcast gray with a fog rolling in from the coast. I stayed in the suburb of Miraflores, which was closest to the ocean, and had a welcome number of places to crash for the itinerant backpacker. I made friends along the way and found interesting places to visit. I went to see the 'huacas' of Lima, some ancient pyramids buried over that were still being excavated to some degree.

A couple days later I hopped on an overnight Pullman bus heading over 1000 kms south from Lima to Arequipa. I was eager to leave Lima and see the city that I had read so much about, and then catch up further south to Cusco and Katherine.

I arrived in Arequipa in the early morning and went walking about. Arequipa was called the white city. It was still mostly built with this white volcanic stone called sillar from the beautiful volcanic cone El Misti which loomed over the city.

I went to the Plaza de Armas, the city's main central square. I thought about walking to the Convent of San Francisco, one of the recognized treasures in this gorgeous, bright city. All of a sudden, I felt a tingling and an urge to go around the next corner into a shop with postcards on a revolving stand outside. Who should I discover there but Katherine?

How can one explain these types of circumstances? We were supposed to try to meet in Cusco, still over 300 miles away, perhaps eight to ten hours by bus. I was in the southern valley lands of Arequipa at 7500 feet altitude, Cusco was up in the mountain highlands at over 11000 feet. Yet amazingly I had felt drawn like a magnet. We kissed, and it was truly magical. It felt entirely natural that we would come together in this way.

We spent the next ten days together. We visited different Incan sites and holy places across southern Peru, including the extraordinary Macchu Picchu and the Sacred Valley. We moved south to Puno and Lake Titicaca, visiting the floating islands of the Urus. We then crossed over to Bolivia from Copacabana and went to La Paz.

Katherine and I shared a room and soon more. Being together was joyous, fulfilling and elevating on so many levels. We seemed such opposites. I was of course the overweight, Jewfro jaded New Yorker, though I had lost a bit of weight in my first year as a PCV. She was a freckled southern California strawberry blonde who spoke softly about spiritual gifts, Society of Friends mystical understandings of the 'peaceable kingdom' and the purpose of prayer.

In this of course she evoked a bit of Kat, who had also been a Quaker from a long line of philosophers and spiritual teachers. Perhaps I was already primed by that experience and drawn to that type of person.

Our time was incredibly energizing, and I felt wholly renewed by this precious soul. After the two weeks, it came time for us to part. Katherine was determined to head south to look for ways to share her skills with the Mapuche and Puehuenche people of southern Chile. Perhaps I could join her there.

I hesitated. I was obligated to return to Ecuador to finish my Peace Corps service, so staying together at that point was not to be. We met up, though, in La Paz with Chris, another friend of hers from Colgate. Chris was heading to Arica, Chile. He was a young aspiring journalist; he had already documented American political and military interventions in several countries, including Gulf-Western corporate misbehavior in the Dominican Republic.

Chris wanted to document the actions of the Pinochet dictatorship, which had been in power for ten years. We would go with him to Arica by train. We would cross the altiplano and the high Atacama Desert and descend into what once had been a Peruvian settlement on the coast. It and other vast territories once claimed by Peru and Bolivia had been conquered decisively by Chile in the War of the Pacific in the 1880s.

I will never forget that train ride on several different levels. First, I was saying goodbye to Katherine and did not know if or when we would next meet. I had resolved, at the very least, to head south to join her in Chile after my Peace Corps close of service in December 1982, but would that still happen? Second, La Paz is already at a high altitude of 12000 feet. The train to Arica, a relic of the postwar treaties with Chile and Peru, rose up to 15000 feet on the border. It was quite the train ride out of La Paz, with many switchbacks. But third was the experience of getting to the border with Chile.

We got to the border in the middle of the night, and we were forced to stumble off the train in the cold to show our passports to the Chilean authorities. They opened my passport, looked at me, and asked in a surly Spanish, "Religion?" I answered, "Jewish." The border guard sneered, "Heil Hitler" making a fascist salute before proceeding to stamp my entry visa. I wanted to kill the guy, but Chris held me back.

Chris had told us on the ride about the right-wing extremism of the Chilean authorities and military police. He reminded me about the open secret of postwar Nazi infiltration. Far too many had escaped Europe to Chile, Argentina, Paraguay, and their respective militaries. And here it was demonstrated right in front of me by one of Pinochet's low-ranking stooges. I was disgusted and angry but looked away at the border guard.

We got into Arica without further incident. Katherine and I spent one more night together, discussing the world, universe, and everything between. The next day we separated, with plans to reunite hopefully the following year one way or another.

A new and challenging opportunity arose in my second year of Peace Corps service. One of the doctors who was initially working at the Buena Fé Ministry of Health subcenter, Dr. Guido Perez, took a liking to my work. He made it a point to introduce me to Dr. Luís Triviño, the cantonal head of health and the director of the main Quevedo hospital. He carried out a supervisory visit to the subcenter.

Dr. Triviño asked me if I was interested in taking my work to another level. I said sure, I would be happy to help. He then asked me to visit the hospital with Dr. Guido (not to confuse with Guido Montes the Buena Fé pharmacy owner curandero!) I went later in the week, meeting Dr. Triviño in his offices. He invited me to walk around and visit the hospital and to see the different sections and offices they had. One big gap was in health education and outreach.

Dr. Triviño invited me to come to Quevedo, and to help the hospital build up a capacity across the entire canton. I could continue to help the health sub center in Buena Fe. He wanted to also use what he saw as my talents and capacity to bring volunteer support to a wider scale. I shared the news with our Peace Corps program manager Martha. She rejected the idea, seeing it as a volunteer leaving their original site without cause.

I thought matters would stay at that, but Dr. Triviño was persistent. He stopped by the Peace Corps offices in Quito. He urged Martha to support an official government request from the Ministry of Health. Dr. Triviño would turn out in time to have a great deal of influence within the MOH. In fact, six months later Vice President Osvaldo Hurtado succeeded Jaime Roldós as President of Ecuador after a tragic plane crash. Luis Triviño was named Health Minister in a new Cabinet.

In Quevedo, Dr. Guido and I began to go out and meet with health staff in different facilities. We also carried out health education trainer of trainer classes in the hospital. We looked for ways to further expand a public health reach for the wider population. I got the idea for a radio health program, modeled on a radio education experience I had read about.

The University of Massachusetts Amherst had developed a successful radio literacy program. They partnered with the Bishop of Riobamba, Monsignor Leonidas Proaño. They were influenced by the revolutionary liberation theology teachings of

Paulo Freire. I would encounter his teachings over and over in my career in Latin America.

We met with the owner of RADIO REY, the largest radio station in Quevedo. They had a broadcast output of 50,000 watts which allowed them to broadcast over a large portion of the entire country. The radio manager was enthusiastic and supportive. I developed an hour-long weekly magazine type format radio program with Dr. Guido. We mixed local music with radio health messages, interviews with local doctors and nurses, and some attempts at humor.

While I had not planned to be a speaker on the show, I was encouraged to do so by the doctors and nurses at the hospital. They said that having a 'gringo' speaking accented Spanish on the radio would capture more attention from the listeners. It would add "credibility" to the messaging. So I did, little realizing that this would bring more consternation to the Peace Corps Country Director and management in Quito!

The show became famous among the many listeners. The radio station got great feedback from listeners. They heard it as innovative and distinct from what they could hear on other radio stations. We followed Health Ministry and WHO policy on any guidance or recommendations we said on the air. We began to get letters from listeners asking questions which I would field to the hospital medical staff, particularly Dr. Guido. It was a big success on that side, reaching a regular listenership at least in the hundreds of thousands.

However, the Peace Corps Country Director blew a gasket. Who was this American voice now appearing on Ecuadorian radio? Was this going to cause an incident with the Ecuadorian government? What was I doing instigating such a high-visibility program? Had this been cleared? I had to turn to Mike Hirsh once again, his deputy, and Martha, my program manager, for cover.

Mike was my advocate, my defender, and he once again saved my butt, as he had done after the Quito jail incident a few months before. Mike would end up becoming a true mentor and friend, who my family and I would meet repeatedly in different countries over the years.

My father back in New York took a sudden turn for the worse in August 1982, a few months before my close of service (COS). My mother told me he had been hospitalized at the Veterans Administration Hospital near Bay Ridge in Brooklyn. His doctor was uncertain if he would make it. My father had been a smoker and a drinker for many years, and though he had quit the damage was done.

He had worked for twenty years as a bartender. At that time, this meant working, as a matter of course, in a heavy smoking environment with a huge amount of secondhand smoke. He had developed colitis and then an aggressive emphysema over time, and it had gotten worse. My sister and I would learn only recently and unexpectedly that he had not only suffered ulcerative colitis but had also been diagnosed with colon cancer. My parents never told us this; I wished I had learned it years ago when I faced my own health challenges.

Luckily, the Peace Corps has a provision for emergency visitation leave under those circumstances. I flew back to New York and spent the next several weeks visiting him in the hospital. It was tough and painful to see him that way, all drawn and gaunt, and having to rely often on oxygen to breathe.

My father's doctor was sympathetic and compassionate. Dr. Finch was English, had red hair and a ponytail, and was married to a Black American woman. He stood out among the VA medical staff. Both my father and mother adored him, and Dr. Finch tried everything he could to make my dad more comfortable.

My dad was able to come back home to my parents' house for long weekends using a portable oxygen tank but then had to return to the hospital for better care. Sitting with my father was, at times, depressing. He really didn't understand me or my sister. Talking to him at times reinforced the distance that lay between us.

We had never been close; he was an emotionally distant father for both of us. He was puzzled and confused by his children as well as the hand life had dealt him. I could count on less than one hand his moments of enthusiasm for either of us. He did not know how to show paternal pride or support to either of us. I did not realize at the time how mean he had been to my sister after I left for the University of Chicago, only learning of it later from her.

Somewhat out of character, he told me he was proud of me and of my service in the Peace Corps. He seemed at times confused and viewed it as some sort of military service obligation. As I mentioned earlier, he himself had served in the Coast Guard during World War II and then in the Merchant Marine for some years before marrying my mother. National Service was validating and important in his eyes, even Peace Corps service.

I didn't waste any breath trying to explain Peace Corps better. I was relieved on some level that at least he was proud and did not make light of it. I also spent a lot of time with my sister and mother. I had been away from home not only during the two years of Peace Corps training and service but for much of my four years at the University of Chicago.

After nearly a month, it seemed that things were a bit less acute, and my dad was out of immediate danger. He had more or less stabilized and was able to return home for longer stretches. It was time for me to return to Ecuador and decide on a path forward. We made our goodbyes and I flew back to Quito and traveled to my site.

I had only about three more months left of my two-year service. But I was in no rush to return to the States. Dr. Triviño asked if I could stay on for another year in Quevedo. He asked me to help the canton build up a health education and prevention program. I liked the idea.

While Peace Corps service was a two-year commitment, there were a few options to propose a third-year extension of service. It wasn't routinely approved or encouraged. In my case, Ned Benner, the Peace Corps Country Director, quickly clarified his feelings. He sent a clear and negative message of "NFW;" for better or worse, he was not interested in my staying in whatever the interest of the host country counterpart was. My 'Question Authority' attitude at times had not left me in his good graces, despite Mike Hirsh's understanding.

The Peace Corps reaction perplexed and left me a bit disappointed. I considered my other options. I had originally joined the Peace Corps with the idea of completing my service and then returning to the USA for a career in health policy and politics. But I had lost any immediate interest in that.

I realized then, reinforced by the sudden visit home to see my dad, that I felt a growing sense of belonging and vocation in what I was doing in Ecuador. I sensed I had a knack for working in community development with people. I examined other opportunities for service in a different direction. I learned a bit about a program in Israel that was Peace Corps-like. It brought together American Jews and Israeli Arabs in Haifa to work together as teams in community peacebuilding. That was also appealing to me, but I wanted first to exhaust what possibilities might exist in Ecuador and Latin America.

Around that time, I received my first and only visitor from the States. Kat, my former girlfriend from college finished school and came to Ecuador. She had always impressed me with her deep commitment to social justice and her Quaker-infused spirituality. It was balanced by a light and cheerful sense of self-deprecating humor. Her ever-

present straight-haired ponytails would dance when she laughed. She spent a week with me in Quevedo, and then used Quevedo as a base to visit other parts of Ecuador.

While finishing school after I left, Kat had gotten involved for a time with an Ecuadorian friend in Chicago called Marcelo Laniado. On learning of her trip to Ecuador, he had given her a formal introduction letter to his folks in Guayaquil. Guayaquil, the largest city in Ecuador, was located on the coast about three hours south of Quevedo. It sprawled along the banks of the brown, sluggish, and wide Rio Guayas.

Towards the end of her stay with me, she pulled out the letter to look at it more carefully as I was going to accompany her for a couple of days to Guayaquil. To our great surprise, it was addressed to Mr. Marcel Laniado de Wind. Wind – my last name. How very odd. She had not noticed before either.

Now, to be honest, this was not the first time I had heard my last name mentioned as present in Ecuador. At some point, I had heard from Don Guido Montes and others, "Oh yeah, there was somebody with your last name in Guayaquil." Perhaps I was too jaded, but from past experiences, I knew what that usually meant. I hadn't believed Don Guido.

Wind was a very uncommon last name. How could there be someone in Ecuador with that name? At that point, I knew of very few people with that last name, even in the States. But here it was, and it seemed a remarkable coincidence. Kat herself was surprised and amazed she hadn't looked at the envelope sooner.

Kat and I took an express bus to Guayaquil, where we looked up the Laniado de Wind family. We found Doña Marta Laniado de Wind, Marcel's sister, in a very affluent apartment building in a rich suburb of Guayaquil. We dropped in on her, exchanged pleasantries, and shared Kat's letter, and she was warm and cordial to both of us. We went over what we knew of the family, and it seemed somewhat plausible that we were distant relatives.

Marta told us that the Laniado de Wind family had migrated to Ecuador in the early 1900s from Belgium and Holland. They headed first to Machala in El Oro province, south on the Peruvian border and a big banana producing area. She thought they came to Belgium first from eastern Europe, probably Poland. She also knew there was a Jewish heritage from the past. She thought that the long aristocratic last name of Laniado de Wind had been originally a simpler one connected with "Wind". This strikingly aligned with the little I knew at the time of my family's origins.

The Laniado de Winds had become banana plantation growers, selling bananas for export to the United Fruit company. Eventually with their wealth they moved to Guayaquil, and established one of Ecuador's major private banks, the Banco del Pacífico.

Don Marcel dabbled a bit in right wing conservative politics. (Some years later he would become notorious as a corrupt Minister of Agriculture in the right-wing nationalist government of Leon Febres-Cordero 1984-1988, a sort of proto-Trumpian right wing populist back in the day.)

Kat was uncomfortable by this; the family's high social and economic status made them part of the Ecuadorian robber baron class. She was disinclined to have much to do with them, viewing them as part of the problem behind Latin America's wider social problems and poverty. I was bemused as well. While surprised, I didn't feel comfortable in my gut with the new connection.

I decided not to pursue any further social connections with the family. While Marta was polite and friendly, she seemed also not moved to do much follow-up. It was just as well, but still quite a coincidence.

As Kat moved on to head south to Peru and her own backpacking adventure, I returned to Quevedo with some grudging respect for Don Guido. He had been right all along. With some amusement I realized I had some wholly unexpected family ties to this country I had come to love. And when you love a place, you also see it through the lenses of expectation and higher standards. You notice when it falls short.

This was true of Ecuador. But it was, of course, that way too for me with the United States. I was as much a patriot as the next guy. I wanted to believe in a benign and charitable role for the United States. I wanted to be able to think better of it and not worse. Yet I became increasingly disenchanted by what I saw of American policy and behavior overseas, as I became more informed and engaged. I was displeased by governmental policy in Latin America as it was being articulated and exercised by the Reagan Administration. I was also turned off by the abusive and patronizing behavior of some official Americans in a country not their own.

This steered me increasingly towards thinkers who articulated critiques of American policies. This is not to say I saw great value in any heavy ideological approach; I didn't see myself as a partisan or ideologue.

I was skeptical of governmental interventions. I saw the logic and need for a more participatory community-based approach to development, humanitarian assistance, and fighting poverty. I questioned what the fundamental barriers to overcoming poverty were and why.

I shared the general PCV suspicion of the work of the U.S. Agency for International Development (USAID). I would, of course, later develop positive relationships with some officials working there. I reasoned that there had to be good people working there as well as others. I saw plenty of signs with the USAID logo connected with different projects, sometimes very dubious ones. I would learn about a plethora of failed projects and program approaches undertaken by the Agency. I did not see myself as eager to work on the governmental side of things in international development, at least for a long while.

But I wanted to see what I could do to build on the Peace Corps experience. Could I learn more about development assistance, foreign aid, and the actions of big donors like USAID and the

World Bank without getting myself entangled in it? Without compromising any principles, at least until I understood better the consequences and characteristics of those sorts of compromises.

In the next chapters, I will describe how I would try to do that. But first, I had the itch to see more of the world around me and the urge to scratch it.

CHAPTER 4

POST PEACE CORPS COMBUSTION

I had to figure out if I was going to be able to stay on in Ecuador after my Peace Corps service ended in December or not. Dr. Guido, my Quevedo counterpart and Dr. Luís Triviño (now the national Minister of Health) were annoyed with the rejection of an extension. Dr. Triviño decided not to worry about Peace Corps. He thought of a better idea.

Instead, he reached out to Anibal Oprandi, the colorful Argentine local Country Director for Foster Parents Plan International (known as PLAN, now called *Childreach*). It was an international private voluntary organization. The main Ecuador headquarters was in Guayaquil. Unbeknownst to me, he told Anibal to find a way to hire me to stay on and help the Ecuadorian Ministry of Health. I got an invitation to interview in Guayaquil out of the blue. I reached out to several volunteer friends who were in Guayaquil, two special education volunteers Lea and Lisa. I was close friends with both. They had an apartment in the city and offered to allow me to crash, which helped save the cost of a pension for a couple nights.

Lea and Lisa were familiar with PLAN and gave me some insights on how PLAN worked, since they had had some past contact. PLAN was one of the original child sponsorship organizations, like Save the Children and others. It was born in England and the USA after World War I, as part of efforts to help the massive amount of refugee children in Europe. They matched needy children with specific "foster parents" back in the USA. These volunteer donors would contribute a modest amount each month, usually under $20. The donor would get a photo of an identified child, a brief bio, and a few times a year a short letter from the child that was translated into English.

By the early 1980s, several child sponsorship organizations had been operating. Some with greater or lesser amounts of trustworthiness to their operations. Some were religiously connected. PLAN was one of the first and was nonpartisan and nonsectarian. They were building a steadily increasing international operation in Europe and the United States.

I met with Anibal Oprandi in early November. He was a tall, white-haired gentleman with all the classic expansive airs of Argentines. He was happy to invite me to come to work for PLAN after my service ended. I would earn a mid-level local-type salary. It was probably about $1000 monthly or 3-4 times the monthly allowance Peace Corps volunteers received. I could supplement that if I wanted to, helping to translate letters between English and Spanish.

The job description was a little unclear. Anibal made clear we could develop that over time. He knew the Minister of Health respected what I had done as a PCV. He thought I could start by helping to improve the quality of PLAN health, water, and sanitation projects. Perhaps in time, I could apply to PLAN's international headquarters in Warwick, Rhode Island—"IH"—and get considered for an international expat job as a program director.

I thought about it. I had a few misgivings about the idea of child sponsorship, but I also recognized I didn't know much about them. It would be good to gain practical experience from the inside. Plus, it was a way to stay in Ecuador and try to make a difference.

I accepted the job offer. I asked Anibal if it would be possible to delay the offer till March of the following year since I was going to travel a bit after my Peace Corps COS. With his very exaggerated gestures and booming voice, Anibal gave his assent.

Looking back, I am a little bemused that I rushed to travel across South America but still missed some great places in Ecuador itself. I managed to visit almost all the different regions of the country, including the Amazonian jungle area. I kept putting off the idea of a trip to the Galapagos islands and never managed to go, at least not yet! They were and are a unique treasure of the country, about a two-hour flight from Guayaquil.

I finished my PC service in early December 1982. I held a series of goodbyes with friends in Buena Fé and Quevedo and then with fellow volunteers up in Quito as I went through the procedures of the closeout of my service. While some PCVs were eager to return home to the USA, quite a few were also looking to travel around South America. I ended up linking up with a couple of friends to start my own journey south of the border into Peru. I readied my backpack and sleeping bag.

I had a copy of a great South American guidebook, which I annotated with different notes on where I wanted to stop. I decided that I wouldn't lock myself into any unbreakable plans but would leave things flexible on how long I would stay in any one place. I expected to travel for at least a few months and wanted to go as far south as possible on the continent, all the way to Tierra del Fuego if possible. I looked forward to unexpected adventures. I would try to connect with Kat, if possible, who was still traveling south, swinging by Cusco again.

Then there was Katherine, who had settled in southern Chile outside Pucón and Temuco. Over the intervening year, to my surprise, I learned she had married an Englishman resident in Chile. My own feelings and passion had changed after a year away from the magical journey we had shared. But I still loved her and hoped to see her again.

Travelling by backpack requires a real commitment to flexibility, patience, and persistence. I wasn't planning on relying on expensive means of transportation. I would take buses where it made sense, trains where possible, and hitchhike where necessary or possible. I expected to walk quite a bit as well.

I was putting my possessions for the road into a medium size orange backpack, including a minimum number of changes of clothing. I would look for cheap ways to wash my clothes every few days if possible, or longer if not. In terms of lodging, I would mostly rely on cheap youth hostels and "pensiones". It was a surfeit of simplicity, reducing things down to the basics and essentials. I would focus almost entirely on my surroundings, on the places I would see and the people I would meet.

Now, four decades later, I remain a bit amazed at what my friends and I could do at that time. We traversed vast distances without the benefit of any of the sort of technology we take for granted today. I had a great guidebook with maps, many tips, and a compact short wave/FM radio I could turn to when needed.

I had a supply of American Express travelers' cheques and some US dollar cash, which I could draw occasionally to resupply my local currency needs. I had these secreted around my person and backpack in different ways to reduce the chance of a casual robbery.

I expected to meet interesting people along the way, and perhaps that helped make it a self-fulfilling prophesy because it certainly proved to be true.

Crossing Peru heading south meant heading down the dusty dry "Carretera Panamericana." The Pan-American Highway made its way down the Pacific coast of South America. Most of the Pacific coast of Peru is climatologically a desert, with a few exceptions. I was eager to cross it without delay. I figured I would stop in Lima to catch my breath but then head back down to southern Peru as quickly as possible.

In Lima, I went to a well-recommended youth hostel in Miraflores, but it proved to be full. Some folks there suggested I try a nearby pension. It had one remaining room with a German woman, Andrea. She had arrived in Lima on the Lufthansa flight from Frankfurt and was planning to meet up with a Swiss friend in Cusco later in the week. We hit it off, and she was happy enough to share her room, which had two twin beds.

We walked around Miraflores to see the neighborhood through the fog rolling in from the Pacific below the cliffs nearby. I talked about my PCV experiences in health, which she found interesting as she was a nurse in training back in West Germany. We went to listen to music in some cheap music halls which didn't charge a cover or harass visiting backpackers.

Andrea was going to fly on to Cusco, and I took note of where she might be to see if we might reconnect together again. This was also a bit of a remarkable thing in hindsight. There were a finite number of places where I and fellow road travelers were likely to be. Still, coincidences abounded on the road, and it was not unusual to cross paths twice or more, even when it seemed so unlikely. I said goodbye to Andrea and moved on two days later, determined to head further south on my route.

Lima remained less interesting to me at that moment. I had just visited Lima briefly the year before, and I was turned off a bit by the grayness and semi-authoritarian air about things. A democratic government of sorts had returned to Peru—as it had in Ecuador—just a couple of years before but it remained wobbly.

I couldn't resist spending more time in Cusco, even though I had also visited the year before. There were so many different Incan ruins and other archeological sites, far beyond what I had been able to see with Katherine the year before.

I was fascinated with the red brick colonial architecture but especially with the people, sights, and sounds of the place. I didn't meet with Kat as I had hoped. According to a note I found waiting for me in the local post office, set up for general delivery, I had just missed her. But I did run into Rina, a fellow former Peace Corps volunteer I knew from Ecuador.

Rina had made friends with some of her fellow backpackers with whom she had been travelling for a time. They were a motley crew – two Israelis, an Australian, a Brit, and a Colombian. She had an on again off again with a boyfriend who was also a former PC volunteer but who had not been crazy with the idea of a backpacking trip.

We resolved to hike a bit in the area around Cusco, and then took the train to Juliaca outside Puno. The train took much longer than expected due to mudslides from heavy rains, and we pulled in about 3 AM. The hot corn drink of "api," favored in the highlands and made from purple or yellow corn, was never so much needed as then. We managed to find space at a youth hostel a couple hours later, to crash for a day before continuing to Tacna.

I had decided to skirt Bolivia, heading south, and cross the border to Chile from Tacna near the coast. Rina was game for tagging along with me to Santiago and seeing where we might go from there. Getting to Tacna, though, was a challenge; there were no buses running due to a labor action. We decided to try our luck at hitching.

Luck arrived, in the form of a huge beer truck from Cerveceria Cusqueña, heading down to Tacna. There wasn't much room in the cab as the driver was already carrying another passenger. There was room for Rina, and I persuaded the driver to let me ride on top in the cargo area. The truck was slow but steady, and it wasn't too terribly uncomfortable for me. The stars were incredible and luckily it did not rain at that point.

Tacna was forgettable. It was a nondescript market town with a lot of commerce and black-market activity. I had thought Tacna was near the coast, but it proved to be inland still and a crossing point for merchants and farmers. They came from Puno to bring their highlands produce, particularly potatoes, to the Chilean border. Rina and I were able to get a local taxi to bring us to the border so we could walk across into Chile.

To some extent, crossing from Tacna into Chile was almost like going from Mexico to the USA, although in hindsight, that may be a little exaggerated. But Chile was cleaner and more organized than the Peruvian side. The transport companies in Arica ran modern buses down the coast south towards Antofagasta, Iquique and Santiago. We bought a ticket for the next day. We luxuriated in spending the night in a modest Chilean pension which had hot water, a delicious treat not always found in Peru.

Santiago was a long trip away, a bit over 24 hours by bus, about 1300 miles. But there didn't seem to be that much in between. A large portion of desert, the Atacama Desert stretched ahead of us. One of the driest areas on earth. We did it in segments, stopping first in Antofagasta, getting a meal and stretching our legs.

Antofagasta was historical – it had been captured from the Bolivians during the War of the Pacific. It was a key train head for the mining operations in the northern part of Chile. We began to hear from people the sort of sing-song accent that the Chileans often had. It was quite distinct from that of the Bolivians or Peruvians.

From Antofagasta we caught a bus on to La Serena, where Rina wanted to stop and check out the beaches and the historic center. La Serena had been the second city founded in Chile after the capital Santiago, in 1544. Some of the colonial center remained from the 16th and 17th century. We walked around and stopped in some cafés off the Plaza de Armas. We found a place where we could drop our backpacks and head to the beach.

Chile's ocean is unlike the tropical Pacific in Ecuador or northern Peru. It was bracingly cold and had strong waves with good places to surf. The Humboldt Current came from the direction of Antarctica, bringing the cold water along the coast. It was good to loll on the beach a bit, though, and refresh from the time on the bus. Later in the afternoon we got a ticket for an overnight bus into Valpariaso and Santiago. We again saved ourselves the time and expense of a pension or hostel.

We found space in the official youth hostel in Santiago and made a bunch of new friends, particularly from southern Brazil. Katherine proved to be in Santiago. She had come up to the capital to try to pursue some legal bureaucratic paperwork about her plans to stay on in Chile.

Katherine was working with an NGO that advocated on behalf of the Mapuche and Pehuenche peoples in the volcanic lakes region of Chile. The military government did not like this theme, so she had to thread her way gingerly through the bureaucratic minefield.

I saw how Katherine was so taken up with the indigenous cause. She was passionate about how her ethnobotanical studies at Colgate could be best to help. I admired her work. We agreed to meet up again in the Temuco area later in the month. Katherine seemed different: she appeared fulfilled and centered. I still loved her, but no longer felt 'in love' to the same degree. It was strange in some ways. We'd both felt an urgency to be with each other the year before and share precious moments together. Now the urgency had passed. We cared for each other, but it was different as our original passion had passed.

Several days of walking around Santiago provided me with a chance to see the city in the context of tumultuous change. Santiago had faced enormous change in the prior decade, following the U.S.-instigated coup. The Salvador Allende socialist democratic government had been overthrown. Pinochet had put in place a severe military government ten years earlier. The military had been steadily tightening its grip on social freedoms.

Opinions were quite divided among the Chileans. Some saw the right-wing military government as Chile's salvation, While others saw it as anathema that had upended the democratic process. I wondered what it would be like to live in such a divided country.

It was eventually time to move on. Our new Brazilian friends were eager to head south to the Chilean lake district, see the Osorno stratovolcano's beautiful snowcap and visit Temuco. Katherine promised to meet up with me to show me Puerto Montt and the gorgeous island of Chiloe. Rina was keen to go backpacking with the Brazilians, and I was also up for it. They had already become good friends. I remain friends to this day, decades later, with one of them who emigrated eventually from Brazil to western Canada.

This area of southern Chile is surely among the most beautiful. Thick green temperate forests, beautiful mountains, and volcanic lakes. It had a coast with the magic of Nordic fjords and so many intricate inlets that provided a deep blue and green filter for everything. I spent Christmas and New Year's going through this area and Chiloe. I finally said goodbye to Katherine, and we promised to stay in touch. Her marriage seemed to strengthen her for sure.

I camped a couple of days in some of the national forests, sharing a tent with our Brazilian friends. Then, I decided it was time to cross the border into Argentina and visit that side of the Andes. The Andes ran like a jagged chain down the border south through the two countries. I was curious to see how Argentina was doing. The military government and Argentine economy seemed to be on shaky ground—far less stable than Chile.

Argentina and the United Kingdom fought a brief but bloody war from April to June of that year over the Falklands Islands. Argentina and the rest of Latin America called them Las Malvinas. The islands had been a South Atlantic British territory since the 1800s. Argentina had always hoped to "recover" them, although it was uncertain when they had ever owned them. The war led to a humiliating defeat for Argentina and was now used by democratic forces to fight the dictatorship.

I liked the idea of heading down along the Argentine Andes and eventually making it to Patagonia. I would then go to what the Chileans called "Atlantic Chile," where what I thought were eternal Chilean glaciers came down the Andes. I would make my way back north towards Buenos Aires, heading through Patagonia and the Pampas.

Traveling in this area required a lot of improvisation as there weren't regular bus schedules. Over the course of one day, we managed to hitch two trucks and a bus and got into Bariloche. It was a remarkable discovery. This Argentine ski town was built like an Austrian ski chateau paradise. It was an unexpected sight, almost like walking into a Twilight Zone episode. This town, with its ski lodges in the Argentine Andes, was midway between the

Pampas and Patagonia. Yet you felt like you must surely be in Europe. Even the chocolate was great.

Whatever the influence of German and other European refugees in Argentina (including many former escaped Nazis and Nazi sympathizers), I think the Argentine lifestyle had co-opted many. The Argentines were often slow-paced and leisurely about their business. They had what the French called 'joie de vivre'. There was ample wine all day, often diluted with water, extending lunches for a few hours.

From Bariloche, we flew several legs by local planes at bargain-cheap prices. I had not started this backpacking adventure with any ideas of being able to fly anywhere. I had thought it would be prohibitively expensive. But Argentina was going through another of its frequent episodes of hyperinflation in local currency. We purchased some flights heading south to Cafayate and Rio Gallegos on Australes Airline at the equivalent of US$5 or $10.

Rina and I arrived in Rio Gallegos later in January. She was a fun traveling partner, cheery and adventurous. This was to be our last leg of our journey together. I had plans to go on to Tierra del Fuego, and she was returning to catch a flight home from Buenos Aires. We landed in Rio Gallegos and looked around the airport to see the best way to the youth hostel.

There was no airport bus, but there were taxis, and the taxis were cheap. We picked one and started chatting with the taxi driver Carlos as we headed into town. To our enormous surprise, he invited us not to go to the youth hostel but to come and stay at his parents' home in town. His parents often rented rooms to travelers. Carlos said they would love to meet two former US Peace Corps Volunteers who had made it out to the end of Argentine Patagonia.

We accepted the invitation, and we were not disappointed at all. Carlos' family were Lebanese immigrants. They were Catholic, but they projected all that you would imagine from classic, over-the-top Middle Eastern hospitality—but with a unique Argentine flavor.

I remember Carlos' mother welcoming Rina and me and exclaiming, "How nice of you to be visiting from South America."

This caused us both to arch eyebrows but with smiles. It reflected the Argentine attitude, true as much in Patagonia as in Buenos Aires, that being in Argentina was as much like being in Europe. As we were coming from Ecuador and the Andean countries to the north, well, THAT was South America. Where all the 'indios' and 'mestizos' lived, and how quaint was that. The Argentine never lost his ego or his faith – even these immigrants from Lebanon – that Argentina was God's country through and through.

We were offered a homecooked dinner, and over dinner Carlos' father asked us, "Have you heard of the penguin colony in Cabo Virgenes?"

Cabo Virgenes was at the mouth of the Straits of Magellan. There, a famous and unique penguin nesting colony had made its way from Antarctica. We had heard about it, having seen it mentioned in the guidebook, but it seemed very off the beaten trail from the town of Rio Gallegos.

"We will go tomorrow in the truck!" Carlos' father announced with wide expansive arms. "It will be an adventure."

Indeed, it was an adventure. Carlos and I rode in the back of the 20-year-old Toyota pickup truck, and Rina rode in the cabin with Carlos' father. The colony at Cabo Virgenes was about 170 kms away on gravel roads. We left at 8 AM and were there at 10. It was incredible. No tourists were visible, with no one around but sheep and a few shepherds. And the braying sound of the jackass penguins, as they were known.

We walked with care out to the nests and along the side of the dunes. The view of thousands of penguins was amazing, as was the smell to be honest. The hunting parents were going in and out of the deep blue water of the straits, bringing fish and other catch to help feed their nestlings. Across the water was the dark dun color of Tierra del Fuego, the Land of Fire.

Through these straits, Darwin in the HMS Beagle had passed 150 years before. It was windy and gritty from the sand and gravel caught up in the wind. But exhilarating. Such an extraordinary adventure, and one we were so grateful for our generous hosts to have offered us.

I can still close my eyes and see in my mind's eye the dark overcast of the stormy South Atlantic on one side, the Straits of Magellan with wind-capped waves on the other, and the cutting grit of the air in this most isolated corner of the Americas. Seeing the penguins here was a unique experience. Yet it was echoed and almost matched when many years later my family and I would come to see their cousin colony at the very tip of the Cape of Good Hope in South Africa.

We returned to Rio Gallegos after a couple of hours, and Rina caught her flight the next day to Buenos Aires. I had another adventure in mind. I got on a bus, heading across Argentina to the border with Chile, toward the Torres del Paine National Park and Puerto Natales. This was at least 6 hours, maybe more, across sheep herding moors and scrub grassland.

Imagine going across Scotland, with rising hills. But soon, you see in the distance the blue, white ice of the awesome glaciers of the Golfo de Ultima Esperanza, the Gulf of Last Hope. This was now Chile, the edge of Atlantic Chile, a land of fjords and channels perhaps like the coast of northern Norway. It was an incredible landscape, and though I tried to take pictures with my camera, I knew it would be hard to do justice.

I made it to Puerto Natales and I could not get over the breathtaking fjords and archipelagos of Chilean Patagonia. It might be an easier feat now for some travelers to get to. Back then you were stretching the limits of accessible travel in this southern reach of South America. Big Sky country indeed, and the gateway of one of the most extraordinary ice fields and glaciers anywhere

to be found.

I spent a few days climbing and circling the nearby Cerro Dorotea and on water tours to the deep blue edge of the glaciers calving into the Magellan waters. I did not have full ice gear to do serious climbing onto the higher glaciers, but I didn't miss them. I was more interested in the majesty of staring at these glaciers as they came down to the port. At the youth hostel, I met Leo, this husky Swiss adventurer with stories to tell about his travels. Together, we crossed over to Punta Arenas and then used that as the launching point to head back to Argentina's own Ushuaia across the straits in Tierra del Fuego.

Ushuaia often gets the sobriquet "the End of the World." Indeed, it is not only the capital and largest town in Tierra del Fuego, but some say it is the southernmost city in the world. It is a center for the Argentine Navy; few tourists make it anywhere near.

In Ushuaia, I saw the magical main glacier, nearly half a kilometer wide, marauding into the town. It dominated the landscape. The port, Puerto Navarino, was a busy humming place. Naval freighters left for the Antarctic Argentine territory claimed by the military regime.

I'd heard it was possible to offer to work and ship out. I was so tempted to hop on one and try to make my way to Antarctica. We were in the window of the Antarctic summer when boats could travel. I also knew that if I did this, it was unpredictable when I might make it back and then return up South America to Ecuador.

I hesitated and decided against it. It was already the second half of January, a little over a month from when I had left Ecuador. I did want to try to get back to Ecuador by March. I didn't know what hurdles or discoveries I would still face on this backpacking expedition. That was even without going off on some side adventure to Antarctica.

I spent the next week or so making my way north through Argentine Patagonia. I visited towns like Comodoro Rivadavia and Neuquén before moving on to Mendoza. Mendoza is a fruit orchard and wine-producing area in the Argentina Pampas, not far from the Andes foothills. It was a beautiful town with a strong siesta mentality, particularly in this warm summer in Argentina.

Shops would close around noon, re-open around 4 or 5 PM, and then stay open until 9 PM. Argentines usually didn't have dinner until 9 or 10 PM, an exaggeration even from Spanish or Italian customs.

I dropped my stuff off at a youth hostel I found and made some friends there. I walked around Mendoza a bit to see the town. I then impulsively joined a couple of Argentine backpackers who were on post-university holidays to drink wine and chill in one of the parks.

Returning to the hostel, I ended up crashing relatively early. I woke up the next morning to a hangover from too much wine and discovered that I had been robbed. The damn backpackers who I had shared a room with had taken my money and my father's old Leica camera. I had been carrying it with me and using it to take photos. My passport was stolen as well. Bastards.

I was stunned by the robbery. I couldn't believe it. This was the first time something like this had happened to me. What were they going to be able to do with my passport? I looked around for all my reserves of cash secreted around. It was almost all gone. I had started easing off and not dividing up my cash as I had done at the beginning of the trip. Of course, no one knew anything. This was a real violation of a common backpacker code. These things weren't supposed to happen.

I had lost close to $500 cash and $300 in travelers' checks. The checks could be replaced at an American Express office, although the one in Mendoza was closed for some reason. The closest alternative, Santiago de Chile, was only 200 miles away or less by bus. But the thieves had also taken my passport, and there was no way I was going to be able to cross the border to Chile without it. I'd have to go to Buenos Aires. But Buenos Aires was three times as far away.

I tried the police with the little information I could share from the hostel registry. Obviously, it might or might not have been valid. The police did not focus their efforts on a nonviolent crime against a backpacker.

I called the American Consulate General in Buenos Aires. The person I reached on the phone was officious and unhelpful. Yes, I was told that American Citizen Services could possibly help me. They sounded very reluctant and annoyed that I was wasting their time. No, there was nothing they could do to help me in Mendoza. They didn't have a consulate there, only a sort of honorary consul who did little. After I tried to ask for help in getting to Buenos Aires, they hung up on me.

This was a serious problem. How was I to get to Buenos Aires? I found about $20, and the hostel gave me some Argentine pesos to help out, but I had no money for fare or passport. To buy a ticket I'd have to show my passport, even if I had money. Ugh!

Another backpacker from Uruguay told me to go down to the train station and explain the situation to the station master. Maybe they could help. The station master did; I couldn't board the train in the usual way without a ticket, money, or passport. But he did allow me to hitch a ride, grabbing space in the luggage car of the train. There were no seats, but some improvised space where I could find a place to sit on the floor without getting in the way.

It was not the most comfortable way of travel. But it was very much in the spirit of how I had started this trip, travel forward by any means necessary or possible.

That said, it was a long way to Buenos Aires—about a 15—or 16-hour train ride. I traveled all through the night, arriving at the main station in the middle of the next day. It was dark for most of it, except for the brief stops at each station and cattle post. There were no windows, but in fact, one of the cabin doors was kept half open.

The humid night air was comforting, as was the sound of the train pressing forward down the rails. I chatted with the porters who came through, who were all kind and generous. Once or twice, they brought me some light sandwiches and drinks from the dining car.

I dozed here and there during the night, but I mostly wondered how things would play out in Buenos Aires. Would the American Embassy be of any help? Would I need to contact my family, causing needless increased worries or burdening them? We pulled into the Retiro train station in Buenos Aires around noon the next day, the center of a big transport complex. Checking my guidebook, I looked for options and found a good pension a short distance away by subway and not far from the downtown Lavalle district.

Buenos Aires is a huge city with British and Italian influences and huge park areas. I found a room with a private shower for less than $5 per day and, after a quick shower, made my way to the American Citizen Services office at the U.S. Consulate and Embassy.

A remarkable disappointment awaited me. After a long interview, I explained my situation and asked how I could replace my passport. After many disapproval looks and harrumphs from the American Embassy officer, he made clear that I was another unneeded burden and pain in the neck for him. After a pause, the officer gave me two options.

I could get an emergency temporary travel document to be repatriated back to the States, but that was the only way to use it. I couldn't go elsewhere. Or I could wait for a new passport to be made and sent down from Washington by pouch and use that to travel anywhere I wanted.

How long would that take? "Well, we can ask for fast delivery, but it almost always takes several weeks, maybe more at this time of the year." Ugh. So, if I wanted to return to Ecuador as planned, I would have to wait a while and cool my heels in Buenos Aires.

Would they be able to help me with a loan of funds while I was waiting for money to be sent from the States? I had received a small portion of my Peace Corps readjustment allowance in cash to make this trip. I was waiting to receive the balance of it.

Could I borrow something as a traveler in distress, just robbed? This drew an even larger glare of disapproval.

In the end, I had to sign multiple IOUs, promising my left testicle if I failed to pay, but the Consulate did lend me emergency funds of about $200. With the hyperinflationary economy in Argentina, I could make this last. But I would still have to be careful, of course. I promised to return in two weeks and check back on my passport and any funds that arrived from the States. It was a dreadful experience.

There was a lot to see and appreciate in Buenos Aires and things were relatively cheap for me. There were plenty of expensive restaurants geared towards well-heeled tourists and foreigners. I could avoid these by frequenting quite a few that were part of the local economy.

I found a remarkable vegetarian restaurant with generous portions and a prix fixe for only $1. I found movie theatres and museums that cost only ten cents to enter. Buses and the metro subway of Buenos Aires were also less than a quarter dollar. I had experience living cheaply as a Peace Corps Volunteer. Here in the very sophisticated city of Buenos Aires, thanks to hyperinflation, I could almost live as cheaply or more.

It was troubling to me how unsympathetic and unfriendly I found the American Consulate during that visit and subsequent ones. It ended up taking almost a month to get my new passport and to get some additional funds. I wondered what American Citizen Services from the State Department were even for. Wasn't it their job to help American citizens in distress for one reason or another?

I wasn't a druggie; I hadn't been arrested for violating any Argentine laws. I had been a little careless with my belongings and had been robbed. But did that justify the hours and hours of bureaucratic games I encountered? And why did it have to take so long to re-issue and send a passport? Over the years I would hear many similar horror stories not only about American Citizen Services but Embassy treatment. Maybe not all the time or even most of the time. But enough to leave a sour taste in the mouth.

By the middle of February, I was ready to travel again outside the country and say goodbye to Buenos Aires. I spent the next week traveling to Uruguay, visiting Montevideo and Salto. Montevideo was a sort of miniature version of Buenos Aires across the big Rio de la Plata estuary. It was as much or more influenced by the Italian immigrants who had come to South America in the postwar decades.

It seemed to be preserved in amber as if in a time capsule, largely untouched by outside influences. Still, I was bemused to be almost assaulted in one or two of the parks by wandering gypsy beggars and fortune tellers. One of them cast a curse on me when I refused to give money to have my hand read by one.

I didn't stay long in Uruguay and did not head out to the famous beach resort of Punta del Este, which had perhaps more fame than the country itself. Perhaps I should have stayed longer. More recent Uruguayan friends have convinced me of the wonders of that country, at least currently.

I planned to head north to Salto. I would cross over the Uruguayan river to the Argentine city of Corrientes. I wanted to see the Misiones province of northeastern Argentina. The Misiones province was gorgeous, and I stopped to see some of the ancient Jesuit redoubts and ruins in the deeply red clay soil.

I followed this road north to see the remarkable waterfalls of Foz do Iguacu. The falls are one of the world's marvels and deserve that reputation, shared on part of the river between Brazil and Argentina. There was a wooden plank boardwalk across different viewing points above the river's tumult, which was breathtaking. I was able to cross into the town on the Brazilian side and capture a bit of the Portuguese vibe.

I remember Niagara Falls from visits when I was a kid, with summer camp and my parents. The Horseshoe and American Falls on the Canadian border are impressive, but the Foz do Iguacu in the tropical setting is unmatched.

Here, I ended up reuniting for a day with Leo, the Swiss backpacker I had met some weeks earlier. It was nice to see him again and catch up. Leo was certainly an interesting character; he shared how he financed his world travel with the sale of carpets.

He would drive his battered Mercedes a few times a year from Zurich to Istanbul, Türkiye, and on to different villages in Anatolia. He would buy high-quality Turkish carpets at cheap local prices in Turkish lira, roll them up in his trunk, and bring back as many as he could fit in the car.

It was about 1500 miles each way, or about a 24-hour drive, so he would take a couple of days or so each way from Zurich. He wouldn't have to declare anything across the borders, and the trunk was never inspected. Each carpet could be re-sold in Switzerland for 5 to 10 times the price purchased in Anatolia. From these sales, he would clear a substantial profit to supplement his income for his yearly month-long travels around the world. Pretty sweet deal.

I considered where next. I was invited to move through southern Brazil to Curitiba and visit friends there. I had heard beautiful things about both it and Florianopolis from some of the Brazilians I had met previously in the Chilean youth hostel and camping. It seemed appealing. Brazilians were such fun people to be around. It was a tough choice, but again, I thought about the unexpected delay in Buenos Aires and my desire to get back to Ecuador sooner rather than later.

From Iguacu I moved on west, crossing into Paraguay at the nearby border with Argentina and Brazil. I then took a Pullman bus a couple of hours across the country to Asuncion.

I decided to drop into the Peace Corps office since Paraguay has a long-standing Peace Corps program. I found out about a cheap pension that was a hangout for PCVs.

I spent a few nights there, making new friends and acquaintances and walking around Asuncion to get the feel of it. It was, at that point, a small and provincial city. The capital of a country like most of the rest of the Southern Cone countries with a right-wing paranoid military dictatorship. Again, frozen in time. In this case, the notorious, thuggish, and corrupt Nazi sympathizer Alfredo Stroessner was in charge. His paramilitaries kept a tight lid on the capital.

Asuncion is located at the eastern border with Argentina. I crossed Paraguay back into northern Argentina. I debated the best routes to follow. I crossed over to Chile to head north rather than through Bolivia. I don't know why, but I had something of an aversion to spending any time in Bolivia on this trip. Perhaps part of me knew that Bolivia would prove to be an important and seminal place for me later.

It was a bit counter-intuitive regarding the general northern direction I needed to go in eventually. I figured I would get myself to Mendoza again and see if there had been any unlikely discoveries with the police from the robbery the month before. I would then cross the short distance over the Andes to Santiago. I managed to get to Tucuman in Argentina and then got on a cheap

Argentine Air Force flight to Mendoza, which made easy going of the distance.

It was crazy, but between hyperinflation and the military government, the Argentina Air Force flew cheap local flights to different cities. They complemented or competed with Argentine commercial airlines. In Mendoza, as expected, there was no news or progress from the police. I got a fast bus out the next day to Santiago, Chile.

I thought I might stop by Santiago to check up on Chris, the rising young journalist with whom I'd become friends after meeting Katherine, who was now established with the Mapuche in Southern Chile. I had heard that the elected former president who had immediately preceded Salvador Allende, Eduardo Frei Montalvo, had died in mid-January. I wondered how that affected the mood among the democratic forces opposing the military government. Little did I imagine what waited for me!

I got into Santiago, found a pension I could stay at, and looked up Chris, finding him at a local café near the Plaza de Armas. It was good to see a familiar face. I shared with him my experiences over the past months traveling, and we reminisced about Katherine. He urged me to stay in Santiago a couple of days and join him the next day at the main Cathedral across the street.

"There's going to be a memorial mass for Eduardo Frei Montalvo there, 40 days after his passing. I'm going to cover it for the Christian Science Monitor, and you can help." He told me. "It'll be interesting to see what the "milicos" do about it, and whether it can help wake up the public."

The "milicos" were slang for the military who had taken over the government. Some pretended to be legitimate when they were simply authoritarian dictators. A little voice told me, "Stay away, stay away!" But having perhaps never suffered from an overabundance of common sense, I promised Chris I'd join. I offered to help him with anything he needed for his own planned reporting write-up of the memorial mass.

The next day, I went early to the cathedral, and it was impossible to get inside as thousands of people were already there. I stood outside the cathedral on the wide sidewalk, where speakers had been set up.

At Chris' request, I interviewed different people to get a sampling of the protest voice among the Chileans. Many were socialists or democratic socialists who had been supporters of Allende.

Many also considered themselves conservatives or moderate Christian Democrats. They had supported Eduardo Frei Montalvo and opposed the leftist or radical bent of the Chilean Socialists. Some had initially supported Augusto Pinochet's arguments for the military coup in 1972.

Eduardo Frei Montalvo began speaking out against the military junta in 1976 and became a target of the Pinochet government. Now, six years after Frei Montalvo's death, they were growing increasingly weary of the military government, which showed no sign of letting up.

The memorial mass started about a half hour late. Cardinal Silva led the ceremony, and everyone listened quietly to hear what he said. When he began to depart from the liturgy and speak to the assembled about the meaning of the day, everyone was all ears. The rumors among the people around were that the Cardinal had warned the government and army.

If any soldiers came to invade the area around the church, the church would not hesitate to condemn and excommunicate soldiers and their leaders. Cardinal Silva never mentioned Pinochet's name. But he warned those who rejected and ignored the peoples' voice, and denied the peoples' rights, and spoke about the disappeared ones, the "desaparecidos." There were almost 1000 desaparecidos, according to the local nongovernment organizations, who had been picked up by the military and never heard from again.

I looked at Chris, and he raised his eyebrows and mouthed, "Be alert."

124

In fact, even as the Cardinal spoke, military armored personnel carriers and other military vehicles had drawn close to the Plaza de Armas. They had stayed just outside the periphery, away from the Cathedral. I could see them at the road crossings at the four corners of the Plaza de Armas.

It was surreal, a menacing presence, but they seemed to dare not enter the actual central plaza. The Cardinal finished his invocations, reminding all that Eduardo Frei Montalvo had been a man of God, true to his principles in the end. He spoke for all Chileans who now rejected the military claims of a right to rule. He demanded the return of a true democratic government elected by all Chileans.

"Be brave!" the Cardinal demanded of those who attended the mass. "Do not be cowered. Do not be silenced. Do not seek violence but demand the rights of all Chileans." The mass ended with some final prayers, and people began to leave the Cathedral peacefully. A few began to mock and attack the military when they left the Cathedral, but others silenced them and began a different chant as they came out to the Plaza.

"We demand the rights of all Chileans. We demand the rights of all Chileans. We demand the rights of all Chileans." That innocent chant was apparently enough. As the mass of people in the Plaza de Armas grew, the chant was taken up. The body of people began to move in the direction of two of the plaza's exits opposite the Cathedral. Placards were raised with a variety of epitaphs and demands.

A siren went off, and with that, water cannon trucks came forward and began to fire at the demonstrators. There was a screech and whine as tear gas canisters went off and were fired into the crowd, causing a panic of people scrambling away. General chaos let loose. With all the exits to the plaza blocked, the crowd reacted like cornered animals. The crowd was uncertain in what direction to go other than to escape the acrid tear gas.

More sirens went off, and the Cathedral bells began to toll. People had still been filing out of the Cathedral's huge wooden doors but now began to turn to retreat inside.

Chris and I ducked under one of the plaza arches near one of the shops, which were now abruptly closing.

"PRENSA LIBRE INTERNACIONAL" he shouted, waving the international press credentials. We bought a couple of bottles of water to soak our shirts which we pulled over our faces, to partially protect from the tear gas.

Someone tossed a Molotov cocktail against one of the APCs, and that led to a volley of discharges of what we realized were rubber bullets. But live ammunition could be next.

We held up cartons to protect ourselves – two shells hit mine and a box nearby. Chris motioned and we managed to slip down an alley while he held up his press credentials from the Christian Science Monitor.

Amazingly we were permitted to go, as the soldiers seemed to either ignore us or be oblivious to us skirting the exit. Chris and I made it out to his temporary office at a pension he was staying at a few blocks away, lucky that we got out with the way things had been.

Chris was going to call in a report of the attack on the peaceful demonstrators and memorial mass. I wished him well as I moved to go to my own room where I was staying.

It was a heady and exhilarating experience. I was proud to see the democratic protest in action up close. I felt energized by the courage of the ordinary citizens speaking out against the military regime. I wondered whether journalism, like Chris was undertaking in Chile and in the Dominican Republic before that, could, in fact, be a calling for me.

Later that year, the democratic opposition in Chile would become louder. More violent protests and demonstrations in favor of the return of democracy. Cardinal Silva would step down and retire. Pope John Paul II replaced him with a choice initially seen and criticized as more accommodating to the regime, Cardinal Juan Francisco Fresno Larrain.

The Catholic Church stumbled a bit with how to support best reconciliation and the obvious abuse of Chileans by the regime.

For me, it was a further reminder of the tug-of-war between the spiritual mandate and the political realities of speaking out against oppression.

It was mid-March, and I thought it was time to head back. I gathered my things and decided to start hopping on buses and other transport to head north along the Pan-American Highway. A couple of days later, I crossed the border into Peru and quickly found myself facing further challenges.

The Niño Phenomenon had hit Peru with a vengeance. The excessive heating of the Pacific off the coast had stirred up massive rains, mudslides, and road blockages across much of the roads heading north. I detoured into highlands routes when the coastal highway was completely blocked. There were torrential downpours in southern sierra provincial centers like Abancay and Andahuaylas, but more road options existed.

At one point, the road was so blocked that the bus could not get through. The only alternative for the passengers was to walk across a rocky, muddy stretch of two miles. This was to get to the other side of the destroyed road and find new transport north. It was difficult, but we made it across. It still took over five days to get across Peru and finally reach the border with Ecuador.

That trip from one end of Peru to the other had been sobering. There had been vast misery because of the Niño phenomenon. Later years would see multiple repetitions of this huge rainfall and flooding season. By then, scientists would understand and describe the periodic oscillation of ocean and atmospheric currents across the Pacific Ocean and what were the planetary effects.

But the great El Niño event of 1982-83 was much broader and deeper than had been seen or understood before. Hundreds of villages were affected, if not more, and hundreds of people were lost to landslides. Mudslides were everywhere, with cars and buses slipping off dangerous precipices and slopes. The coastal highway had been cut by portions of the Pan-American highway breaking off and sliding into the Pacific.

The indigenous communities in the Andean highlands and valleys felt the greater misery. When roads and paths were demolished, the people would sometimes trek for miles out of their way. I was frankly unaware at that time of things like climate change, but I soon came to understand.

In hindsight, this Niño cycle of ocean currents and rainfall changes was an early, unheeded alarm clock over the greater devastation that was yet to come of Global Warming and Climate Change. I was happy to have seen the Chilean glaciers when I had, as they would not last much longer.

I returned to Ecuador and looked forward to the next adventure awaiting me.

CHAPTER 5

●◆●

HOW PLAN SET MATTERS AFLAME

Guayaquil was as dirty and suffocating as ever. I returned to check up on my Peace Corps volunteer buddies after having been away on my three-month sojourn. Lea and Lisa were happy to see me again. We went out for some typical Ecuadorian "chifa" food and ample beer to celebrate.

I then went to meet with Anibal Oprandi, who was at that time visited by the so-called sheriff of Guayas province, Abdala Bucarám. Abdala was wearing a typical coastal guayabera shirt outside the pants and demanded a bunch of things of PLAN projects. He had a trim little Hitler moustache across his upper lip. He was red-faced and sweating with puffy cheeks and paunch. He strutted back and forth trying to intimidate the Argentine Anibal Oprandi.

Anibal was unflappable. Even when Abdala in his high-pitched hoarse voice pulled a pistol out of the paunch of his pants waist and insisted "AQUI MANDO YO!" – Here I am the boss! Anibal managed to suavely and soothingly calm Abdala down. Anibal promised to "consider" infrastructure projects Sheriff Abdala wanted for the Guasmo slums of Guayaquil.

Abdala Bucarám was a scion of the political Lebanese immigrant family that had founded the center-right populist party, CFP, forty years earlier. His father, the party's founder and patriarch, Assad Bucarám, was always careful to sidestep any insinuations of personal corruption. He was widely seen as a long-suffering populist opponent of military rule.

Abdala was brother-in-law to the debonair and sophisticated former president Jaime Roldós – who had died in 1981 in a mysterious plane crash near the Peruvian border. He had developed his own political movement and cult of personality, tied to the tragic memory of Roldós, a sort of JFK for Ecuadorians. But Abdala was also part of the new generation of Bucaráms who were far crasser in their populism. They enjoyed hand over fist corruption, which did not stop them from having thousands of devotees. As Sheriff he was a major power broker rivaling the mayor or governor of the province. He held responsibility over much more than the police power.

Anibal finally turned his attention to me and my somewhat bemused expression after Bucarám's departure.

"Bienvenido, bienvenido." He told me, welcoming me back. "I have some new ideas over the work we want to ask you to do." He had met with Henk Franken, the Dutch director of the new PLAN program in Bolivar province. Henk needed help.

Anibal thought I could be even more useful there rather than in the "catch as catch can" environment of the Guayaquil slums of Guasmo. He suggested, "Why don't you travel up to Guaranda, the provincial capital, and meet with Henk and see if there was a meeting of the minds?"

I was game and open to anything. I wasn't particularly familiar with the province. I understood it was neighboring the highlands provinces of Ambato and Riobamba, a smaller version of both. It had lowlands tropical communities as well as mountain ones. After living in coastal Ecuador for the last two years it might be an interesting change.

I knew that Annie and Daniela, two PCV women with whom I had become friends in Guayas during my second year, had moved to a small town called San Simon outside Guaranda. Both women had together gone through the horrible experience of rape by a pair of coastal youths after nine months in the country.

The Peace Corps had offered them a choice of returning home to the States or a site change to a safer highlands community. They had bravely decided to stay on and were roommates in a shared house in the new safer site. I sent a telegram to Annie and Daniela to let them know I was coming soon.

A couple of days later, I said goodbye to Lisa and Lea and moved my modest belongings to Guaranda, initially staying in a small hotel off the town square. Because of the seven hills and valleys surrounding it, Guaranda had the rather ambitious nickname of 'the Rome of Ecuador'.

Guaranda was a lovely tidy town with cobblestone streets in the center, rising sharply on a hillside. But even being generous, it was hardly a Rome. But it did have a mostly intact colonial character. The buildings were only a few stories tall, so you could easily see the surrounding countryside.

Most impressive was the formidable view of the top third of the snowcapped volcano Chimborazo, visible from much of the city. Chimborazo was a gorgeous mountain about 15 miles away; it was in fact the highest peak in Ecuador. The peak of Chimborazo was 6263 meters or 20,550 feet high.

Some mountain climbers say it was, in fact, higher in the atmosphere than Mount Everest, given the planet's equatorial bulge. I adored the beauty of the white gleaming ice in the clear sky above Guaranda—like a giant ice cube. It was mesmerizing.

I met with Henk Franken the next day and discovered Annie and Daniela had already vouched for me with Henk. They knew him and had been working in partnership with PLAN since settling in San Simon.

Henk was a tall, direct, and candid Dutchman. While he was at times skeptical of Anibal and his approach to things, he respected American Peace Corps volunteers. He was happy to take me on to his staff. He offered me the job of Program Advisor/Trainer, working within the health department of PLAN Bolivar. Depending on how things went, he suggested that he might expand that role in time.

Henk made clear that he was the only expatriate hire at PLAN Bolivar and relied on his senior Ecuadorian staff in key roles. He didn't want my coming on board to upset staff dynamics; I got the message and assured him that was not in the cards.

During the first two weeks of coming on board with PLAN, tragedy would strike at home for me, but I would find out about it too late to be able to do much.

Henk asked me to travel to the Amazonian jungle of Ecuador and manage a previously arranged exploratory meeting with an indigenous people's federation in Napa province. I spent a week and a half in the eastern jungle of the country.

It was a fascinating trip that I hoped could lead to a PLAN partnership there. But back in New York, during early April, my father's emphysema suddenly worsened, and he died in his sleep at the Brooklyn VA hospital.

My mom and sister sent me a telegram with the information, but it went first to Quevedo, where I had lived before. It was forwarded somehow to the PLAN offices in Guayaquil and then on to Guaranda. I did not receive it or find out about things until a week after he had died and several days after the funeral.

I called and reached my sister and mother; it was a difficult and painful situation for all, but not unexpected. I had fortuitously been able to reconnect with my father and say goodbye the previous September. We decided together that it made little sense at that point for me to return to New York. The funeral had already been held with my grandparents, a few of my father's family members, and friends. I promised to travel back to the States to visit sometime in the coming year.

I grew to build deep ties with the PLAN staff. I worked closely with Luísa, the head of the health department for PLAN, and Luís Torres, the Administrator and chief operating officer for the office. They were a little uncertain of where I was coming from and whether I intended to come to PLAN as some "know-it-all" American. That was not the case; I wanted to learn and grow and be as helpful to them as possible at the same time.

Within the first weeks,, we developed trust. I made clear I was not coming in as Henk's new deputy or senior advisor, although I hoped to earn that role and more.

It was a big office with over 60 staff including 25 extensionists or promoters. These promoters, young men and women, would take motorcycles out to visit their assigned communities and families.

Henk was a revolutionary in that he encouraged hiring these community promoter jobs to young women. Luís, as administrator, had been skeptical that women could do the job. They came to prove him wrong.

It was an innovative and pioneering example of overcoming gender differences and traditional roles. One that worked its effect not only within PLAN and its employees but also with the thousands of beneficiaries and participants in the PLAN program. It was even more amazing that they could do this in a conservative Latin country with the mores of the Andean highlands.

I came to appreciate the remarkable way PLAN worked in nearly 300 different communities across the province, ranging from the altiplano highlands to the coastal lowlands.

Under the child sponsorship approach, each donor who came on board made a commitment to contribute $20 or more per month. A modest amount was spent on program administration, salaries, and overhead.

Under Luís, PLAN Bolivar expanded the number of participating children and communities monthly. It had developed an ambitious public works approach. It used the annual budget from child sponsorship for community development budgets for each community. They would support broad-based infrastructure needs. PLAN would not just support individual family assistance to the sponsored children.

The available budget was significant. It grew as new children and communities were signed up. The contributions of a European or North American donor family represented an annual investment of $200 per year. With a community of 50 children enrolled, this was a potential budget of $10,000 per year. About 10-20 percent of that was set aside for direct assistance needs for the child including special assistance with school supplies or clothing to help incentivize their staying in school.

An annual budget of $8000 or more for a community represented a significant amount of money. This could mean rehabilitating school classrooms, building latrines, or wells. For larger communities, the building of water projects and rural electrification. It was rivaling if not surpassing what was possible from the provincial and municipal governments. And it was hugely more than any resources I had been able to find as a Peace Corps volunteer.

I learned an immense amount in the nearly two years I spent with PLAN. I spent much of the next two years, traveling on motorcycles and old jeeps along countryside dirt and gravel roads. I visited community promoters and community leaders in villages from 900 feet altitude lowlands up to 17,000 feet, often a couple times a week.

PLAN was a development arena for me. I deepened my understanding of community engagement and participation. I saw the potential for human upliftment.

It was a human development laboratory where I tested different ideas and concepts in adult education. I received real and meaningful feedback in real-time, and I came to appreciate what worked and what didn't. PLAN and other friends in Guaranda also provided a safe space of great camaraderie, solidarity, and meaning. It helped me to really develop a further foundation for the vocation I felt my life was calling for.

Luís Torres was a mover and a shaker. He was not a perfect angel, of course; that was an open secret. He had political ambitions for the future, though he denied them. Building up this sort of program for the somewhat neglected province would not be a political liability; quite the contrary.

While Luis was honest, there were occasional signs and discoveries of corruption, such as engineers who seemed to be making side deals with contractors and suppliers. We sometimes discovered petty corruption from some of the promoters. People were dealt with when these discoveries were made. Usually, they quickly departed when confronted with an embarrassing prosecution and dismissal. It wasn't possible to usually prosecute with the local court system, which was sadly compromised.

During my first year under Henk, I revamped our promoters' health and community development training program. I tried to apply what I had learned in the Peace Corps and beyond.

Annie and Daniela turned me onto the Food First movement. I borrowed materials they had collected on nutrition and community learning to complement my own. I visited Riobamba to follow up further on the indigenous literacy efforts that I had heard about as a Peace Corps Volunteer.

While in Peace Corps training, I had heard a bit from Ed Scholl about the "Red Bishop," the revolutionary Bishop in Riobamba Monsignor Leonidas Proaño. I knew that monied and upper-class Ecuadorians despised him, in large part because he refused to try to "westernize the Indians." He dedicated himself to helping to protect the traditional indigenous values and culture.

Monsignor Proaño supported literacy efforts in Spanish and beyond. He promoted literacy work in Quichua and other indigenous languages in the neighboring province since 1973. The local indigenous language Quichua was a highlands altiplano legacy of the Quechua Incan presence in Ecuador that came fifty years before the Spanish.

The Monsignor's life work inspired me, and I sought to look for ways to expand it within the many indigenous highlands communities of Bolivar. I took time to learn the basics of Quichua with the help of some PLAN promoters. I could at least offer greetings and engage in extremely basic conversation.

Luis introduced me to a group of revolutionary Jesuit priests. They built rural cheesemaking works in half a dozen communities across the province. Their work had begun at some ancient salt mines in an area appropriately known as Salinas, about 90 minutes from Guaranda, and had expanded to other centers.

I loved the incredible cheese these villages produced. And I saw how much in demand they grew to be in Quito and elsewhere. It gave me valuable insights into how to support income-generating projects that would benefit rural villagers. Most importantly, I realized how essential business enterprises are to development.

The Jesuit efforts provided real jobs and reliable income to many families. Their communities thrived. They saved and invested savings in health and education. They were able to sell their cheese in big cities far away. The families and communities became self-reliant. The best students had opportunities for college and higher income professions. It was a virtuous circle.

Meanwhile, my social life was an active one as well. While Guaranda was not exactly hopping as a city I had plenty of friends. I quickly became close friends with Ronnie Reitz, who was a remarkable fixture of the community.

Ronnie had been a Peace Corps volunteer in the 1960s. He had married into a local Lebanese immigrant family with three sisters who owned a textile store and haberdashery. He worked at the store, which was the best in town and a popular stopping place for volunteers. He was a hoot with stories and tall tales when I would pop my head into it in Guaranda's central plaza. He would invite me over every other week or so for some delicious meals, usually with Lebanese desserts one or the other sister would make.

Ronnie was an example and model for some of the volunteers. He had completed his Peace Corps service and returned to stay on. I could imagine the same.

I was earning a salary in local currency that approached $1000 per month, which was comfortable compared to Peace Corps volunteer sums. I had access to vehicles. I had been allowed to take out a motorcycle to use for work and after hours. After about six months, I was able to borrow old Toyota jeeps to get around when needed outside of Guaranda.

I loved the outdoors around Guaranda and the nearby pine forests. It was like being on a branch road off the Avenue of Volcanoes in Ecuador. Chimborazo's stratovolcano heights loomed right over the city. Driving towards Ambato an hour or so away I could see the breathtaking cone of Tungurahua. Heading north towards Quito I would soon encounter the perfect snowcap of Cotopaxi, sitting above Latacunga. Cotopaxi must be one of the most beautiful snowcaps in the world, akin to Mount Fuji in Japan.

Further on, just adjacent to Quito, were Pichincha's two peaks cones, Wawa (Baby) Pichincha and Ruku Pichincha. North of Quito was the massive Cayambe. For me, the snowcapped volcanoes were perfect metaphors for the challenges we face if we are prepared and willing to do so. Those snowcaps could also sit as ornamental reminders of what had been left unfinished if you didn't pursue the challenges.

I dated some local girls and found this fun but a bit limiting. Casual liaisons filled only some needs. I didn't expect long-term relationships to happen there in Guaranda.

I became good friends with several Peace Corps volunteers in the province and dated a few of the women amicably off and on over time. Even so, I hesitated to date PC volunteers in Bolivar Province or Guaranda. I thought it might complicate friendships and be disruptive.

Then I met Cindy. She was a Peace Corps Volunteer, also in rural public health, but two years behind me, so her COS date would be at the end of 1984. She lived and worked in a village in the neighboring province of Cotopaxi.

I forget who introduced us, but when we first met, she had been dating another volunteer for some time. That relationship had ended, and I was interested. Cindy had amazing blue eyes, a quick mind, and obvious social commitment. She also had an extraordinary singing voice, particularly for folk music. I asked her to share any cassette recordings of her singing.

In our first conversations, she mentioned that she was Bahá'í. I wasn't sure what that was, but I thought a girl from Hawai'i at the University of Chicago had said the same thing, or maybe not. I wasn't sure. I remembered they had a big temple of some sort near Evanston, just off Lake Michigan. I had never gone inside the unusual but admittedly impressive building, north of Chicago.

She lent me a few books that she had about the Bahá'í Faith, and it did not make a huge initial impression. I skimmed them through somewhat carelessly and made positive noncommittal answers. I wasn't sure about what I was reading, but I definitely wanted to get to know Cindy better.

I introduced Cindy to Mary Fiksel, the new Canadian PLAN assistant country director. After a year, she replaced Henk Franken, just as a new Dutchman named Herman de Koek replaced Anibal Oprandi in Guayaquil. I was curious about Mary's opinion of Cindy.

Mary was a remarkable person who profoundly affected me at the time. She seemed a bit on the hippie mellow side. At the time, I saw her as an attractive and compelling woman, ten years older than me. It wasn't a connection in any physical or carnal way but on some sort of spiritual level which I could intuit but not fully understand.

Mary was born in Montreal to Holocaust survivors. In her early twenties, she went to an ashram in India to study eastern philosophies. She was briefly married but left that marriage. She returned to study for a graduate degree in nutrition at Tufts, working as a nutrition advisor for UNICEF before joining PLAN.

I described Mary as hippie-like and that may sound a bit uncharitable. Mary and I had some interesting overlaps; she had come from a Jewish family but had abjured Judaism for the most part. I could never have imagined then what would happen in her life, which I only recently learned about writing this book.

I met her elderly parents during the year I worked under her in Guaranda when Jay and Lea Fiksel came for a visit. I helped Mary as much as possible with some logistics connected with their visit. They were loving parents, a little puzzled by her previous flirtations with India and Buddhism. But reassured that she was now in a stable position in an international organization like Foster Parents Plan. They seemed grateful to me for being somehow a grounding and positive influence in Mary's life. I didn't see myself in that way but somehow Mary had conveyed that to them.

I loved Mary's wisdom and insights. We had long conversations about life and its inevitable surprises during lengthy field visits in the PLAN Chevy Blazer. She valued my bicultural fluidity and ease with language. She helped solidify my sense of vocation and commitment to organizations like PLAN.

Mary was fascinated by Cindy as well and made all these faces asking if we were dating or not and why not. She seemed like a Buddhist Jewish yenta at such times, which made me laugh. Cindy and I did begin to date and see each other at least a couple times a month. I wondered where things might go.

In an interesting turn of fate, I had been checking in with the USAID Ecuador office in Quito from time to time, particularly the health office. USAID was the local headquarters of the U.S. Agency for International Development. USAID had poured millions into infrastructure and other projects in Ecuador over the years.

I knew USAID was connected with the U.S. Embassy, but at that point, the connection was at times arms-length. Just like the Peace Corps, USAID occupied its own office building and was not on the Embassy grounds. I was slightly suspicious of USAID and its role in official development assistance.

I had read many critiques of USAID and World Bank assistance in the developing world. I was leery of any agenda they might have. I did not believe I would ever want to work with them. Little did I know at that point how that might change.

PLAN Ecuador received a health sector institutional strengthening grant from USAID. It complemented PLAN's own funding. I thought it made sense for me to remain in regular contact. Henk and then Mary had strongly encouraged me to do so. I had made friends in the health office with Ken Farr, Jay Anderson, and one of their water and sanitation engineers, Herb Caudill. Herb was a highly respected technical expert among the Ecuadorian institutions known to PCVs. He had lived in Quito for many years. I also met Ken Yamashita, who was then on loan to USAID from the CDC. He would eventually go on to a very distinguished career with the Agency.

One day, I was in Quito for a short visit and stopped by USAID to share some updates on our training of health promoters in the province. Jay had a special request.

"Would you be willing to lead a group of health promoters from Chimborazo and Bolivar provinces to Otavalo?" he asked. "Specifically, to Radio Bahá'í Otavalo, about an hour north of Quito?"

Jay told me I could take a couple of staff members from PLAN Bolivar for an opportunity for a mutual exchange of experiences and lessons learned, and USAID would pay for it. Bahá'í – this must be linked with the Bahá'í movement Cindy had talked with me about. Sure, I said. Happy to do so.

I led a group of about 20 or 25 to Otavalo for about 3-4 days. I always liked Otavalo as a place to visit. It had a unique group of indigenous peoples with their own distinctive culture, costumes, and food and a pleasant small city. It was fun to return to, particularly for an official work-related reason.

Radio Bahá'í was located on the edge of town. It proved to be a remarkable and eye-opening experience for me. The radio station was one huge nonprofit private development project. Over the course of ten years it had captured over 85% of the rural and most of the urban radio market around Otavalo. The commercial competitors were left to compete for the remaining scraps.

The station organizers were Bahá'í teachers or "pioneers" from abroad. They created an authentic radio community education project. The station programming was enriched with local music and culture. They provided educational messages in health, literacy, agriculture, small animal husbandry, etc. It used the magazine format I had copied in Quevedo from the University of Massachusetts Amherst's experience in Riobamba. It seemed, in fact, that many of the most innovative students and faculty from the Amherst school of education were also Bahá'ís.

One of the most popular programs was called "LA VACA PERDIDA" – "The Lost Cow." It was a sort of radio bulletin board for rural villages all around Otavalo to share community service messages around for each other. These included the inevitable ones small farmers would ask, 'have you seen my cow?' And other similar messages.

Radio Bahá'í complemented radio broadcasting with an active community education and promoter program. They cooperated with the local government ministries to bring them and their experts in an inclusive manner.

The radio station had started with small seed funding from the Bahá'í World Centre in Haifa, Israel, and donors from the United States. It had gone on to win competitive grant awards to expand the rural education services from Canadian CIDA, Swedish SIDA, and USAID. They also received grants as well from other private foundation sources.

The Otavalo team took my group to different villages to see how the radio program fit into village life. We observed how it complemented the curriculum at primary and secondary schools in the area. We saw how crop extensionists and health center doctors relied on it to reach out to the hundreds of thousands of rural villagers in the area.

There were Bahá'í religious symbols and material visibly around. But at no time did the radio center staff or volunteers talk to us about the religion or try to inculcate any missionary type message. It was thoroughly professional, and inspiring to all the participants.

We were all impressed when we learned that the Otavalo radio station was, in fact, part of a hemispheric development education network targeting indigenous communities. There were radio stations in southern Colombia, one in southern Peru in Puno, one in the Bolivian altiplano near Caracollo and Oruro, one in southern Chile near Temuco, one under construction in the Guaymí indigenous lands of Panama, and a rural Black hamlet in South Carolina in the United States. It was an outstanding array of development initiatives.

I came away deeply affected by the experience. I wasn't particularly drawn to know much more about the religious teachings of the Bahá'ís, which I later shared with a sympathetic and curious Cindy. However, I was intrigued by the vision, purpose, and principles that these Bahá'ís were offering and demonstrating through their efforts.

I was impressed with the linkages with the UMass Amherst School of Education and wondered if I should consider graduate work there myself at some point. The idea of a participatory education platform for a holistic approach to human-based development was compelling. I wanted to try to adapt this to the work of PLAN and other nonprofit community development organizations.

I was also moved by the resonance of the spiritual teachings within this development initiative. That had been an important driver in the liberation theology efforts that I had learned about as a Peace Corps Volunteer. It also seemed consistent with the Society of Friends' writings about the 'peaceable kingdom' that I had gleaned from Kat and Katherine in the past.

That USAID supported this Bahá'í effort was a bit unexpected, but they recognized success wherever it came from. The success was measurable. There was clear improvement in the indicators about the use of health, education and agriculture extension services from government ministries in the area. Also, the level of prosperity in the villages we visited was visible and impressive. How much of this was due to the program was unclear, but it seemed likely to have a strongly positive effect.

When I shared these experiences with Mary back in Guaranda, she was supportive and encouraged me to look for deeper meanings. She considered herself still a student of Buddhism and used a Buddhist lens to examine life options all the time. She wondered where I wanted to go in life; she was happy to have me stay on, as well as Cindy, but sensed that I needed to grow somewhere else.

During much of the year, I had begun to apply for international hire positions with Foster Parents Plan. I hoped to move up into an expatriate Assistant Country Director role in Ecuador or some other country program. Yet PLAN senior staff who visited from headquarters always seemed to demur. They said they valued my contributions and efforts with the PLAN program in Ecuador. They had good recommendations from Mary, Henk, Anibal and Anibal's successor Herman de Koek. But it never seemed to go anywhere.

Finally, during the field visit of their senior program director from Warwick, Rhode Island, in late 1984, he confided in me. I was unlikely to be hired for some time, and this was due to no specific fault of my own.

PLAN International was a growing international network with many unique concerns. Though the HQ was historically in the USA, the larger share of revenue and donors now came increasingly from Holland.

Consequently, there was a large push from the Board of Directors for hiring to be more diverse. Had I been Dutch, I would have had no problem; Canadians would also have been fine. There was a growing need to add more female staff—had I been a woman, I might also have had greater success. But as a White American male, I had a very uphill battle considering the demographics of the organization.

I considered my options, weighing them separately with Cindy as well as Mary. I decided as December began that it was probably best I travel home to New York after New Year's. I could catch up with my mother and sister and look for future employment opportunities. PLAN was jerking me around a bit. They made no move or invitation to have me fly back to the States to interview. This was despite open applications that I had understood were or should be competitive.

Cindy encouraged me to send out my resume and apply for jobs where I could demonstrate the substantial experience gained. Mary thought the same. I let Mary know that while I was leaving, Cindy was getting ready to complete her own PCV service.

Mary reached out to Cindy and let her know a job was available with my departure in January if she was interested. She invited Cindy to help with program evaluations and translated donor letters for the sponsored children's families.

Mary generously offered a severance pay package that would cover my airfare to New York and about four months of salary. She felt PLAN HQ had given me a raw deal, and while under no legal need to do so she wanted to do more than just help me along.

Mary's generosity and spiritual encouragement were frankly unusual for someone in her position. It was unexpected and I gratefully accepted.

I had no idea at the time that Mary would continue her work for PLAN only for another year or two in Africa but then leave PLAN to take up a hugely different calling in her life. Mary took up formal ordination orders as a Buddhist monk in Burma, renaming herself Ayya Medhanandi. As I mentioned earlier, I had no idea that she took this path until I began to prepare this book.

As Ayya Medhanandi Bhikkhuni, Mary was the founder and guiding teacher of Sati Saraniya Hermitage, a forest monastery for women in the Theravada tradition. Her biography notes that as the daughter of Eastern European refugees who emigrated to Montreal after World War II, she began a spiritual quest in childhood that led her to India, Burma, England, New Zealand, Malaysia, Taiwan, and finally, back to Canada. In 1988, at the Yangon Mahasi retreat centre in Burma, Ayya requested ordination as a bhikkhuni from her teacher, the Venerable Sayadaw U Pandita. This was not yet possible for Theravada Buddhist women. Instead, Sayadaw granted her ordination as a 10-precept novice nun on condition that she take her vows for life. Ayya's monastic training in the Burmese tradition began.

When a military coup closed the borders to foreigners, Ayya felt called to more seclusion and solitude in New Zealand and SE Asia. After nearly 20 years as a novice alms-mendicant nun, in 2007, Ayya fulfilled her long-held wish for full ordination. She took her bhikkhuni vows at Ling Quan Chan Monastery in Keelung, Taiwan. On invitation from the Ottawa and Toronto Buddhist Communities, Ayya returned the next year to her native Canada to establish Sati Saraniya Hermitage.

I found out about all of this online just a couple of months before the writing of this book in 2020. It left me touched and humbled. I realized that I had spent over a year with her at a critical time in her own life. She no doubt had pondered the closure of her materialistic life in international development. And her future profound spiritual journey.

Have you ever come to realize that someone you worked with or were friends with years ago ended up taking a radically different path? I had never seen someone go through such a transformation.

I arrived in New York in mid-January. I mailed my resume to several different organizations I identified through listings I had collated. Two days after arrival at my mom's apartment, I was contacted by Loren Finnell. He was the New York representative of the Arizona-based NGO Esperança and suggested an interview lunch in Manhattan near Grand Central Station.

Esperança was, in some ways, a spinoff organization from Project Hope and included a number of people who had worked there. It was founded as a Catholic-aligned private voluntary organization to support Father Luke Tupper, a Franciscan medical missionary priest and physician in the Amazon.

For many years, it operated a hospital boat on the Amazon, bringing health services to the tribes and peoples living on the river. Eventually, a land-based primary health program at Santarem, Brazil, was established. A two-year pilot project was conducted in the Chaco lowlands of neighboring Bolivia. Esperança needed a new project director for its Bolivia program who could bring the program to a new level of growth and vitality.

By the end of the Manhattan lunch, Loren offered me the Bolivia job. He invited me to visit him in Larchmont to learn more about Esperança and his work as a Senior Advisor and Representative of the PVO. I was flattered to be offered a substantive job within days of my arrival; I could not believe I was offered the job even before our lunch was over. I asked for at least a few days to think about it. Loren made noises initially that the offer might disappear if I did not pick up on it that moment, but he then agreed to wait.

I did not tell him that the afternoon before I had been contacted by the human resources office of PLAN International's HQ in Rhode Island. It was both cheering and annoying; the day after I arrived in New York they finally called. Would I kindly be available to fly up to Warwick for an interview with them? I was pleased but rueful at their cheekiness - now that I was in the States under my own steam, they wanted to interview me. Regardless, I agreed, scheduling the flight and interview for later that week.

PLAN flew me back and forth from LaGuardia airport in New York the same day. I spent a day interviewing them at different levels and thought for a moment that something long-term would materialize with them. But this was perversely still not to be. I learned a few days later they were still not ready to take me on as an international employee, despite the welcome and full day of

146

interviews that had seemed to be a virtual onboarding to the organization. I told them not to fret – I had already accepted the position of Bolivia Country Director with a different NGO. I was peeved again briefly, but also convinced that Bolivia was the right choice.

Esperança was certainly a little unusual among many organizations. It was a nonprofit private voluntary organization based in Phoenix, what the IRS calls a "501 [C] 3" charity. They were not located in New York or along one of the two coasts in the USA. They were in the Southwest, which was unusual. They were a modest sized operation, officially nonsectarian although with deep Catholic roots. They had wisely brought on the entrepreneurial Loren Finnell in New York as an advisor and consultant on retainer. This saved them the need to worry about a formal office in New York or elsewhere on the East Coast.

I didn't fully grasp it then, but Loren was an inspired choice as a representative on retainer. Loren Finnell had been in the Peace Corps—Ecuador, as it turned out—in one of the first groups, 1964-1966. I think that is when Ronnie Reitz from Guaranda joined. Loren then went on to work with International Voluntary Services. From there, he was one of the founders of Private Agencies Collaborating Together (PACT), one of the first networks among private voluntary charities overseas.

I contacted Loren and told him I would accept, and Loren arranged for me to come up by train to Larchmont for an initial briefing. We called into the Phoenix headquarters of Esperança and Chuck Post, their Executive Director. He then invited me to fly to the Phoenix headquarters the following Monday. I could get to know people of the organization and go through the paperwork there. It was all moving amazingly quickly – my karma seemed to be pointed in their direction. I wrote to Cindy and Mary to inform them about the quick developments. Soon I would be on my way to Bolivia.

CHAPTER 6

BOLIVIAN BONFIRE OF THE VANITIES

I was proud of the sudden job offer in Bolivia, and what it spoke to my experience and capabilities. But I soon learned all the other reasons for my rapid recruitment and onboarding, beyond the apparent karma of the moment.

Esperança was working in the Chaco of Bolivia – not the usual photogenic altiplano highlands of countless tourist posters. It was the only international private voluntary organization (PVO) working in the region, a very isolated and remote area. This in a country that itself was also a bit isolated and remote to the outside world. The Chaco was far from any city and extremely far from the capital.

Look on a map: the Chaco – also known for decades as the "Green Hell" - is a vast depopulated territory of southeastern Bolivia. In the early 20th century, it had been much larger, including a big chunk of what became the western lobe of Paraguay. Paraguay and Bolivia fought a series of bloody battles called the Chaco War from 1932-1935.

The war was largely invisible and unknown to much of the world. It was instigated largely because of the belief of many that it might hold big oil deposits. The Bolivians lost huge amounts of land here as they did elsewhere in past decades after encroachments from Brazil, Peru, and Chile. This was not an area that I figured was the easiest to recruit for.

Loren Finnell, who was in New York, did his best to help Esperança build a program team in Bolivia. There was a healthy dose of synchronicity about my recruitment and selection by Esperança. By an interesting coincidence, Loren was himself a Returned Peace Corps Ecuador volunteer. Esperança supported a part-time country representative in Sucre, Bolivia, Hank Beder. He was essentially a logistics manager for anything Esperança needed purchased or done to support the project in the field. He was also an RPCV from Ecuador; his wife Miriam was Ecuadorian. Here, I was recruited and brought on board, as well as a recent RPCV from Ecuador.

Esperança had hired Ana Marie, an older, no-nonsense Arizona public health nurse, almost two years earlier as project manager. She had served for several years on the famous Project Hope hospital ship. She was, in some ways, from a different era, and she never really managed to learn Spanish particularly well, if at all.

When Esperança recruited Ana Marie to scout out project sites, she sought partnerships from the Catholic clergy above all. She looked around the country and saw plenty of international nonprofit voluntary organizations working in and around La Paz, the biggest city. There were also some organizations around Cochabamba and Sucre, which boasted scenic and comfortable places to live. Sucre was the legal capital of the country though the functional seat of government was La Paz.

Ana Marie went further afield, and to this day, I can't imagine how she made it all the way out to Camiri and the Chaco. But she was looking for an area no one else worked in. She won over an invitation and support of the Catholic bishop in Camiri and a pair of Italian brothers who were Franciscan priests, Father Fulgencio and Father Roberto.

The brothers lived a rather splendid life in isolation and comfort at the Catholic Parish house of Macharetí. This village was a tiny cattle station in the middle of the Chaco region of Chuquisaca province. About 300 miles south of the eastern lowlands city of Santa Cruz de la Sierra and 100 miles north of the Argentina border. In other words, in the middle of nowhere.

The Bishop provided Ana Marie with a sturdy old Toyota jeep that seemed almost indestructible. He also made available a small house with a few rooms in the village. Ana Marie started a small-scale health project from there, not much different from many Peace Corps volunteers. Her crusty southwestern manner gave her charisma and authenticity to the local villagers. But she was unlikely to be in a great position to expand the program much beyond that. She was also eager for retirement, having signaled that since late 1984.

Loren and the Esperança Executive Director, Chuck Post, knew they needed to build credibility with USAID. This was important to expand the program to the next level. With Esperança an active member of the PACT network, PACT included Esperança in an NGO "Block Grant." That grant had provided modest seed funding from 1983 to help Esperança launch a program in Bolivia.

Now there were expectations that the PVO might qualify for direct USAID funding. The PACT network participation and the fact that Esperança was in the middle of nowhere left the PVO well-positioned and competitive.

It could apply and compete for one of the first USAID Child Survival grants. The grants were intended to spur a new serious focus on reducing infant and maternal mortality in the countries of Latin America, Africa, and Asia. For me, at least, it seemed to be a good example of being in the right place at the right time.

In less than a month, I was on my way to Bolivia, heading first for La Paz and then onto Sucre, Bolivia's legal capital. There seemed to be something magical about it. For some reason, I had largely side-stepped Bolivia previously during my travels across South America.

Hank and Miriam picked me up, and we began to make plans for how I would travel to Macharetí and the Chaco project site. We reached Ana Marie in Macharetí using a ham radio setup in Hank's house.

Ana Marie was friendly on the radio but gave us a heads-up that road conditions in the area were terrible, if not impassable. It would be best to find a way to fly if a small plane were headed down to the Chaco region, or if need be, fly to Santa Cruz and take the train down from there. But then, things got even more complicated in the next couple of days.

A major national strike that had been brewing and threatening for months finally materialized. The Bolivian Labor Confederation suddenly shut the country down. It was a very militant body with Maoist communist leadership. They were protesting against a range of government economic measures. In fact, it was an open secret that they were trying to topple the government.

Bolivia and its economy were once again veering into hyperinflation, and the value of the Bolivian peso was dropping like a stone. One day, it was worth 10,000 to the dollar; the next day, 50,000 to the dollar. The currency seemed to have no bottom. It would reach two million pesos to the dollar during my first months there.

The practical consequence of this was that there was no way to leave Sucre. Few shops were open; the central market itself would open for only a few hours each day. There was total chaos. I was going to cool my heels and wait with Hank until things calmed down.

With Hank's radio, we managed to reach a ham radio operator in California. He did us the favor of a phone patch to Chuck in Phoenix, and we gave him a rundown of the status of things. We would have to be patient.

This went on for days. Craziness was in the air. One morning, I was walking down to the market to help Hank and Miriam pick up some basics for the house. I found a neat mahogany walking stick for sale with a llama head on it. I liked it, and after bargaining a little, mostly for the fun of it, I bought it from the vendor. I had simple sandals on and a linen shirt.

As I was walking through the market, this crazy man with a scraggly beard spotted me and started shouting at the top of his lungs in Spanish, "Saint Joseph! He is here. The Father of Jesus is walking among us in our market! Saint Joseph!" People stared, and I tried to get away as fast as possible, with this crazy man following me and shouting.

In the afternoon, after lunch, I went out again to the central square of Sucre, to sit in the sun and people watch. I hoped the crazy man had other ideas. This time, I heard some gunshots in the distance, and wondered what was going on.

Two young Bolivian students came up to me, and hissed at me, "Alfonso, what are you doing here?" I looked confused, and they said, "The milicos, the military are looking to round up student leaders. You have to hide!"

I answered back in Spanish, "I'm not Alfonso, my friend; I have no idea what you are talking about."

Either my words or the traces of my gringo accent made them nonplussed.

"Damn, you are the spitting image of Alfonso Alem, the student labor leader. Be careful gringo, make sure you carry your passport in case the police stop you!"

With that, they ran across the park and over to the next street. I rolled my eyes; I did have a photocopy of my passport with me, as I had left my original with Hank. That would have to do.

By the time the week ended, I was getting a little bored. I had walked around almost the entire colonial center of Sucre and saw what there was to see. The two museums were, in any case, dilapidated and not well kept up. I finished reading what I had been carrying. Hank had some reports and project material for me to read, but I also wanted to look for something to distract me a bit.

I stumbled upon a tourist brochure in their house. I noticed the back page of the pamphlet had a list of religions present in Sucre. At the bottom of a list of Catholic and Christian churches was written "Bahá'í Community." Hmm, Bahá'í Community. I remembered it from the materials Cindy had shared with me, and what I had seen at the radio station in Otavalo Ecuador. I thought they might have stuff to read. There was a phone number and an address.

I called the number from Hank's home phone and had a very pleasant conversation with this woman for some minutes. The call was filled with pleasantries until I began to get the idea she might not be, in fact, the "Bahá'í Community" I was trying to reach.

I asked her directly if she was, and she laughed. "Oh, sorry, my dear, this is a wrong number. Others also call me sometimes. To talk to the Bahá'ís, well I don't know their phone number, but you can go down to the Badi School on Calle Junin. They can connect you with the Bahá'ís."

Late the next morning I decided to walk down to the Badi School and see what was up. It was a midsized elementary school with many classrooms. Only a few kids were around with their parents, I imagined due to the national strike.

I went into the main office and saw a rather ungainly, very tall, and pale, reddish blond man who looked up and greeted me in Spanish. I answered him back and introduced myself in Spanish. We exchanged pleasantries, and I learned that he was Bruce Fox, the school's owner and director.

I mentioned I had seen the name Bahá'í community in a tourism pamphlet and had been curious. I looked along the walls at a wide collection of books. By this point, Bruce had done a double take and realized, wait a minute, this guy is American.

"Why are we speaking in Spanish then?" he asked in English.

"Well you started, and I followed your lead." I answered.

We both laughed. I explained that I was sort of captive in Sucre to the national strike and waiting to get down to my new job responsibilities. I wondered if he had any books in English I might borrow since I had little to do for now.

He looked at his watch and stood up. "Come, come join us. Let's swing over to my house; we can chat there, and let me invite you to lunch. You can meet my wife Teresa."

153

"Are you sure?" I asked, a little surprised. "I don't want to be an imposition."

"Not at all, not at all. It's a treat for me to speak with someone again in English, a native English speaker at least. It's a rare treat. Just a few blocks away."

Thus began a bit of a journey that was unexpected, unsought, and even unimaginable. One separate from but inevitably interwoven with my journey to and through the Bolivian Chaco.

Bruce was married to a Bolivian woman and had two adopted children at the time. He had traveled to Bolivia about 10 or 15 years before, arriving in Sucre, and never left. In addition to those at the school, his library and living room were filled with books.

Badi school was not just a Bahá'í school. Bruce and Teresa launched it to offer a qualified, competent private sector alternative to public primary schools. It included many aspects of Bahá'í teachings in the curriculum, and some, although not all, the teachers were Bahá'ís. They seemed to be attracting a growing clientele. They mostly came because of the perceived quality and commitment to performance. They also avoided some of the perceived anachronisms of the Catholic private schools.

Bruce was what I later learned Bahá'ís called a "pioneer": not so much a missionary but a self-supporting settler in another country. He wanted to share by modeling his life and experience as a Bahá'í with others. He was not going to "evangelize". That was frowned upon, if not forbidden, among Bahá'ís. But he was going to be available to answer questions and provide resources to seekers and those with questions.

I certainly didn't consider myself a seeker. I was curious, though. I had some questions for Bruce. But more than anything, I befriended the family, who were warm and welcoming. I was welcomed over the course of the next couple of weeks by an eclectic group of Bahá'í pioneers and believers in Sucre. There were many Bolivian Bahá'ís, some of whom had first heard of the Bahá'í Faith decades before. Among the international pioneers were Persians, Americans, Colombians, Haitians, Germans and more.

I had originally asked Bruce if he had any English language novels or other books to borrow. He later guiltily admitted to me he had told a white lie when he apologized and told me all he had were Bahá'í books. If I wanted to borrow any of them, I was most welcome. So, with a little reluctance, I did.

There really wasn't much to do in Sucre in the evenings. A common practice was to walk down in the evening to get the night air and go people-watching at the so-called "locodromo." This is hard to translate, but it loosely meant the 'racetrack for the crazy ones'.

The locodromo was the evening ambience of the broad sidewalks of Sucre's Plaza de Armas or central plaza. All the single men mostly walked in a counterclockwise rotation around the plaza. While all the young single women walked in the opposite direction. It gave ample opportunity for flirting with eye contact while chaperones trailed at a safe distance behind. I wasn't looking to flirt with anyone, but I joined the circuit around for the night air.

The term 'locodromo' was a pun of sorts since in Sucre's colonial 17th-century center, the Casco Viejo, as it was called, one of the nearby buildings to the Plaza de Armas held the National Insane Asylum. I had no idea how often the inmates there escaped or whether they themselves also chose to frequent the 'locodromo'.

In any case, I would borrow a few books from Bruce and go through them at a time. I read through them quickly. I would then go back to the Badi School or the Fox house or the house of other Bahá'ís to borrow more books when I finished the earlier lot.

I grew increasingly surprised, mystified, incensed and exasperated with the books I read. I began to draw up some charts and tables with notable points quietly. I wanted to better organize, understand, and assess the claims of the Bahá'í Faith. This included going carefully back through the books Cindy had originally lent me back in Ecuador. I read them with more care now and attention to detail.

Much of my reading was impressive, spiritually uplifting, inspiring, and moving. I found it difficult to accept the scope and breadth of the claims being made by the Bahá'í teachings and their place and context in history. It is not that anything was bad. On the contrary, everything I read seemed too good to believe and left me wondering why I was only now reading about all of it. I was of half a mind trying to disprove these claims and digging up any contradictions.

Let me pause here and say that I am not trying to proselytize or evangelize on behalf of this Faith. Far from it. I am trying to categorize and explain how the Faith ended up affecting and shaping my sense of meaning and purpose, and the vocation I wanted to pursue.

You have probably never heard of the Bahá'í Faith. I hadn't myself before, and I was coming to view it as one of the world's best-kept secrets. What were these teachings that I found almost too good to be true? Let me briefly cite from some different sources, including one of many websites out there: http://WWW.BahaiTeachings.Org.

THE BAHÁ'Í

The Bahá'í Faith, the world's newest independent global belief system, arose in 1844 in Persia. It was a time of global messianic expectations among both the Christian West and the Muslim Middle East. It claimed to fulfill the past prophecies of all the major global revealed religions, e.g. Judaism, Christianity, Islam, Zoroastrianism, Buddhism, Hinduism, and more. It teaches fundamentally the oneness of God, the unity of humanity, and the essential harmony of religion.

Bahá'ís believe in the independent investigation of the truth, the equal balance of science and religion, peace, justice, love, altruism, and unity. The Bahá'í teachings promote the elimination of superstition, the elimination of clergy and a special religious class, the equality of the sexes and the elimination of all prejudice and racism.

Just about anywhere you go on the planet, you'll find Bahá'ís. The Encyclopedia Britannica claims the Bahá'í Faith is the world's second-most widespread religion after Christianity, spanning the globe and working to unite it. Bahá'ís have no clergy or churches, gathering together in democratically led communities and welcoming everyone.

The millions of Bahá'ís in the world come from every ethnicity, nationality, tribe, age, racial group, religious background and economic and social class. Gentle, peaceful, warm and welcoming, diverse Bahá'í communities exist just about everywhere. Bahá'ís accept the validity of each of the founders and prophets of the major world religions. They believe in progressive revelation, the unique Bahá'í principle that views every great Faith as a link in a single spiritual system progressively revealed by God to humanity.

Bahá'ís follow the teachings of Bahá'u'lláh. He proclaimed the Bahá'í Faith during the middle of the 19th Century, and who taught world peace, the oneness of all humanity and the essential unity of all religions.

Bahá'u'lláh's timely mission was to take each of these grand religious traditions and show how they are in fact interconnected. They are part of one great process of spiritual evolution. It has all now positioned us to forge a planetary civilization uniting all of mankind, over a period of the next ten centuries.

After the proclamation of his Faith, Bahá'u'lláh suffered forty years of exile, torture and imprisonment. All for announcing that a new revelation had been born. This great divine educator and messenger, despite the persecutions he bore, then wrote a series of epistles to the political and religious rulers of the world from his prison cell.

Those letters, called the *Tablets to the Kings*, openly announced Bahá'u'lláh's station and mission. The intended recipients were the American President, Queen Victoria of England, the Czar of Russia, and Napoleon III of France. There are independent confirmations of this at least from the Queen's household and that of Napoleon III. The tablets warned the world's leaders that humanity faced disastrous consequences unless they laid down their weapons. He commanded them to suspend the armament race and to convene to unite the world and end warfare.

Believers tell an interesting story about these Tablets, specifically the recipients. When Napoleon III received his letter, he exclaimed to his private secretary in disgust, "Hah! This writer says he speaks on behalf of God." He threw the letter down dramatically to the floor. "If he is God, then I am Three Gods!"

When Queen Victoria received her letter, she mused about it and passed it back to her privy secretary. "If what He says is true, then it will endure and last. If it is not, then it is of little importance."

When Bahá'u'lláh was told of this in the responses he received some months later in Palestine, he is said to have blessed the British monarchy and promised it would endure whatever challenges it faced. He said Queen Victoria's descendants would recognize him. Her granddaughter, Queen Marie of Romania, would, in fact, become a Bahá'í forty years later. Of Napoleon III, he is reported to have said in 1869, "The French monarch will rue the day for his arrogance and insolence. Verily soon the streets of Paris will run with blood and his head will be called for."

Bahá'u'lláh called the entire world to collective action and to unity, and that call, Bahá'ís believe, inaugurated a new age of spirituality, harmony and human maturation. Essentially a mystical Faith, the Bahá'í teachings focus on the soul's relationship with the eternal, unknowable essence of God, and recommend daily prayer and meditation to everyone. Bahá'ís believe that the human spirit lives eternally. They endeavor to illumine their souls with spiritual attributes—kindness, generosity, integrity, truthfulness, humility, and selfless service to others.

Bahá'ís accept, respect and revere all the world revelations and distinct religions as well as the sacred traditions of the prophets and teachers of indigenous peoples whose names written history may never have recorded. The Bahá'í Faith encompasses, embraces and advances the past teachings of all those great Faiths, and Bahá'ís view Bahá'u'lláh as the most recent of these divine teachers.

Bahá'u'lláh called each of these divine messengers and teachers "Manifestations of God"—perfect mirrors of the Supreme Being's love and concern for humanity, each of them destined to inspire entire civilizations based on their spiritual teachings and advance the collective maturation of humanity during their dispensations.

That these principles and beliefs somehow emerged from the backwater of Persia in the middle of the 19th century, at a time of global religious reawakening and receptivity, seemed well-nigh unbelievable if not miraculous. That the Founder of this Faith, and his appointed successor, would proceed to address themselves to all the peoples of the world, and the governing authorities of kingdoms and republics, in a prodigious flow of religious and social writings and epistles with social teachings that were so future-leaning for their time, seemed remarkable if not anachronistic.

That they called for social advances that not only were unimaginable for Persia and the Middle East in the 1800s but were even many decades far ahead at the time for the leading countries of their time in Europe and North America, stretched my understanding and imagination to the limit. And that all of this would be unknown to so many seemed also so difficult to swallow on so many different intellectual and spiritual levels.

The son of the Founder, Abdu'l-Bahá, continued and expanded on his father's teachings. His father designated him the 'Center of the Covenant', a perfect exemplar for people to follow after the passing of Bahá'u'lláh in 1892.

In 1912, Abdu'l-Bahá traveled across Europe and North America for nearly six months. He was by that point hailed as the 'Persian Prophet' and was widely acclaimed in the national and local press at the time, which newspaper clippings and microfiches clearly show. We know he spoke at many leading universities, churches and synagogues across the United States, particularly focusing on racial equality and racial healing. He gave a widely respected address on this at Howard University in Washington DC. He spoke as an invited luminary at the fourth annual conference of the NAACP in Chicago.

When Abdu'l-Bahá arrived in San Francisco, as in other places he talked about the need for peace and ending international conflict, and then his remarks took a notable prophetic turn. He warned his audience of a coming conflict that would leave the streets of Europe bathed in blood. He urged mankind to learn its lessons from that conflict.

Abdu'l-Bahá warned prophetically that a further and more devastating war would follow the first. Only then, motioning to the city of San Francisco, he said paraphrasing, "In this lovely city by the bay, the flag of Universal Peace will finally be unfurled." This remarkably foreshadowed both the Great War which would start two years after his sad remarks, World War II, and the San Francisco United Nations Convention 33 years in the future.

There I was, in Sucre, Bolivia, reading serious books and publications that attested to this history and these truths. These included the works of researchers, often carefully citing their sources. There were remarkable notations, excerpts, and quotes. Despite my best efforts, I could not help but feel myself struggling to be increasingly intellectually convinced. But what would that mean?

The Bolivian National Strike went on and on, ultimately lasting a month. During that period, I read at least 15-20 books. I shared meals and hospitality with many of the Bahá'ís in Sucre who I befriended, in part to be less of a burden on my hosts, Hank and Myriam. With almost no exception, no one pressed me about whether I was a believer or not.

But I did feel a profound awakening or curiosity that I recognized as the sensations of a tentative but growing seeker.

I was not looking for a religion for a start. I was searching for a way to better bring meaning to my own deepening vocation in community development. I wanted to understand the principles so I could be much more effective in my work. I found myself intellectually drawn into the thought processes of different Bahá'í writers. I found the hierarchy of history that was increasingly appealing.

I found this disruptive, disturbing and unnerving. I was not looking to become a follower of this Faith. I had come to Bolivia with a job to do and wanted to get on to doing it.

Let's leave that for now. I'll discuss my life choices and the chain of circumstances later.

BACK TO BOLIVIA

By this point the Bolivian peso had devalued to somewhere close to 1,000,000 to the US dollar, and still falling. You practically needed wheelbarrows of currency to buy anything substantial. Yet there was a brief respite in the labor action, and stores, markets and businesses were trying to temporarily re-open. For how long was anybody's guess.

Finally, there was a flight I could join to Camiri, and Ana Marie promised me that she could arrange to pick me up from there and bring me back to Macharetí. This was a particularly good thing. I also learned with Hank that the Executive Director of Esperança, Chuck Post, the Medical Director, Bill Dolan, and a Phoenix NBC TV affiliate film crew were going to come and fly to Bolivia in a month to shoot film for a documentary about the work of Esperança. I needed to get settled to be able to help with that.

As I was making my goodbyes, Bruce and some other Bahá'ís offered to lend me another two dozen books or so for the trip, to be returned whenever possible. The books included pieces on Bahá'í principles, holy writings and scripture, Bahá'í history and biographies, and Bahá'í writings of social and economic development and the progress of the world. I took them in a crate and added it to my luggage for the journey onwards. I had no clear sense of when I would make my way back to Sucre again, nor what was waiting for me in Machareti.

Arriving in the Green Hell of the Chaco was surreal. After a forty-minute flight in the small plane, we landed in a pasture just outside of town. It belonged to the Bishop of Camiri, as indeed much in town appeared to.

Ana Marie was there waiting with her Toyota Hilux 4WD pickup truck. The locals called it a Toyota Mosquito because it was smaller than other Toyotas. It also had the rear elevated a bit, fancifully like the rear legs of a mosquito ready to bite. We dropped my things in the back.

Ana Marie was with a driver and two volunteers from Machareti. We all exchanged greetings and best wishes. Given the small size of the mosquito cabin, I volunteered to ride in the back of the truck with a male volunteer. Ana Marie nodded approvingly but warned me to be ready. "The road has been washed out a lot. It took nearly three hours from Machareti, and hopefully, we won't get stuck."

We headed south, and the lush green vegetation I had first seen around Camiri changed quickly into a green-brown savannah. There was a rich dark brown chocolate roadbed, sometimes thick with mud.

I've heard the Chaco described as a savannah often enough, but it really became over time a sort of spiny forest as well, punctuated by huge baobab trees and cacti. It wasn't that hot then, but I was told it was very changeable. The winds were blowing in a "surazo" from the south. It was a southern cool wind often with a bit of rain, that could also drop the temperatures quite a bit from the 80s or 90s or hotter to the 50s.

It was a bumpy ride. I got to thinking after the first hour or two that Ana Marie had made sure to hit some of the bumpy tracks more enthusiastically. As a welcome baptism by mud for me. We made it through in any case without getting stuck, although there were a few close calls.

During my first days in Macharetí, Ana Marie introduced me to the Italian clergy at the parish house. I also met the political leadership of Macharetí and Dr. Carlos, the director of the small Ministry of Health hospital in town. We visited about a half dozen neighboring communities. She had done some advance outreach, meeting and greeting community leaders and representatives.

Ana Marie gave me a complete overview of her health education work. It reminded me of some basic Peace Corps health initiatives.

Ana Marie had tried to make available vehicle support to get the doctor and the nurse's aide to do a certain amount of outreach outside the facility. As a six-bed hospital, it was mostly facing the occasional trauma from farm work or bar fights. It needed to expand its capabilities to better make inroads in the reality of maternal and infant mortality. A lot of the latter was coming from the inevitable effects of diarrheal disease and respiratory illness.

I had a chance to see the records of a modest community loan program Ana Marie had launched. Unfortunately, she had never adopted the practices of successful programs, such as enforcing repayment terms and interest. With hyperinflation, the dollar value of the loans had become virtually completely de-capitalized.

The loan program had started with a $10,000 injection from the Esperança HQ, but it had lost about 90% of its value. I did not see a way for that to recover. I was more concerned with turning around a perception that some might have of the program being essentially a giveaway. I had seen enough of different village revolving loan programs to understand the risks of moral hazard. If village groups and borrowers feel there is no real obligation to take the loan seriously then they won't from the start.

This loan program, advocated by the Italian priests, was very paternalistic. It was set up more as a charity than as a development initiative.

Ana Marie had made some efforts to locate agricultural inputs at a discounted wholesale price to complement the revolving loans. Without competent and available technical assistance, better supervision, and some way of overcoming the pernicious efforts of hyperinflation, it struck me as simply too little and a distraction from the core work of Esperança.

The communities near Macharetí were an interesting mix. Some communities were made up of mestizo settlers who had come to the Chaco looking for land after the Chaco War. Many of these included ranchers who had built up cattle holdings.

There were also some hamlets and smaller collective made up of indigenous Guarani people who lived in the Chaco. They sometimes migrated between ranchland and hunting in Bolivia, Paraguay and Argentina.

There were also a number of Quechua and Aymara indigenous migrants who had left impoverished and dry lands in the highlands. Many were grouped in the neighboring village settlement of Camatindi. The migrants from the highlands came for the opportunity to grow corn, soybeans, and other crops. There was some overlap, but also important cultural differences that we had to consider with any programming.

Several nights a week I was invited up with Ana Marie to the Parish House. Meals were simple but very generous for the clergy. While I tried to be sociable and engaging, the conversation with Father Fulgencio and Father Roberto struck me as sterile and much of a dead end. The two brothers had lived in Machareti for over fifteen years and, as such, were very set in their ways. Life in the Parish House was not luxurious, but comfortable. I thought it surprising that they had acceded to the arrival of Esperança since, from my point of view, the potential of the PVO program was surely to be disruptive over time.

We didn't have electricity in the project house, at least at first. We had some truck batteries with a hook-up to allow them to recharge in a vehicle for use with the short-wave and ham radio setup. There was a hookup connection to the Parish House, which was about 400 feet away. When they had their generator on for a few hours each night, we could take advantage of that power.

For light outside of those circumstances, we used LNG tanks with elevated lamps. When ignited, they provided illumination. It was a rustic arrangement, to be sure, but it was also a time and place much less dependent on powered devices. We didn't have computers or cell phones at that time, but at least we had running water and a flush toilet in the house.

I rather liked the simpler lifestyle, even if it meant compromises and adjustments. When the night skies in the Chaco were clear, they were often gorgeous. I wished I had a telescope since I saw such a stain of stars across the sky. At times, I could understand how the ancients had named the Milky Way.

I continued to read a bit from the Bahá'í books at night, pondering some key philosophical concepts and metaphors. It was like I was tugged in two directions. I found myself intellectualizing what I would read and focusing on chewable bites that I could analyze and classify.

At the same time, I felt a stirring and emotional warmth that would grab me. It would startle me and discomfit me. I was uneasy about surrendering to that. I felt on safer ground looking at the philosophy, the history, and the biographies from a historical, if not cultural, anthropology lens. It was tough to reconcile.

I learned of some Bahá'ís who had started health education initiatives about eighteen hours or more to the north. They had been in Montero, north of Santa Cruz de la Sierra. I thought about the logic of reaching out to them at some point and sharing experiences and lessons learned. I felt attracted with exploring whether aspects of my work could be consistent with the values and approaches that these Bahá'ís espoused.

I wondered with whom I could talk with and share what I had found in my reading. That opportunity was actually coming sooner than I expected.

The month after I arrived, the NBC Phoenix affiliate TV crew producer-cameraman Howard Shepherd and his soundman flew into Santa Cruz de la Sierra, Bolivia, for a documentary field visit, together with Chuck Post and Brother Bill Dolan, the Medical Director. Chuck had been an IBM salesman for many years and had come on board to bring private sector expertise to the PVO as Executive Director.

Brother Bill was cut from the same Franciscan cloth as the founder of Esperança, the somewhat mythical Father Luke Tupper. A tall Irish American Catholic from the southside of Chicago, he was an accomplished physician-surgeon. He was also a Franciscan monk, and he wore a monk's habit, making him an unusual sight.

Brother Bill had previously served and completed medical and surgical residencies with the Indian Health Service in Alaska and in the lower 48. He had also served in Brazil with the Santarem hospital\primary health care center supported by the PVO. He seemed young, no more than 15 years older than me, and was gentle, kind, and impressive.

Chuck and Brother Bill arranged a small plane charter from Santa Cruz to fly them into the Chaco, with a pickup a week later. We spent much of the next week making site visits and holding community health and education activities while Howard filmed. No one had strong Spanish language skills. Chuck had the rudiments of Spanglish from life in Phoenix while Bill spoke Portuguese from his lengthy time in Brazil.

Howard filmed a lot of stand-up interviews with us and with community representatives. He wanted to offer a feel for the work of Esperança and shot footage in the communities and the area we worked.

Howard intended to film at least 12-15 hours of videotape. From this, he would extract material for a number of video products, including shorter advertising segments of the organization and longer segments for a documentary to air on NBC.

The four of them were invited to stay in the most comfortable rooms up the hill at the Parish House. At night, I would usually join them for dinner; Ana Marie less so as she was getting ready to pack up her things and leave Macharetí after two years. She had goodbyes to make. The rest of us sat and decompressed after the long days of filming.

One night as I sat with Chuck in the night air outside his room, I mentioned the Bahá'í contacts I had had and the books I had been reading.

In hindsight, it was an odd thing to do. Chuck was still getting to know me; I had been hired almost sight unseen in February. Here I was in the middle of our project zone, talking to him about spiritual and religious matters from a virtually unknown religion or cult. What could he think? Yet I felt moved to do so.

Chuck nodded positively and commented to me, "Well, you know I'm a pretty conventional guy, long time in IBM and all. I'm not a particularly good Catholic myself. But this Bahá'í sounds very interesting and a powerful motivator for you. I think it must be an incredibly good thing for you. Good for you to have found it."

I was a little taken aback, but also deeply reassured. I was not coming off as some weird flake or cultist. He was not at all suspicious of these comments of mine; on the contrary he was supportive.

After a bit I went to chat with Brother Bill. I shared similar thoughts with him about the deep meaning and affinity I found with Bahá'í teachings. I mentioned that there were interesting links with Christianity, Islam and Judaism.

To my surprise, Brother Bill's eyes lit up and he seemed deeply intrigued. "Do you have one or two books that you might be able to share, Alonzo? I'd like to know more myself."

I told Bill I would be happy to do so and was pleased and surprised by this universally positive response. I had mentioned a little bit about it to Ana Marie in previous weeks, but she had been very skeptical and not at all interested, so I had changed the subject.

I passed to Bill a couple of books the next day that I knew specifically spoke to Bahá'í teachings in a Christian context. I mentioned to Bill as well about the Montero project, that I had read about. Perhaps since he was planning on stopping at the offices of USAID and UNICEF in La Paz he could find out more about it, time permitting. I showed him a project report by one of the project managers, someone called Eloy Anello.

Before the crew left, Bill took me aside to return the books. I wondered if he had looked through them, and he said he had.

"You know, Alonzo, reading about the Bahá'í Faith brings a memory back to me," Bill intoned. "I went to seminary school in Quincy Illinois, and I remember the Brother teaching us a class on comparative religions. We were talking about the relation between the different religions in the world and the holy mother church. We went over different aspects, and then I remember one of the other novitiates had a question." He paused and looked meaningfully.

"'Brother, what about this Bahá'í temple north of Chicago, by Evanston? What should we make of it?' The brother teaching the class nodded, and sat down, and put his hands across his big

Franciscan belly. He then turned to the class, and said to us, 'My sons, the Bahá'ís are very good and very special people. They are doing God's work on this planet. That's all you need to know about them. Don't ask me any more questions about them.'"

I laughed. "What do you think he meant, Bill?" I asked.

Bill smiled and leaned his head back, and said, "I think he was afraid he would lose some of his clients, some of his students, if he went any further." We both laughed.

He continued, "It's a good path you are on, studying the Bahá'í Faith and asking questions. It is bound to be a positive one to continue. I think you should give the Bahá'í Faith a great deal of consideration."

I was amazed, even more taken aback by Bill than I had been with Chuck. Here was Brother Bill, a hugely sensitive and deep Franciscan monk, leading a life of charity, service and Catholic example. But he was advising me to think seriously about becoming a Bahá'í. It was not at all what I had expected.

The next month or two was busy. I was still getting to know people: community leaders, volunteers, and other stakeholders. I was also trying to better understand the varied economies of survival in the Chaco.

The ranchers, not generally large herd holders, were trying to raise cattle and find access to where they could sell their meat. That usually pointed to the rail line that ran from north to south from Santa Cruz de la Sierra to the Argentine border.

The farmers were primarily subsistence farmers. Some were considering soybeans as a possible option, as there was a soybean oil processing plant in Villa Montes. That was in the Chaco of the neighboring Tarija department (province), about 100 miles to the south.

I could see that the success of a primary health care project required also looking at other areas and needs for the communities. This included the economic production and generation side as well as basic education.

Meanwhile, I plugged away at the project on the ground in Macharetí and neighboring communities. I received great help from Dr. Carlos, the medical director of the modest hospital there and many community volunteers. Some had been recruited by Ana Marie, others I had motivated to join us.

After Ana Marie had left, I had a sobering moment one day when I woke up in the pre-dawn morning hours with my chest completely closed. I couldn't breathe. I couldn't bring air into my lungs at all.

I stumbled outside the house in the dark and somehow made it into the truck. I drove wildly the half mile or so to the hospital and banged on the door, waking Carlos. He quickly realized that I couldn't breathe. He got me into a cot and quickly applied what I learned was epinephrine. Within minutes I was able to start bringing air into my lungs.

"Are you ok, hermano?" he asked me with concern.

I nodded and calmed down. It had been some sort of asthmatic attack. Perhaps provoked by allergies to some new pollen or something. We never quite figured it out, although I did start taking allergy medicine during that season. It was scary. It had never happened before, and thankfully never happened again.

Esperança had received word it would receive a grant it had applied for under the new USAID Child Survival program, which would be launched later in the year. This would mean a big injection of resources to complement the funds the PVO had available and would allow for expanded hiring. But I thought we had to consider new partnerships and new ways to work beyond just primary health care.

My best way of communication with the home office was through telex. It was cheap and fast, much more economical than trying to make an international phone call, even if that were possible. In most Bolivian cities I traveled to periodically over the next few years, I could find a telex machine in the hotel I was staying in. I would arrange to have a message tapped out on a ticker tape to run through the telex machine. Or more often they would let me go behind the counter to type them myself.

My telexes to the USA went through the rudimentary MCIMail email system that offices had in the USA. Similarly, when Phoenix knew I would be at a given hotel or city, they could send a message back to me as a telex from MCIMail.

Time went on. After a lot of thought and a bit of prayer and meditation, I found myself thoroughly and intellectually convinced that I had to become a Bahá'í. But what of the heart and the soul? I did not easily bring myself to prayer, but I applied myself to it, as if it were an exercise to build up a weak and flaccid muscle.

I chanted some of the most powerful and evocative prayers and meditations and asked God to give me a sign. I know that sounds a bit hokey and conventional, but I reasoned that I needed to declare to the Divinity, to whatever spirit of creation and creativity was out there, that I was ready and receptive, that I would open myself to accept the challenge that was put in front of me.

That night, I dreamed of Abdu'l-Bahá, the son of the Founder of the Faith, the 'Center of the Covenant'. He looked kindly and warmly at me and beckoned at me to come join him. There were no words, no message that I could remember afterward. I felt infused with a sense of welcome and recognition. I sensed a promise that whatever my weaknesses or baggage that I had from my life so far, this was a choice I was being offered and encouraged to take. If I could bring myself to do so.

I realized that even if I fell short of what you'd expect of a good Bahá'í, that wasn't the point. As the saying goes, it was the journey not the destination that mattered. An apprenticeship and Example to follow. Hopefully, I could and would stay the course; God willing I would find the strength within me to do so.

Thus, I made the choice and commitment to join the Bahá'í Faith and be part of that spiritual fellowship. On the next one of my weekly expeditions to Camiri, I went to the telephone company office and to let them know I had decided to join. I first called Bruce Fox in Sucre and then the office of the National Spiritual Assembly of the Bahá'ís in La Paz. Both were surprised and pleased.

When I wrote my mother a letter about the choice I was considering before I had fully decided - her reaction was not unexpected. First, she responded positively that it sounded like a nice thing, and if this made me happy then she was for it.

Then I got another letter a week later, telling me that she had asked some friends and people she knew about what the Bahá'ís were. She told me that I was crazy to go into this. They are persecuting the Bahá'ís in Iran and other Muslim countries, she had learned. You can't do this, she said. First, they will kill you for being Jewish, then they will kill you again for being Bahá'í. I laughed to myself – after all how many times can they kill you anyway?

A few weeks later she would write about my sister's path, as she was on the point of becoming an evangelical Christian. It was perplexing and she was clearly bemused at that point, and she had heard a story of a rabbi who had said, "Don't worry, the Bahá'í Faith is good for Israel. It's the next best thing to being Jewish." She had more or less come to terms with my decision as well as that of my sister back in New York.

There were no rituals or rites associated with becoming Bahá'í; no baptism or need for clergy to endorse a personal decision. It was just a phone call to a startled but happy Bolivian volunteer in La Paz. I was startled in part because the La Paz National office had received its first word from Bruce Fox a couple of months before, guessing I might call. Then again, a few days later, a call from Eloy Anello, asking them to pass on a message to me to contact him if I called. It was all very serendipitous.

Eloy Anello was an American Bahá'í who had been – like Bruce – living in Bolivia for about ten years or so. He had come from California with his then-wife Lynn, both with master's degrees in public health and determined to work in their field in Bolivia. On the professional side, Eloy had worked for UNICEF as a consultant off and on, and on the USAID-funded Montero health project north of Santa Cruz. He was also a respected volunteer Bahá'í itinerant teacher.

After getting the message and the details about Eloy, I called him at a Santa Cruz phone number. He welcomed me into the Bahá'í fold and said he hoped I could come to visit him in Santa Cruz. He told me about a remarkable encounter he had had some weeks before.

As Eloy described it, he had happened to be in the offices of UNICEF in La Paz, picking up some papers he had left with another friend. He heard someone talking in Portuguese in the reception area. The Bolivian receptionist was having some difficulty. He saw a tall Caucasian Franciscan monk, obviously not Bolivian.

They first spoke in Portuguese, exchanging names, switching to English when it was obvious both were Americans.

"I'm Eloy Anello, helping out here. How can I help you, Brother Bill?" Eloy asked solicitously.

"Eloy Anello? Excellent, Alonzo Wind told me about you." Bill answered with satisfaction.

Eloy said he had been stunned. "Alonzo Wind, I just heard about him this morning from some Bahá'í friends."

Bill leaned forward with a conspiratorial smile, tapping his nose. "Oh yes, he is one of yours."

Eloy blinked with surprise. "What do you mean?"

Bill nodded and said, "I mean he is a Bahá'í. He just doesn't know it yet. You should sign him up."

Eloy shared that he still had to shake his head in amazement. He was almost a little paranoid. Here was this impressive man in Franciscan robes, a surprise visitor. He was telling him about someone else who had just been the topic of a curious phone call just a half hour before. He couldn't get over it then, and as he recounted the story to me on the phone, he still marveled at it.

"Please come to Santa Cruz de la Sierra when you can. We are getting ready to launch a university and I would like to show you what it is about," he encouraged.

I had been in Bolivia for nearly four months, and I thought it made sense to get a sense of what Santa Cruz offered. I also had a delayed purchase list of some project supplies. Hank Beder and his wife were no longer in Sucre, playing a logistics role. They, too, had moved on.

It made sense to take advantage of what would be a more accessible commercial center for the Chaco. Finally, I learned that representatives of PACT would be in Cochabamba for a gathering of NGOs. As PACT had been an earlier booster of Esperança's work in Bolivia, and Cochabamba was a short plane ride from Santa Cruz, it would make sense for me to meet them. I made plans to travel the following week.

The trip to Santa Cruz opened a huge new world of possibilities for me and would prove consequential for the future of the program in Bolivia. I met Eloy, who took me under his wing and introduced me to many other remarkable Bahá'ís residing in Santa Cruz, Cochabamba, and La Paz.

The Bahá'í community members had depth, diversity, and dedication, which inspired me. I learned from Eloy the unique story of the Bahá'ís in Bolivia, and the special laboratory that Bolivia represented. In the heart of South America, it was more isolated from the outside world. Yet it offered opportunities to advance community human-centered development.

In 1982, the governing body of the Bahá'ís of Bolivia, the National Spiritual Assembly, approved the creation of an organizing committee. The committee's primary objective was to form a legally constituted NGO to serve as a center of Bahá'í social action and human development.

This would be called FUNDESIB, the Foundation for the Integral Development of Bolivia. FUNDESIB would host a steering committee to create a new university in Bolivia as a center of Bahá'í education and intellectual thought. It would be called Universidad Nur or Nur University. "Nur" means "Light" in Persian. By early 1985 the steering committee had managed to overcome a tremendous number of bureaucratic hurdles and initial government resistance to get a Presidential decree authorizing the establishment of Nur.

The month before my call, Eloy and the other Bahá'ís in FUNDESIB officially announced and opened Universidad Nur. It was one of the first private universities in Santa Cruz de la Sierra and Bolivia itself. It was also one of the first Bahá'í-led private universities outside of the faith's birthplace in Iran.

Nur started small, with a few classes in business administration and management in a rented building in downtown Santa Cruz. It had an initial enrollment of a few dozen. The first rector for the pilot planning phase was a Bolivian academician with the basic business and government pedigree required. He was not very empathetic or strong in outreach. He was replaced within a year with Manoucher Shoaie, a Persian émigré who was dynamic, charismatic and multi-cultural.

The new university's board of directors brought Canadian, American and other expat curriculum designers and other experts to set out the requirements for a freshman class. Over the course of the next few years they would build out each succeeding class.

Bolivians responded positively to the new venture and enrolled. They saw it as a way to disrupt and overcome an often dysfunctional public university system—one where students frequently saw their education interrupted due to labor strife and funding cuts.

Within three short years, they would attract the students, investors, and municipal support to build a home for Nur. A newly constructed building they owned, stocked with equipment, media, a library and classrooms and an increasingly more diverse academic offering that reflected both the needs of Bolivians and the social teachings of the Bahá'í Faith.

When I arrived in Santa Cruz, Eloy Anello met me at Nur where he kept an office. Eloy had been one of the dozen official founders of Nur but was in some ways *primus inter pares*, first among equals, as a driving force behind it. He was visionary about what the University and FUNDESIB could potentially achieve. Eloy wanted me to understand how these had been shaped by his own study of the Bahá'í teachings as well as his experiences in public health and development. As I mentioned earlier, he had been a key advisor to the USAID-funded Montero health project, and he told me about his first introduction to it.

"When I came on board the project, I asked about the project strategy, the project design, and what had contributed to it. I was given copies of the USAID project papers and the project approval documents," he shared. "These seemed superficial to me. I wondered aloud, but where did the thinking come from to design the project in this way in this particular location? I asked if I could look at the earliest project files and see what else had been behind."

He looked at me.

"Did you ever hear about the famous German historian and archaeologist Heinrich Schliemann?"

I said the name rang a bell from college. "Something to do about Troy?"

"Exactly," Eloy affirmed. "In the 1870s, he found the remains of what he was able to identify as King Priam's chambers in the city of Troy from the Greek myths from Homer. It had been sought for decades, but he found it. What was even more interesting was what he found as he dug.

"Underneath the city of Troy, he found layer beyond layer of previous ruins of Troy. In total there were something like seven different Troys over thousands of years, on the same site. The city would be destroyed over and over, but eventually it would be rebuilt again and again."

He looked at me and motioned a collection of papers on his desk.

"So it was with the Montero project. The further I dug, the more I found previous projects that had been carried out in the same area as the Montero project. It was like Schliemann's Troy; the more I dug, the more I found one project after another over many years that had been started in the same area.

"They often had the same objectives, trying to do the same thing. A project would end, it would finish its financing. But then a few years later it would be like they had forgotten the old project and would start all over again and do a new project again."

I frowned.

"I am not saying all USAID or other donor projects are always like that. But frequently the people who finance these projects pursue limited objectives. They are trying to achieve a certain number of project outputs in return for the inputs of the donor cash they put in."

Eloy paused for a moment, and then continued.

"But they never really manage to change things fundamentally. There's no transformation involved. They aren't looking to the basics. How do you undertake a process of human-centered development, and fuel a process of permanent transformation?

"As Bahá'ís, we don't have any magic answers or solutions. We do have the writings and the essential principles that come out from them. We use these to guide a continuing circle of questioning and exploration. To see what we can do to help communities transform themselves permanently and gain better and richer lives."

I nodded. I could see how these sorts of questions and approaches could benefit the Chaco project over the longer term. I also saw how this philosophy harkened back to the sorts of questions I had dating back to the time I was a Peace Corps Volunteer, trying to find greater meaning in my work and in my developing vocation.

It reminded me of repeated dialogues with friends and fellow Volunteers, from my time as a PCV in Buena Fé and Quevedo. As well as a Program Advisor with PLAN International, befriending, coaching and mentoring successive waves of PCVs and in thinking about development and greater meaning with Mary and with Cindy.

Eloy's key partners at Nur were the rector, Manoucher, and the Canadian Administrator Jeremy Martin. Eloy was the visionary and strategist. Jeremy in many ways was the nuts and bolts operations chief who pulled it all together. Both Jeremy and his Bolivian wife Mary Rodriguez and their children welcomed me warmly and showed me ample hospitality.

Eloy and Jeremy assigned Oscar Rojas as an initial counterpart from the university for the Chaco project. Oscar was a Peruvian Bahá'í émigré sociologist in Santa Cruz who had a long history working in social action movements and consciousness-raising. Oscar would travel down subsequently on the train and join us to get a direct understanding of the social issues we were facing in the Chaco.

While in Santa Cruz, I also familiarized myself with other official USAID development projects in the eastern region of the country to better appreciate the state of the art of health projects in Bolivia. Eloy was, in fact, a part-time advisor to a new USAID health project called PROSALUD. It was managed at that time by a large US-based firm called Management Sciences for Health (MSH).

Eloy introduced me to the PROSALUD project director, a Bolivian public health physician called Carlos Javier Cuellar. I also met other public health experts on the MSH-PROSALUD staff, such as Pilar Sebastian, Marta Merida, Antonio Arrazola, and others. This, too, proved to be a fateful moment of synchronicity that would offer an important boost to the work of Esperança in Bolivia.

Carlos was a disciple of one of his professors at his MPH program in Belgium, Dr. Peter Piot. There was a saying of Piot's that I remember him paraphrasing as a mantra when I met him. "Effective public health and primary health care services for the people, be they poor or working class, may not have a price but they do have a cost." What Carlos was getting at was the centerpiece of the MSH-PROSALUD. How do you ensure sustainable high-quality primary health care services accessible and available to all?

Bolivia's Ministry of Public Health had a network of health care centers and hospitals. They were overcrowded, poorly staffed, and equipped. They rarely had sufficient medicine and supplies and were generally ineffective at public health in any serious way. This had been even worse through the political and economic crisis and hyperinflation Bolivia had faced for the past year.

MSH proposed developing a network of high-quality, low-cost, self-financing primary healthcare clinics. PROSALUD would apply the best private-sector approaches to health management. They envisioned creating a sort of HMO for Bolivians, with subscription payments by working—and middle-class residents of communities in and around Santa Cruz. There would be some initial subsidies and a system of cross-subsidization. It was a novel idea for Bolivia, and I would soon learn for the developing world as a whole.

I became friends with the MSH-PROSALUD management team. We promised to stay in touch and look for ways to share ideas and experiences. It wasn't clear what would be the overlap between my job with the Chaco project and what they were trying to start in Santa Cruz. But we shared together with the friends associated with Nur and FUNDESIB a sense of promise and potential.

Before returning to the Chaco, I flew to Cochabamba to meet with Carlos Castillo and Daniel Santo Pietro from PACT. I discussed with them options for the future of the Esperança project. I knew that Esperança would be starting the USAID Child Survival project soon. It seemed to me that there should be ways to increase the opportunities for organizational learning. This was always a priority for PACT and its members. As well as the range and scope of the Chaco project.

I met representatives from Save the Children Canada and other NGOs with activities in the Cochabamba area. And I took advantage of staying another day in Cochabamba to visit with Dr. William K. Baker and his wife Ann Marie, one of the Bahá'í founders of Nur and FUNDESIB. He had started his own small-scale community development learning center. Their son Bobby helped at times with the center; their daughter Crystal was married to the Universidad Nur Rector.

Dr. Baker's modest center had pilot efforts on alternative technologies to conserve water and build mini greenhouses. This would enable people to cultivate tomatoes and vegetables in the altiplano highlands of Bolivia. It had facilities to support community education.

Returning to Santa Cruz I checked in with Eloy again before boarding the train south to the Chaco. I mentioned the conversations with Daniel Santo Pietro and the connection with PACT. Eloy saw an immediate opportunity for more synergies.

"You should come with me to the Bahá'í International Youth Conference in Lima Peru in August. I am going to speak, and it'll be a great opportunity for you to get an even broader understanding of the Bahá'í world. Also, Farzam Arbab will be there."

"Who's Farzam Arbab?" I asked.

"Farzam Arbab is the founder and director of FUNDAEC. It is a Colombian NGO called the Foundation for the Application and Teaching of the Sciences. FUNDAEC is a Southern NGO member of the PACT network. In many ways, we modeled FUNDESIB in Bolivia on some aspects of FUNDAEC in Colombia. Moreover, Farzam is a mentor of mine who is an important teacher in the worldwide Bahá'í community."

I was intrigued and said I would try to see if I could get the time off. Before returning to Macharetí, I had a prearranged check-in with the Esperança HQ in Phoenix to take advantage of the availability of phone lines in Santa Cruz. I briefed Brother Bill and Chuck on how the meetings had gone in Cochabamba and in Santa Cruz and got very favorable feedback from them both.

I asked if I could take vacation time for a week in August to travel and Chuck approved it and gave me some surprising updates on staffing. They had heard from me about Cindy back in Ecuador and had decided to reach out to see if she was available to come on board. In that way they could help boost manpower for the project economically.

Cindy had accepted and kept it a secret so that they could surprise me. She was going to travel to Bolivia in November. They had sensed we were a couple or had been a couple and perhaps this could be a boost as well for our personal lives. I was pleased but surprised; it was unexpected.

In early August 1985, I travelled to Lima, Peru, and attended the large Bahá'í International Youth Conference for Latin America. It was co-sponsored by UNICEF Peru and the Bahá'í community of Peru.

The Conference was being held as one of several to highlight the International Year of Youth, and the upcoming International Year of Peace in 1986. Luckily, the UN definition of youth was fairly flexible and included people under 30. I made plenty of new friends there among the hundreds of participants from all over Latin America, many of whom were Bahá'í.

Meeting Farzam Arbab together with Eloy Anello was a tremendous milestone in my life, one which I would only gradually come to understand. Farzam was a bit intimidating. He was then the Executive Director of the Colombian NGO FUNDAEC, and as Eloy had noted a couple months earlier also a PACT member.

Farzam was a Persian Bahá'í émigré who had moved with his family to the United States in the late 1950s. He graduated from Amherst College in Massachusetts in 1964 and then went on to receive a doctorate in physics from UC Berkeley in 1968. He had emigrated shortly afterward to Colombia as a Bahá'í pioneer, teaching at the Universidad del Valle.

In the early 1970s, he and several other physicists at that school founded FUNDAEC in Cali, Colombia. FUNDAEC's mission was to develop new ways to teach applied sciences to rural farmers and peasants in the Valle de Cauca area, which bordered what would become some of the most vicious drug-infiltrated areas.

Farzam Arbab was then serving on the Board of Directors for the PACT network. The network brought together about 20 NGOs from the U.S. and Canada and a "global south" grouping of 20 NGOs from Latin America and Asia. He was intrigued by the synchronicity of my appearance.

While Farzam was a little skeptical of Esperança, which seemed nominally Catholic and somewhat 'provincial' in outlook within PACT, he saw in my arrival a vehicle to strengthen multiple NGOs. He saw a potential opportunity for institutional learning that would perfectly align with PACT's objectives and benefit several organizations.

Farzam suggested we work collaboratively. We would develop, over several months, a joint proposal for NGO strengthening and the transfer of lessons learned. I readily agreed. He encouraged me to also continue to read from the Bahá'í writings. He echoed Eloy in strongly recommending the books "The Secret of Divine Civilization", "Some Answered Questions" and others from Abdu'l-Bahá. Both said they found continuing relevance to the modern work of community development in these and other writings.

I would continue to receive from Farzam copies of many brilliant articles and speeches he would give over the years in the future. He would eventually leave Colombia to go to Haifa Israel and the Bahá'í World Centre. He would be first named to the International Teaching Centre there. He was later elected to the nine-member supreme global body of the Bahá'ís, the Universal House of Justice.

In September 1985 at the request of the Daniel Santo Pietro, the PACT representative, I helped carry out a workshop in Cochabamba Bolivia. It was for a group of Bolivian NGOs to develop a learning program of workshops and inter-organizational exchanges. It helped boost Esperança's visibility as an organization operating in Bolivia. It also helped enhance my insights and understanding of the situation facing Bolivian NGOs.

This NGO learning program also gave me great insights into what we might try to develop with FUNDAEC in Colombia. It would serve as the inspiration from which PACT would later propose to USAID the funding of an NGO network in child survival and primary health care. PACT—with my help—would later propose this consortium to USAID and other PACT members operating in Bolivia.

However, in a sobering learning experience, I watched how the technically strong PACT proposal ultimately lost out to a USAID-instigated bid developed and supported by the U.S. PVOs in the country, sidestepping PACT. This had apparently been done because of some cost-saving ideas at the USAID Bolivia mission.

It did not seem at the time like the most ethical or fair-play approach by USAID. However, there is no denying that USAID's 'midwifery' of this project ultimately produced the successful PROCOSI Child Survival consortium that continues to function today, many years later.

BUILDING THE BROADER BOLIVIAN PARTNERSHIP

Cindy arrived as promised at the end of November, and we enjoyed the anticipated reunion. Mary had been reluctant to see her leave Guaranda and PLAN Bolivar province. She herself did not plan to remain much longer and had hoped for some continuity for the incoming new director.

Cindy had been unsure whether staying on in Ecuador or going to Bolivia would be best for her own professional aspirations of service. She was surprised by how circumstances had come together for my decision to join the Bahá'í Faith. I am sure she had never expected that outcome given our interactions in Ecuador. I think part of her was proud of my decision and whatever part the early exposure she had given me to some Bahá'í writings had played in it. But I also came to believe that she was doubtful and unsure of it. It seemed to take some wind out of her sails, perhaps literally.

Nevertheless, Cindy took to the environment of Machareti quickly. She made friends with many of the locals. She added an important element of authenticity to meetings with mothers' clubs and other women's groups. We gingerly explored re-igniting the romantic relationship that folks in Phoenix had seemed to expect. We set it aside for a time to see how things would settle out on the work and on the personal and spiritual sides.

Cindy's arrival was preceded by Don, a public health pediatrician from Redondo Beach California. He joined with the start of the USAID child survival project in October. I was happy that things were going forward with project staffing.

Among our first challenges was recruiting a Bolivian technical staff—doctors, nurses, and health educators—to form the core of our efforts for the Chaco Child Survival project.

We tried to advertise for resumes, but that did not lead to anyone we felt confident in. Don had the idea of an unusual recruitment approach, given the difficult conditions of the Chaco and the need to fully test the mettle of any candidates. With the help of Universidad Nur, we opened applications for a pool of candidates for a public health management short course.

Participants knew that we would hire the best of those who participated. It was demanding, and perhaps a little stressful. It was clearly unusual and placed a burden on those participating to show what they could offer the Chaco Child Survival Project. We weren't 100% sure it would work. We didn't know if the right sort of people were going to be available or interested in participating in the short course. It would be under the banner of the Universidad Nur Post Graduate School.

In fact, the recruitment approach worked quite well. We offered jobs to the top six or seven participants based on their contributions to the course. A great indicator of how successful the approach was the staying power of the graduates. These participants formed the core of what would now be known as "Esperanza Bolivia." They stayed on through and beyond the three years of the first Child Survival Project.

In the subsequent independent USAID final evaluation, it noted the unusual approach to spending the first year of the project on recruitment and commented favorably on the Esperanza Bolivia team's successes in the communities.

The evaluator, Dr. Fred Hartman, commented that it had led to one of the most effective and successful primary health care projects he had ever seen. That was saying a lot. He strongly recommended renewed funding by USAID. Esperança would win a follow-on Child Survival Project grant to further build Ministry of Health capacity across the Chaco.

Meanwhile, as part of my duties as Bolivia Country Director, I traveled to Santa Cruz about once a month and to the de facto capital of La Paz every four months. I stopped in the USAID offices in La Paz two to three times a year, and I became friends with much of the health team at the USAID mission.

Some of these have remained lifelong connections. Paul Hartenberger, the head of the USAID health office, would become a mentor to me and encourage and support me at key moments of my career. Not only while in Bolivia but at several points later on.

Charles Llewellyn, Sigrid Anderson, and Bambi Arellano, among others, all USAID Bolivia staff at the time, were also models for me. But Paul Hartenberger stands out the most.

It became something of a running joke in La Paz that I must have come into town on my horse for meetings. That was the perception of someone living way out in the cattle-raising areas of the Chaco. I would also use my visits as opportunities to follow up with key Bolivian ministries if we had some ongoing issues to discuss, which was most of the time.

Bolivian government officials usually had a love-hate relationship with the Americans. They wanted American resources and support, but we were usually seen as meddlers and dangerous instigators of social forces they struggled to contain.

I was in a somewhat special position compared to most country directors of other US PVOs. I did not live in La Paz. I made the rounds and touched base with people associated with the NGO development community and USAID whenever I was in the city.

I was the youngest of my peers, not yet 30. I was at least ten years younger than any of the other PVO Country Directors who would gather and take part in the meetings of PROCOSI or USAID. I chose to deflect questions about my age for exactly that reason.

From my yearly or semi-annual follow-up with Loren Finnell, I knew that there was important value in building an NGO network like PROCOSI. Loren had played an early role in supporting NGO networks in different countries, including Costa Rica. He had been a Deputy Director of PACT. He was a tireless advocate of the value added of bringing together civil society and NGOs to work together in concert.

Loren in fact expanded from his consultancy relationship with Esperança to create his own organization by 1987. He called it the Resource Foundation.

The mission of the Resource Foundation was to go beyond the limited consultancies he provided to the small PVOs of the world like Esperança. He created a one-stop shop to identify a wide range of funding resources for nonprofits. It was customized to their particular needs and abilities. I think he had modeled this a bit on the Foundation Center and other philanthropy centers.

Over time, the Resource Foundation specialized in full-service fundraising and fund management facilities for Latin American nonprofits and NGOs. Loren attracted a wide and diverse group of social investors and funders. He looked to ever more creative innovative mechanisms for supporting social ventures in Latin America. I learned a lot from Loren as did our Bahá'í Bolivia institutional partners.

FUNDESIB signed up early on as a member. They sought the Resource Foundation's efforts to identify alternative funding streams for the Chaco program in Bolivia. As well as other FUNDESIB Bahá'í projects under development elsewhere in Bolivia.

(As an aside I recently learned about Loren's untimely death last year. I had lost contact with him to my deep regret. I looked up his Wikipedia biography. I learned of the many humanitarian awards and recognitions he would subsequently receive. I was especially pleased to see that the Resource Foundation is still alive and well and honoring Loren Finnell's legacy. A good 33 years later, with an active and informative website and a new generation of staff carrying forward his commitment to service).

As PROCOSI took shape, I made it a point to play as active a role as I could in the oversight and governance of the Child Survival network. I would try to make any meetings that were scheduled for the country directors. This would usually coincide with a quarterly meeting of the network board of directors. PROCOSI grew and thrived as a USAID-instigated initiative.

The Bolivia Child Survival Network became technically and managerially renowned. It had over 20 member organizations, between US-based nonprofits and Bolivian organizations. It became a powerful exchange that contributed hugely to public health knowledge, expertise and capabilities.

PROCOSI went on to win several USAID grants after the first grant ended. I checked their website. They are alive and well and describes themselves as a network made up of 24 non-profit organizations committed to the right to health in Bolivia. They regularly verify the quality and transparency of affiliates and members through high standards and maintain a selective membership roll.

Esperanza Bolivia survives and thrives today as a successful spinoff operation. The core leadership is made up of people we had trained and hired. They went on to form a duly registered Bolivian NGO.

It provides me with one of the most satisfying memories of my work in Bolivia. Esperanza Bolivia is still a member of PROCOSI. Its executive director, a public health nurse named Palmira Villaroel, sits on PROCOSI's board today, over 32 years after I first hired her.

The Esperança-FUNDAEC institutional strengthening and learning proposal I developed for PACT was endorsed by Farzam Arbab in Colombia and the Esperança Phoenix headquarters. The PACT Board approved it for funding.

In January 1986, with that approved funding, I led a group of five Bolivian NGO representatives to Colombia. Two came from local hires we had made for the Esperanza\Bolivia team, two from FUNDESIB and one person representing Universidad Nur.

For four weeks, we studied the FUNDAEC Tutorial Learning System program near Cali. Farzam and his colleague Gustavo Correa urged we study the system by taking the modular classes as if we were actual community participants.

The Tutorial Learning System was known in Spanish by its acronym 'SAT'. SAT was a pioneering effort to develop a modernized, scientific rural economy focused curriculum. It was to offer a huge boost to the skills development of peasant farmers.

Rural farmers gained little for their families from traditional primary and secondary schools. SAT included learning cycles tied closely to village life, the agricultural calendar and participatory learning approaches. It had a modular system of learning which offered in essence a "practical literacy." This met far better the vocational needs of the communities we worked in. It had been cross validated and tested in a range of communities in Colombia.

Farzam Arbab and Gustavo Correa at FUNDAEC created a sister organization, CELATER, to expand SAT to several Latin American countries. This was a way to address the inequities of education for rural communities.

It's hard to convey the excitement it gave us, to imagine how SAT could be adapted and adopted at different levels within Bolivia. I saw it as a valuable addition and complement to the primary healthcare work under Esperança. I thought it would mesh well with what would be significantly expanded under the second USAID Child Survival project.

This Colombia visit and cross-fertilization of ideas was super fruitful. It led to a direct formal partnership between Esperança and FUNDESIB in the Bolivian Chaco. We received a one-year grant from PACT to FUNDESIB. It was to help establish a rural technology and agricultural extension program to parallel the Esperança health program. This latter program was expanded with the help of the two consecutive USAID Child Survival Grants.

The PACT funding helped both agencies win multi-year funding from the Inter-American Foundation. We also got funding from the PL-480 Secretariat. This was from the Bolivia Social

Investment Fund, co-administrated then by the Bolivian government and USAID from the US Embassy.

Within two years of my arrival, the Chaco program had grown from a pilot project to a major development initiative. We reached a large number of rural communities across the Chaco regions of three provinces.

We had several different funding channels. Much of it, particularly the Esperança health program, remained heavily dependent on USAID funding. It was hard to get around this. I saw it as a vulnerability and risk, and there was no easy solution for that.

Globally, USAID would become, for a time, an increasingly dominant donor across much of Latin America and the developing world. When you are the only game in town for funding social initiatives there are consequences. The USAID agenda, determined by the U.S. Government, often crowded out all others. A lack of competition in a market economy creates distortions, high prices and reduced innovation. The same thing happens in the market of ideas in poverty reduction and development assistance.

However, even so, the Esperança program would keep growing and develop a reach far beyond the Chaco program. I could not imagine then that what we were building as a program would survive and develop a lasting organizational structure decades later.

Our team's growth with the USAID child survival program funding and the addition of FUNDESIB meant we had to shift the project headquarters. We had to move from the parish house annex of the cattle station of Macharetí to the regional town of Villa Montes, about an hour and a half south.

Villa Montes had electricity, a market, a large hospital and a formal train station. It was at a crossroads, connecting with a road that went up to the capital of Tarija province (or department). It was perhaps not as big as Camiri three hours or more to the north of Macharetí in the lower southern reaches of the Santa Cruz province. But it was closer and offered greater accessibility for the project zone that now ran south to the Argentine border at Yacuiba, and north beyond Macharetí to Camiri.

We located living space for both anticipated Esperança and FUNDESIB staff. Instead of renting, we purchased a house for $18,000, which offered room for joint offices, training space, and a semi-divided living space for Cindy and me.

In negotiations with the telephone company office, I was able to get them to install one of the few telex machines in Villa Montes in our offices. This was a key pre-computer means of communication with the outside world, particularly with the Esperança HQ in Phoenix. I would punch out a long ticker tape message and transmit it. It would arrive at the Phoenix offices or other locations in the USA we wanted to reach as an MCIMail email.

For the Villa Montes headquarters, we purchased computers and printers, probably among the first available in the region outside of La Paz. Through a USAID-supported program with Apple, we received a donation of two first-generation MacIntosh computers.

Under the Child Survival program, I purchased two IBM PC XTs and a Kaypro portable computer that was less of a laptop and more of an industrial-size lunch box. It was high technology for back then, but all this allowed us to do things we'd only imagined before.

Villa Montes in Tarija Province proved to be an excellent choice for other reasons as well. At that point, the president of Bolivia was from Tarija. Was it a coincidence that when International Direct Dial (IDD) capability came to Bolivia in late 1987, the national telephone company installed the wires first in the provincial departmental capital of Tarija and then in the next largest town of Villa Montes?

I cultivated the telephone company's local staff. They were proud to see an American health and development project headquarters in Villa Montes. I convinced them to install one of the first ten phone lines in the Esperanza Bolivia office. From the tremendous isolation we had originally faced, we suddenly had a phone that allowed for international direct dial.

Other cities in Bolivia, including La Paz, had to contend with organizing phone calls through operator assistance. The phone company forgot to install any equipment to meter phone usage and bill during the first six months of "pilot testing." We had IDD for free during that time. Nice budget savings, and a real treat to be able to easily call not only the home office but family in the USA.

FUNDESIB's multinational Bahá'í board was impressive and thoughtful. Other American Bahá'ís provided important contributions. In addition to Eloy Anello, John Kepner was a long-standing pioneer who had married in Peru. He had launched a language translation and other businesses there with his wife Pati and her family. He pursued a master's degree from the School for International Training in Vermont and brought valuable expertise and common sense to the table.

Dr. William K. Baker had been a scientist and industrial chemist working with Kodak in the United States. He and his wife decided to emigrate to Bolivia in the late 1960s. Sabino Ortega and Andres Jachakollo were indigenous Bahá'í community leader. They brought authenticity to understanding community dynamics, as well as social and economic realities in rural Bolivia.

Teresa Mendez was a young Bolivian lawyer in La Paz. She understood clearly how to navigate the official governmental recognition and approval process. Athos Costas was an Argentine Bahá'í community leader who had emigrated to Bolivia in the late 1950s.

The FUNDESIB Board identified key counterparts for Esperança who would join us in Villa Montes. The leaders selected were inspired and gifted. The FUNDESIB Bolivian promoters who were hired had valuable and complementary perspectives and leadership skills.

Garth Pollock and Ken Roedell were two Californian pioneers who had each lived ten years or more in Bolivia. Each was a remarkable, largely self-taught character with unique approaches and personalities. Garth had worked for several years on helping the Radio Bahá'í station in Caracollo Oruro, Bolivia, get off the ground. He helped it develop technically and programmatically. It was a more modest version of the Otavalo station I saw in Ecuador.

Garth had developed a deep bond and affection for the indigenous people of the Bolivian altiplano. I think initially it took some adjustments for him to develop a comparable appreciation for the people of the Chaco, although he did. Garth was a close lieutenant of Eloy's in problem-solving community participation and governance concerns in Bolivia.

Garth took on more of the external representational face of FUNDESIB. He dealt with me on partnership questions with Esperança. He fleshed out the program objectives and goals of different FUNDESIB funding applications. Though I don't think he was especially tall, I came to feel about him as something of a "gentle giant." He had heard Eloy speak about Bolivia in one of his talks back in California and decided right out of high school that he wanted to help out.

Garth may have had a little bit of community college, but he was thoroughly self-taught and from the school of hard knocks. A gentler soul would be hard to find. He had an innate talent for interviewing and recruiting Bolivian agronomists and educators. Whenever FUNDESIB personnel issues might come up, he was always self-effacing and modest. He could handle a critical conversation with deft and kindness.

Ken Roedell was lanky and had a face that reminds me now of the director John Waters. He was a bit herky-jerky and restless where Garth tended to soothe. Ken was recruited from Florida with his Chilean Bahá'í wife and kids. He had lived in Bolivia and Chile for a number of years before returning to the USA to finish his college degree.

I always remembered an anecdote Ken shared with me early on. He described how he made his way around Bolivia when younger, crowded in Bolivia microbuses and other public transport. He talked about how he avoided getting sick by always carrying in his pocket fresh cloves of garlic, which he would pop into his mouth like lozenges. Did he remain healthy from the bio nutrient effect of the garlic? Or as a result of people edging away from him? This always seemed to be an open question.

Ken was, at times, quirky, but he had very definite ideas of things that could and should be done on the community level. He seemed to bring a Bay Area Whole Earth Catalog understanding of alternative technologies and crops. Ken threw himself into guiding the fieldwork of the FUNDESIB promoters in Chaco. He conducted itinerant research on mung beans and cowpeas as viable crop alternatives for local farmers. These had been unknown to them.

Ken was also a big proponent of soybeans and eating soy in different ways as a healthy choice for his family, in many ways ahead of their time. Ken and Garth jointly supervised the FUNDESIB field promoters, who included talented, experienced experts in agronomy and small animal husbandry.

Lionel Ichazo was a graduate of the very highly regarded "Zamorano" school. Lionel had a scholarship to go there but had returned to a Bolivia in crisis with few available jobs for talented professionals.

Zamorano was and remains an international university in Honduras that brings together young people from all over Latin America. They get the opportunity to become leading professionals, capable of transforming companies and organizations facing challenges in the region. Challenges such as natural resources management and conservation, rural transformation and creating internationally competitive agricultural and agro-industries in Latin America and the world. It was the Pan-American Agricultural University in Honduras, founded in the 1940s by the United Fruit Company. It was a social investment growing out of their banana and pineapple plantations.

Lionel was joined by Noe Quispe and Carlos Cortez, who had great backgrounds working with indigenous and migrant farmers. They had both studied in Santa Cruz.

FUNDESIB recruited the creative Xavier Gomez-Garcia as a social promoter and educator. He was a talented poet and writer, artist and community educator. He had an incredible ear for the unique stories and oral traditions of the people of the Chaco. Xavier helped to shape the teaching techniques and adult learning technologies the team would use. I was so impressed with his efforts that I helped Xavier publish a book of short stories and reflections on the Chaco in May 1989, called "Desde el Chaco." We did it to honor and promote broadly the Chaco, which had such a history of voicelessness and invisibility in Bolivia.

Another great FUNDESIB recruit, directly from the Chaco villages, was a youth called Regis Viveros. Regis had actually started with Esperanza, doing some odd jobs and helping as a volunteer. He had little in the way of formal education but a lot of common sense, practical skills, and a great personality. When we set up the Villa Montes office, he also helped as a part-time custodian, ensuring that vehicles were ready before heading out to the field and helping to clean.

Eventually, Regis asked if he could go on field trips with the FUNDESIB promoters. With the help of Esperanza, Nur, and FUNDESIB, Regis would eventually go back to school, advance in his studies, and win a scholarship for university study in Colombia. Regis' success was notable and memorable, but it was also one of several great individual success stories.

All was not always sugarcoated successes. Like any venture in life, there were some painful hurdles we had to cross. One major headache I remember came in the form of a visit I received in a Villa Montes restaurant one day. Cindy was out in the neighboring communities that day and likely to run late. I was grabbing a bite and planning to take home some food to the house so she would not have to worry about preparing something if she were hungry.

A casually dressed man approached me and asked in Spanish if he could sit down. He had an obvious American accent, and I told him we could speak in English if he preferred. He looked relieved.

"You are Alonzo Wind, am I correct?"

"Yes, I am."

"And you are the director of the Esperanza Bolivia project, correct?"

"I'm sorry," I said. "Do I know you? Where are you from?"

He offered a forgettable name and ignored the second question.

"We are hoping to take advantage of your project to be able to visit some different communities and get a sense from your staff what is going on."

I was annoyed. "I'm sorry, WHERE are you from? And what are you talking about?"

"I'm from the Embassy." He said this in a way that made me doubt that was precisely the case.

"And that means?" I asked.

"We want to appeal to your patriotism. We just need to collect some information."

I looked at him, up and down. He was thin and wiry with hair cut fairly short.

"Look, I don't know who you are, but please leave me alone. I don't work for the U.S. Embassy and neither do you."

He took off, and I was left perplexed by the encounter. What was going on?

I mentioned the run-in to Cindy when she got back that evening, and she got indignant. "You have to report this. How dare they?"

"I don't even know who THEY are." I pointed out. We decided to drop it. But two days later I heard from Garth Pollock, from the FUNDESIB team, that he had been approached by some weird gringo who was asking a lot of questions.

"Did you answer anything?" I wondered.

"No, when I asked where he was from, he kept dodging and evading the question. I told him I was busy and to check with you."

Don, who had been listening to us talk, said "I saw the same guy, and he was trying to get me to answer questions also."

Ugh, this guy was really screwing around. I asked Garth if he was busy. "Let's go look for this guy," I suggested. There were only a couple of places he was likely to be in Villa Montes. There weren't a lot of hotels to pick from.

It wasn't that I or we had any secrets to hide. But we were an independent private voluntary organization operating in the country without any sort of hidden agenda. I didn't want us associated with something that could hurt us in some way. Bolivians were paranoid in that respect with Americans still, and for good reason. We were non-governmental and going to stay that way.

Garth and I tracked down the guy pretty easily. He was in a bar next to the best (and only) hotel in town.

"Look, Johnny or whatever your name is. Get out of town. I don't want to hear you pestering people with our project. We don't owe the Embassy or anyone else any special favors, and I don't want to know what you are up to. But if you don't get your ass out of Villa Montes and stop asking questions of our project, I will go to the police chief. He is the father of one of our project staff. I will start letting him know about your behavior and actions here, in case he doesn't already know."

The guy stood up and made as if to push at us. Then he stopped and clearly thought the better of it. We left and I didn't hear from him again, although it wasn't over.

Two days later, I got a telex from USAID La Paz requiring my presence as fast as possible. This was not an easy feat. That night, I had to board a 'ferrobus' to Santa Cruz, a sort of converted Blue Bird US school bus mounted on train tracks. It ran several times a week as a "rapid" service from the Argentine border, and it took twelve hours to get into the city from Villa Montes.

I flew on to La Paz on the one-hour flight midday and stopped into Paul Hartenberger's offices without changing, since speed seemed to be of the essence. Paul was the head of the USAID health office.

Paul told me that there was a problem with the newly arrived U.S. Ambassador Robert Gelbard. He was known as the "drugs and thugs" Ambassador from his prior role fighting narco-terrorists. His wife Aline, who was a demographer, had been 'inserted' into PROCOSI as a special advisor in a way that had raised some eyebrows.

Gelbard somewhat imperiously called in the USAID Mission Director. Without preambles he had demanded my immediate expulsion from Bolivia as persona non grata. He had told the Mission Director that I had interfered with a military intelligence captain and had had a drunken bar fight with the guy.

Paul knew me and was certain this was entirely untrue. He had told the Mission Director as much. He needed me to come and tell my story; we went a few floors to the Director's suite, and I was able to recount what had actually happened.

Paul reminded the Mission Director that I was not an employee of the U.S. government. I would be entirely in my rights to resist any attempt to distort or abuse a USAID-funded program for intelligence purposes. Such an action threatened not only Esperanza Bolivia but all USAID-funded activity in the country and needed to be sharply resisted.

The Mission Director nodded and asked us to leave, as he was going to call the Ambassador.

It was a stressful week, but Paul reassured me that I had done good. I just wanted to get to a hotel and take a shower to get the filth off in more ways than one. The episode was annoying, but I hadn't worried too much that I would get what we called then the "Braniff Award" and get kicked out of the country. But you never knew. I called the Phoenix headquarters to fill them in on it all.

Another painful situation arose from the old Jesuit priests in Macharetí. They had become increasingly aware of the presence of more Bahá'ís working on the joint Esperanza and FUNDESIB projects. They felt threatened and grew alarmed that Bahá'ís must surely be like wolves in sheep's clothing, and proselytizing. That was a totally false presumption. Bahá'ís did not act in that way and never viewed themselves as missionaries. Bahá'ís taught by example and only explained the tenets of the faith when they faced someone truly and sincerely interested and asking for more.

They had sent word to the Esperança headquarters through the unfortunate channel of the former project director, Ana Marie. She lived in retirement in Arizona. The executive director in Phoenix checked with me. He then politely but firmly rejected the priests' request that we cut ties with FUNDESIB. It didn't stop there.

Padre Fulgencio and Padre Roberto then complained to the departmental branch of the Ministry of Health Chuquisaca offices in Sucre, making up a false and unfortunate accusation. A few months later, we learned of a cryptic decree demanding that we stop our health and religious propagation activities.

It took a long bureaucratic process to overcome this. We had to suspend the project activities in the communities that were part of that political subdivision of the Chaco for a time. Community leaders complained—we asked them to direct their ire to the Ministry of Health as well as to the two troublesome old priests.

Eventually, we managed to overcome the headache, but it took time and wasted resources.

On a personal level, Cindy and I had flirted back and forth about reigniting and then dousing the flames of a romantic relationship, only to have it flare up again a few weeks later. It was admittedly an intense situation to be with someone you were working with day after day. We fretted about that, but it was hard to deny the passion and strong feelings we shared.

We'd been close in Ecuador and it was tough to let that go. We shared so many things in common in terms of work and outlook on life.

Finally, in May 1986, Cindy and I decided to get married. I had proposed a few months before and had been turned down. She had then come back to me and told me that if I still wanted to marry she would agree. It was a little over a year since I had arrived in the Chaco and about a year since I had decided on becoming Bahá'í.

This elicited many congratulations from project staff and the folks in Phoenix headquarters. Many of them probably rolled their eyes over the on-and-off-again situation with an exasperated sigh of "Finally!"

We decided we would wed in Rochester New York, Cindy's hometown, that August. Our mothers both approved, albeit with some misgivings over how we would organize something so quickly. While the decision to wed and the setting of the date was rapid, this was not unusual within Bahá'í experience. We were not ones for a long engagement. We had known each other and dated each other off and on for a couple years since our time in Ecuador.

It did come together very nicely with family and friends from both sides attending the simple garden-setting Bahá'í wedding. Friends of ours from Rochester, Chicago and New York came. My sister and mother travelled up from New York City as well.

We had a traditional quick honeymoon at Niagara Falls followed by a road trip across Canada to Toronto. It proved ill-fated.

There were obvious missteps and miscues on the honeymoon despite the lovely wedding. In hindsight if we'd been mature enough, we would have perhaps not made some of the mistakes we made. I know I made more than my share of them. I do not want to get into these sorts of personal details here other than to say that things between us had begun to unravel from the start.

We returned quickly to Bolivia and our work. Both of us throwing ourselves into that, rather than trying to figure out what had suddenly splashed cold water on our previous ardor.

We took a longer holiday at yearend, spending a month touring southern Chile and Argentina. It provided a valuable break for both of us, a chance to recharge our batteries and to come to better terms with the changes in our relationship.

We had seen that there were promotions for Chile coinciding with the latest return of Halley's Comet after 76 years away. It was a geek-out opportunity for both. There were some theories that the 1986 visit would be as brilliant or more so than the previous 1910 visit to the inner solar system.

Arica Chile offered prime viewing opportunities with less light pollution and clear skies, so we thought we'd make a bigger trip to include southern Chile and Buenos Aires.

Halley's Comet ended up fizzling out a bit. What was visible from Arica Chile was not much more than a faintish lit smudge in the night sky, with no great definition of the comet tail. At least we saw something through binoculars and telescopes. Our trip was also a bit of a wash. We had happier and less happy moments, and it was not clear at all to me what was causing this emotional back-and-forth.

One happy moment came when we arrived in Buenos Aires. We managed to reconnect with Rachel, a Peace Corps health volunteer in Ecuador five or six years earlier, in my PCV group.

Rachel was then a refugee counselor for the Hebrew Immigrant Aid Society (HIAS). She worked to address the plight of Jewish refugees in Argentina for HIAS. We had a good time refreshing friendships. I had always considered Rachel to be a sort of big sister full of Brooklyn Jewish sensibility, even though we were the same age. I confided in her and she gave me sympathy and good advice. We've remained in touch and good friends since.

Shortly after our return from holiday, in early 1987, Cindy and I made a site survey mission to Ecuador on behalf of Esperança. There, I contacted some NGOs and consortia to explore opportunities to build on the Esperança experience in that country. Cindy contacted a former friend from her Peace Corps life, an Ecuadorian sociologist named Amilcar Alban, who she thought might be a good prospect for Esperança. She then went on to familiarize herself for a week with the FUNDAEC program in Colombia.

I flew to Panama and Costa Rica to look into NGO exchanges there and visited the famous Quaker community of Monteverde. My old friend from college, Kat, had joined that community and was teaching in the local schools as an environmental educator. It was a time of reunions and old friendships, to deepen perspectives on where things were and headed.

Cindy and I returned back to the Bolivian Chaco and sent our report. Eventually however the Esperança Director and the Board of Directors in Phoenix decided to not pursue grant funding for an Ecuador program, or elsewhere in Latin America.

Cindy basically oversaw the development of community outreach efforts and training on the ground. She was highly effective in that role. She was a constant promoter of women's empowerment and leadership, and the women in the communities where we worked loved her for it. She was a great foil not just for me but for Don and the other program staff. She knew how to ask the tough questions to stir up creative responses and new approaches to tackle problems at the grassroots.

The folks in Phoenix headquarters and Brazil were impressed with Cindy. We traveled together twice to Phoenix for wider organizational meetings. We also traveled for a week or two to Brazil to support an exchange between the sister programs.

We tried to overcome the relationship blues. Cindy decided to leave Bolivia at least temporarily in late 1987. She went to the Palo Alto-San Jose area of northern California. With leave from the Phoenix headquarters, I joined her for two months to try to undertake marriage counseling with her.

We both made major efforts to improve marital communication and reconcile. In the end, we decided that we simply should not have married when we did. There were different reasons why.

Working together and living together 24/7 was poison; I definitely don't recommend it. Our relationship had simply never evolved sufficiently from when we were friends with benefits in Guaranda. Our lives had changed radically. Working together first in Ecuador and then in Bolivia created special stresses.

I think my decision to enter wholeheartedly into the Bahá'í community paradoxically destabilized things for us too. We had failed to communicate and discuss what kind of lives together we wanted to have and share and on what terms in the future. The wedding somehow kicked off a chain of distress and uncertainty, from which we never recovered.

I returned to Bolivia and Cindy filed for divorce, remaining in the Bay Area. The divorce ended up taking effect almost two years to the day we wed. We had no children and no side complications or conflicts. The marriage termination was as painless as possible in terms of processes. It was painful and demoralizing from the emotional toll on both of us.

I can't say I had any regrets in time. I realized that I had somehow been caught up in an infatuation, first in Ecuador and later in Bolivia. I don't know if she viewed it that way. Yet this infatuation mesmerized me even more because of all the logical reasons that seemed to exist for us to get together and stay together. It was further reinforced by my/our work colleagues and supervisors who also thought it made perfect sense for us to be together. Until it didn't – like a candle snuffed out.

It would be easy to expect and understand a crisis of faith ensuing. For hadn't I been introduced to the Bahá'í Faith by Cindy herself? Why had our efforts to build an enduring relationship been undermined, or sabotaged, and by what? It was humbling to be brought up so short.

During our trip to Chile and Argentina, the vertiginous swings back and forth between us led me to implore God for divine assistance. I had felt some help manifested in Buenos Aires through the instrument of Rachel's appearance and her counsel, as well as her kindness with Cindy. I thought this was meant to help us in some lasting way, but that was my will and not the higher will I sought to divine.

I suppose if I had had a truly spiritually enlightened soul, then it would have been clearer to me how to proceed. My faith should have strengthened my discipline and self-awareness. I did not see how to overcome the marital crisis or bare my soul further. Things were too dim to enlighten me.

I struggled with faith and discipline and the paradoxes I faced. A big paradox that troubled me was that as I tried to more closely align with Bahá'í thinking, and talk in Bahá'í terms with Cindy, the more she seemed to drift away. Was I guilty of hypocrisy? Had I done something terribly wrong?

So often, these spiritual tests that assail us seem to boil down to a basic mystical question of will. While we are creatures of free will, we are called to divine and submit to that larger Will. Yet our own will and temptation constantly tug at us, and it becomes difficult to discern which direction in life is the best.

I had felt that so much of my life had been spent swimming upstream against the current. I had thought that much pain and anguish would be lifted by finding a Higher Will and Purpose and hewing to it. And yet, for me, at least, that Higher Will could be sensed only dimly, like a peripheral vision. It is said that "Many are called but few are chosen".

We should all possess the capacity of sensing the presence of God and a Higher Will. And yet there is never a guarantee to that. I marvel at those who seem to have it easy. They talk about the divine will, the higher will, and how they can see it and choose to follow it. Perhaps that is the gift of some.

I found that it is a lot easier to convince yourself that you are following the Higher Will, when it magically matches your own. Was that Higher Will calling me to scrap my work, my vocation, and leave the project? To find an environment hopefully more conducive to building the marriage we had promised each other. I did not hear that message, nor see things pushing me in that way. I thought I needed the discipline and belief to remain true to and stay on course, however uncomfortable it might be. My friends seemed to say the same. Time healed.

I chose to stay on in Bolivia and put the time to good use. Over the next 18 months, I further developed the Esperança partnership with Nur University. I also built deeper ties with the PROSALUD team, the growing self-financing primary healthcare project of MSH. It would ultimately become one of the most effective USAID projects and a successful Bolivian non-profit.

In October 1988, MSH announced a month-long seminar course on health management in Boston for project leaders. It was a global course with about 35 participants from a half-dozen countries. I was able to join four other colleagues from Bolivia, including Diane, a good friend who worked at PLAN International in La Paz, and Juan Carlos, a public health physician from the Ministry of Health. We developed a life-long friendship from that experience, as well with Ellen Eiseman and some of the other MSH trainers and facilitators who led it.

The professional and personal relationships with MSH, PROSALUD and Nur helped me develop the Bolivia portion for an Esperança proposal for a separate USAID Health Management Matching Grant. We won the grant to expand a learning program to upgrade the health management skills of public sector and NGO managers. We linked the Esperança programs in Bolivia, Brazil, and Guinea-Bissau. That latter country in West Africa was picked because it was Portuguese-speaking, with a great deal of ties to Brazil. We did not include Angola or Mozambique at that time due to the ongoing civil wars in both countries.

The Bolivia component of the grant was the primary element, the anchor for the rest of the program. The grant financed a management training program of 10 workshops in key areas NGO managers had identified as weak areas. We carried these out in three of Bolivia's departments, Santa Cruz, Tarija, and Cochabamba.

Don and I developed the program and supervised the budgets and sub-contracting. We hired trainers, recruited outside consultants, and helped teach. We recruited several leaders from PROSALUD to help us with workshops and training, including the director Carlos Javier Cuellar and Pilar Sebastian. The workshops covered Strategic Planning, the USAID Logical Framework, Human Resources Management, and NGO Budgeting and Finance.

An immensely popular series covered 'Human Scale Development' with Chilean NGO leaders Manfred Max-Neef and Antonio Elizalde. We identified Manfred and Antonio thanks to Eloy Anello's ever-active cross-fertilization. Eloy loved to bring people together to build on their distinct experiences.

Manfred and Antonio and their Development Alternatives Center (CEPAUR) developed a conceptual approach for social development. It was need-oriented, self-reliant, endogenous, ecologically sound, transdisciplinary and based on structural transformation. They analyzed human needs, scale and efficiency for projects. They focused on unemployment and local development financing. This was truly cutting-edge stuff in 1989.

It is sobering that some of the current development dialogue between big donors today turns to concepts that CEPAUR described as Human Scale Development over 30 years ago, with support from the Dag Hammarskjöld Foundation. I was and remain proud of how we promoted this development dialogue in Bolivia. Through the workshops and fora we offered, we influenced hundreds of participants if not more.

One day in Santa Cruz, about six months after the divorce had been finalized, I met Judy. She was an English Jewish woman backpacking through Bolivia. She had somehow stumbled into the Nur University offices.

Judy was a pharmacy manager in Cambridge UK, perhaps ten years older. She was interested in the primary health care and health management teaching we were adapting for the program. She was intrigued by Universidad Nur and its principles. We immediately hit it off, and it went from friendship to a bit of a rebound romance for me. She was a tonic for me. I felt appreciated and loved in a way that I had scarcely felt with Cindy for a long time.

When her trip to Bolivia came to an end, I decided to take vacation time, and we took a working holiday to Honduras in Central America. We flew first to Tegucigalpa and from there to La Ceiba and then made a hopscotch trip by small plane to Palacios. This village, on the Mosquito Coast of Honduras, was the home of Asociación Bayán, a small NGO and hospital founded in 1986 by Barry and Marilyn Smith and their three daughters and Houshang Sabripour.

Barry and Houshang were Bahá'í public health physicians. Barry had been for five years a USAID Foreign Service Officer working in the health sector. Jaded with USAID, he left the Foreign Service with the dream and vision of building a community health program in Honduras. He reached out to me regarding our SAT experiment in the Chaco and asked for my help.

Judy and I visited the small NGO hospital and joined the Smiths and Sabripours on some site visits to neighboring communities by canoe. Returning to Palacios, we both helped with a brainstorming session to assist the Bayán team in developing a fundraising and project proposal to expand primary healthcare services in tandem with the SAT approach to rural learning. It was fun and exhilarating to share our experiences in Colombia and Bolivia, and I was so impressed with what Barry and his family and team were doing on the Mosquito Coast. Asociación Bayán is still going strong; Barry would become a close mentor, and he and I would subsequently work together in several different countries and adventures in Nicaragua, Angola, and Nigeria beyond the scope of this book.

After four or five days there, Judy and I took a long weekend to revel in the tropical Bay Islands off the Atlantic Coast of Honduras. We spent a week enjoying the English Caribbean atmosphere of Utila and Roatan. Utila is said to be populated by the descendants of Captain Morgan and other pirates. Roatan was especially populated by these maddening little black gnats and flies. Still, we snorkeled and enjoyed the bathtub-warm waters of the Caribbean.

From Honduras, I joined Judy on her trip back to Cambridge England. We drove all around East Anglia, the isle of Ely, the Lake District, Leeds, York, and the North Country of England, and Judy introduced me to her parents in Hull. I loved England and enjoyed so much Judy's company.

Judy urged me to stay on longer and half-joked that she wanted to make me into a "kept man." I was tempted and felt pulled in different directions. It would be so comfortable to ease myself out of the Esperanza Bolivia group of projects. I even toyed with picking up my studies again at the Nuffield Centre for Health and Development.

But in the end, I felt I had to go back, that there were things still left undone in Bolivia. I felt that my calling was there, and though I loved Judy as a friend, we weren't fated to go further. Judy wasn't interested in having children, and I did not want to close that door. We parted as close friends, and I returned to Bolivia.

The successful Health Management Matching Grant program grew and expanded. We increased the number of workshops and participants. We deepened partnerships with the Ministry of Health in several provinces. The program continued with a high rate of participation from Bolivian NGOs and the Ministry of Health offices, even after my later departure from Bolivia.

Ultimately, it led to several postgraduate modules in human development at Nur University's graduate school, and, as I had hoped, the curriculum for a master's degree in public health and a master's degree in development.

Nur University would formally launch Bolivia's first graduate schools in 1994. Beginning in 2000 the university received direct awards and grants from donor agencies. In 2001 Nur was evaluated positively by donors and the Bolivian government as a "full university". The next year it was selected as a 'Center for Educational Excellence' for the Andean region. This was an initiative launched at the Summit for the Americas, supported by USAID.

Universidad Nur continues to offer an MPH program and other masters programs to this day. A legacy of the original Esperança Bolivia matching grant training program, something I also remain quite proud of.

For its part, PROSALUD became even more of a model public-private partnership. The extraordinarily successful program funded by USAID grew from two primary health centers in 1985 to fifteen centers in 1990. By its 25th anniversary it had become Bolivia's premier health care provider. It grouped 23 health centers, five clinics in nine cities across Bolivia. Far outgrowing its humble beginnings in Santa Cruz.

PROSALUD recently celebrated its 35th anniversary. Certainly, key senior staff like Carlos Javier Cuellar and Pilar Sebastian deserved much, if not most, of the credit for its launch and growth. I was happy that we had been with them for part of that key time.

As I see it, the Esperança matching grant program provided a timely boost back for PROSALUD as a successful Bolivian NGO and consultant group. It also helped support the launch of the Bolivarian University program in development in Santiago Chile, under Antonio Elizalde and Javier Duhart.

I would remain in close contact with both Carlos and Pilar. Carlos became a senior executive at different American projects, then consulting groups and major development organizations. Pilar herself was recruited to lead an important USAID program in Nicaragua which I would supervise years later.

After five eventful years in Bolivia, I was ready to move on. Garth Pollock from FUNDESIB was selected by Esperança's Phoenix HQ to serve as the Administrator or Country Director in Bolivia. This seemed to me a warm endorsement of all we had gone through to build the alliance with the Bahá'ís of Bolivia and the Esperanza Bolivia program.

Dr. Bill Dolan chose to leave his orders as a Franciscan perhaps in part as a result of his contacts with the Bahá'ís in Bolivia and subsequently elsewhere. Before we both moved on, he wrote me and discussed future options. I was getting antsy to do new things, to take on different responsibilities. There was no obvious place to move on to within Esperança. I had told Bill I planned to leave by early May 1990.

He sent a letter which I've reproduced:

April 25, 1990
Mr. Alonzo Wind
Esperanza Bolivia
Villa Montes Bolivia

Dear Alonzo:

As your five years of service with Esperança draw to a close, let me express to you my personal thanks to you for your commitment, labor and concern for the people of the Chaco in Bolivia. Your assignment has been one filled with challenges. There are few individuals who wish to contribute their professional skills to health and development activities in the Chaco. You have persisted and have contributed to excellent Esperança endeavors in the area of child survival and human resource development for the Oriente of Bolivia. All of us at Esperança are most grateful.

The scene from the Emmy Award winning video of you bouncing in the back of the pick-up truck over the "international" highway of Bolivia is rather striking in its symbolism. Life in the Andes is not a smooth ride on a super-highway, but rather a grinding, pothole-filled pilgrimage. You have undertaken that Chaqueño experience with gusto. Your blood sweat and tears have helped make our brothers and sisters in Bolivia a healthier and happy people. You have indeed left your mark.

Once again let me say thank you for your half-decade of work on behalf of Esperanza/Bolivia.

I am happy to hear that the details of transition are moving along. As we discussed by phone recently, please let me know how we here in Phoenix can be of assistance for future employment or academic endeavors. I am sure our paths shall cross, considering the ever-expanding networking within our global village.

Should you need anything, please let me know. I extend to you my best wishes and admiration for all success in your professional career of international health and development.

God bless.

Sincerely

Bill
William V. Dolan, M.D. FACS
Program Director

I realized at the time that, somehow, there was something utterly unique and special about what happened in Bolivia. I did not fully appreciate to what extent nor grasp the implications of what it meant. But Bolivia was in many ways a finishing school for me. It was the completion and consolidation of a key chapter in my education.

What remains truly remarkable about the Bolivia experience for me is the legacy and duration. The lasting power of these groups and organizations that we helped to engender from 1985 to 1990. Was there something in the water? What made it such a unique time and place? Was it the role of the Bahá'ís? From the perspective of time, I remain convinced that this was an important contributing factor. Not the only one, but in many ways a catalytic one.

I was once again left wondering and wrestling with my next steps. I wanted to build on the accumulation of experience and scar tissue from Bolivia and Ecuador.

It had been a decade of tumultuous times for me, but that was hardly unique. Major things were happening elsewhere in the world. Just half a year before, the Berlin Wall fell, and with it, the Soviet Empire throughout Eastern Europe collapsed. The collapse of the apartheid regime in South Africa seemed imminent, and major changes were likely across that continent.

I didn't want to go running after the next shiny thing, but my personality was such that I wanted to do something new and different. At the same time, I was also trying to divine whether there were any clear signs of a Higher Will and guidance for the next steps.

As I prepared to leave Bolivia, I flew up to La Paz to say goodbye to friends and associates there. I visited Paul Hartenberger at the USAID offices and asked his opinion. Paul had been there for me through difficult times and good ones, and I deeply respected his advice and outlook on life.

"Look, I have the perfect idea for you. You should join USAID."

I rolled my eyes. "I don't really think I want to work for USAID in Bolivia. And I have been here for five years and am looking for other things to do."

"Not here." He said. "You think I'd want you here screwing things up with your cowboy Chaco ways?" he joked. "No, in Lima there's been a drawdown of American Foreign Service Officers because of the terrorism threat from Shining Path. But they need someone. I just heard yesterday from the Population Officer there that they are looking for a Personal Services Contractor (PSC), to join the USAID Peru Mission."

I must have looked doubtful.

"Look, I know you don't want to work for the U.S. government. But working as a PSC is a limited commitment, usually two years. And they need someone with a strong project management background." He leaned forward with a conspiratorial look in his eyes.

"Besides," Paul said, "it's a good way to learn the folkways of the enemy." He laughed, and I joined him.

Paul knew that I couldn't help but be a bit suspicious of working for the U.S. government as opposed to a private voluntary organization. But it was true that I would be able to learn what USAID was like from the inside if I pursued this opportunity.

Paul convinced me to apply. We used his ancient WANG terminal that connected with the internal USAID email system, and he sent word to Lima. Paul was always very hands-on and wanted to get things moving. He reached the health office and managed to schedule a telephone interview for me the very next day from his office.

To my great surprise, I learned that Ed was there. He had been in my original Peace Corps training group ten years before but had dropped out. He worked at USAID Peru as a Child Survival Coordinator also on a PSC contract.

USAID Peru envisioned having a total of three PSC Child Survival Coordinators filling the gap of departing career American officers who could not be posted at that time. Amazing, full circle, I thought. The interview went well, and I thanked Paul for his efforts. I received a conditional job offer. While in La Paz,

I took advantage to say goodbye to many close friends and colleagues with whom I had shared so much over the last five years. Some were in USAID; some were in US PVOs, local NGOs and consultancy groups in the very extensive development ecosystem there.

I left Bolivia to return to the United States, joining my mom and sister in Brooklyn. I would end up having to spend about three months in the States to go through the security clearance for the job, as well as medical appointments for medical clearance.

The security clearance process was relatively nonobtrusive, since it was only for what they called at that time 'Limited Official Use' but it still took time. I has in a holding pattern until they let me know I was officially cleared.

It proved to be time well spent. Some of it was on personal rest and recuperation. I used the time to travel across the country and visit a bunch of old friends from Chicago, Texas and California. My sister had decided to become an evangelical Christian around the time I was joining the Bahá'í Faith. She was now engaged to be married and I would be able to participate in her wedding in Brooklyn.

I had been away from the United States for much of the decade. When I left to join Peace Corps Ecuador in 1980, I had no idea that I would remain so long overseas. I had joked with some that if Reagan were elected in the 1980 campaign, I would not return until he had left office. I had meant it somewhat jokingly but here it was the middle of the term of Reagan's successor President George H.W. Bush, and I was returning for the first time in ten years for a lengthy period.

It was also the summer of Saddam and his invasion of Kuwait. The beginning of Operation Desert Shield. Gulf War Part I.

When I visited with people, and they would ask about my work, I think I spoke in abstractions that they had a hard time understanding. I could recognize the telltale signs of someone's eyes glazing over.

I developed a shorter and shorter narrative for those asking me to explain what I had been doing for ten years in the Andes, between Ecuador and Bolivia. Only a few sought to find out or ask more.

The usual lack of interest in knowing the details of a life overseas did not affect my sense of purpose. I was a little frustrated that people seemed to prefer to hold onto their assumptions and prejudices.

The people living in Latin America were easily lumped together in shorthand with other "Mexicans." Their poverty was hopeless; what did I think I could do? The inspiration I had drawn from Bahá'ís I had encountered in Bolivia and elsewhere was even more alien to most.

Eloy contacted me again. He was teaching a class to 20 NGO leaders from Peru and Bolivia at the School for International Training in Brattleboro, Vermont. Would I be interested in serving as a guest lecturer for a couple of days in the seminar?

I was happy to re-join Eloy and felt myself recharged by the experience. It was also another opportunity for synergy and synchronicity. It gave me the chance to learn more about what was going on in Peru before getting the full green light to start the new job. I drove on with him to Amherst and met Eloy's brother Frank, who worked at the School of Education there.

That summer, I traveled a bit to revisit old friends and recharge my batteries. I visited Chicago and some friends from university who were still there. I went out to San Francisco and Marin County to catch up with another friend from college, Kris, who had become a union organizer and leader. I even went up to Bellingham, Washington State, to spend time with Janet and her husband, Brad, on their horse farm.

I also had invaluable family time. I was able to spend time with my mom. It had been seven years since the passing of my father, but she had never taken an interest in anyone after him. She had stopped driving, which concerned me. I didn't know what I could do.

A year after we moved to Georgetown in Brooklyn, she bought a used car, gaining some level of independence and mobility. But it was stolen and trashed, and my parents did not replace it.

For a time, my mother drove my father's car as he sickened, but it seemed like she only used it to drive back and forth to the hospital. Eventually, she and my sister sold it. My mother insisted she was comfortable taking the bus wherever she needed to go or getting car service if that was necessary. But she refused to consider getting another car.

My mother seemed happy despite all she had gone through. My brief marriage disappointed her and encouraged me to date more. She was happy with the impending wedding of my sister and particularly happy with how serious and loving Yvonne's fiancé was.

I was able to spend time with the two of them in the run-up to their wedding in August. I learned more from my sister about what she had to face with our father. I felt bad that I hadn't been around, but my sister shrugged it off. She knew I had my own path to blaze. She was philosophical about our mother. She recognized that our mother was set in her ways. Why worry about that? Or insist on anything different?

I was grateful for the understanding of my sister. My father had been alienated from his family to our dismay. While she and I did not see eye to eye on religious choices, I appreciated her solidarity and loved her unconditionally.

Yvonne's Brooklyn wedding was a lovely one with lots of family, particularly on my sister's husband's side, and a huge number of their friends from both. Yvonne and John were clearly deeply united with their own religious faith and were part of a big community of friends.

CHAPTER 7

ALL FIRED UP FOR SOMEPLACE TO GO

I pondered the ten-year journey I had been on since college. I had left for Peace Corps Ecuador training in August 1980. After nearly five years in Ecuador and five years in Bolivia, I was leaving in late August 1990 for Lima Peru.

Each of the locales I had worked in had been formative experiences. First with Peace Corps as a rural public health volunteer, then with PLAN Bolivar Province as a special program advisor and trainer.

With Esperança Bolivia I had been able to play a role in the success and development of many other important development initiatives. Including the PROCOSI Child Survival Network, Universidad Nur, FUNDESIB and as a partner with PROSALUD. Were there some common threads to these successes, apart from me being lucky to be in the right place at the right time? All had been significant and hugely successful enterprises.

I had come to live among and learn from different communities and peoples, appreciating their values and foibles. Unlike most Americans, I knew Latin America, specifically South America, was far from a homogenous blur. It was a complex and kaleidoscopic mosaic of many different cultures, belief systems, and practices.

In Ecuador, I had come to live first at the slowest pace among the coastal lowlands peoples of Ecuador. As a Peace Corps Volunteer, I came to appreciate the dynamics of those families who lives in the precinct and cantonal centers vs those who lived in the more outlying and isolated settlements. I could see the differences in diet and habits between those living in more fertile and productive lands and those who lived in semi-desertified areas. When I moved to a mountainous province, with

217

communities ranging from high to low altitude areas, I got to appreciate the differences in family customs, language fluency, and attitudes toward outsiders, among other questions.

In Bolivia, living in the Chaco in an area much influenced by cattle raising, it was noteworthy the differences between communities that had been long settled by herdsmen and their families and that of Quechua-speaking immigrants from the highlands, who attempted to adopt new crops and diets.

My Peace Corps service and my work with the two PVO\NGOs shared some commonalities. I feel that I brought unbridled energy and enthusiasm to each of them. I believe this communicated itself to the people around me. I'd like to believe it was infectious and contagious. My peers and counterparts knew I was throwing myself without hesitation into the work of each. I sensed that it encouraged them also to try to do the same.

In each locale, I always tried to listen to people. It was active listening not passive. I would ask them questions and explain what I was hearing and perceiving for confirmation and validation.

Active listening isn't easy these days. The topic is covered extensively in different types of leadership training as people rise in their functions and responsibilities. This is in part because there's a persistently annoying tendency among many who are in conversations to not be active listeners. They may ask questions of each other and seem to be listening, but during that period of listening, they are thinking about what they are going to say next. Nowadays, of course, other distractions also rob us from where we focus our attention, such as cell phones and the like.

I would learn and see later in life how in government work, all too often, that approach to listening was common. The expected choreography of meetings by diplomats and senior officials. Each would go into a meeting prepared with their talking points and often strayed little from their scripts. A meeting would be deemed 'successful' if you managed to raise all your points. Whether a meeting would lead to any creatively positive or significant outcomes was beside the point. Or as the saying goes, 'Good enough for government work.'

As a Peace Corps Volunteer, and then as an NGO development worker and practitioner I always sought to look for ways to involve all. The broadest possible group of stakeholders. We looked to expand the circle at any opportunity; we wanted to build networks and connections and not walls or dividers. This sometimes led to unexpected synergies and reinforcing connections. Not always, but often enough to make a difference both in Ecuador and Bolivia. It helped our programs grow and reach more people and have more influence.

Finally, it never occurred to me in any of the positions I was in to reduce myself or limit myself to only one sector. I wasn't interested in working only in public health. I wanted to use public health or any other valid entrée into promoting opportunities for improvements in peoples' lives.

As a Peace Corps Volunteer, I had looked to include vegetable gardens and small animal husbandry besides basic health education and sanitation. I worked with mothers clubs as well as schools and other community associations. I didn't want to just work with the Seguro Social Dispensario if working with the Ministry of Health subcenter meant being able to reach more people.

At PLAN, I saw that a broad approach of integrated rural development was already in place thanks to the Ecuadorian administrator. I learned from this how progress in different areas could add up to progress in others. I applied these lessons when I was director for Esperanza Bolivia.

Yet as I rose higher in my professional life and advanced over the years since, there seem to be fewer and fewer opportunities to allow this. Funding is almost always very narrowly targeted. With USAID funding, there are formal earmarks and strict rules on how resources may be used. It must be closely tied to specific pre-determined indicators. The logic of this was to increase accountability and improve reporting to Congress of U.S.

taxpayer money. Indeed, every year new burdensome requirements seemed to be added by Congressional committees.

I had to wonder about how much was lost when grant funds were not only so narrowly defined but almost exclusively available in only one sector. It took away any flexibility within the projects on the ground to flexibly respond to the needs of the communities being served. It also psychologically put project workers into a mental strait jacket about what could and could not be done.

To paraphrase Rumsfeld, at that point in my life, I didn't know what I knew, and I didn't know what I didn't know. But I did have the sense, talking to peers and colleagues, that I had been around some uniquely thrilling successes. How would that translate to work later on, I wondered.

What else had I personally learned? How had I personally grown? Had I gained meaning and purpose in my life? Those weren't easy questions to answer.

On the personal and emotional side, the fragments from my relationship and brief marriage with Cindy were still there, as was the sense of failure associated with it. I thought I should have been more self-aware and more able to freely communicate feelings and worries about the relationship we thought we had going forward.

I had a few dalliances and brief romances afterward, but nothing that really seemed to be any more solid than what had gone on before. The friendship and romance with Judy had been more memorable than others, but they lacked a real foundation for a family.

I had made meaningful and what I hoped to be lasting friendships with many people from both Bolivia and Ecuador, locals as well as expats. Both countries had meant a great deal to me and had been difficult to leave. I felt like I would be forever connected in important ways to both countries, and really to the whole region.

I felt comfortable living in South America; I felt no urges to go elsewhere. At the same time, I looked at people like Eloy, Garth,

John, Katherine and others, who were likely to never leave their adopted homes. They had made life choices to give up everything behind them and to commit to a life of service for a given country. Both Eloy and Garth had told me they wanted nothing so much as to bury their bones in Bolivia. I wasn't sure I was quite ready for that type of commitment.

Yet the spiritual connection and kinship I felt with Bahá'ís seemed real and substantive. I felt like I had gained a sound foundation and ideology for meaning and purpose in my life. Over several years I had met serious and thoughtful Bahá'ís from all of Latin America and other parts of the world.

I'd met a couple of weird and odd people from time to time, and I remembered a statement that Cindy had attributed to her grandmother, who had been Bahá'í. "The Bahá'í Faith is a bright light that shines outwards. And like all bright lights you attract every variety of strange bugs."

Overall, many Bahá'ís had impressed me by their steadfastness, their patience and sense of vision. The grandeur of the Writings in describing the past and the future facing mankind had no competition.

I wondered how worthy I was to join that company. I had challenges and tests all the time which reminded me that I was a mere apprentice, and that I should not even claim to yet be a Bahá'í.

Nevertheless, I had made a nine-day pilgrimage to the Bahá'í World Centre in Haifa Israel. The trip had further deepened my sense of belonging as both a Bahá'í and as a Jew. The one did not negate the other. I learned while there of the unique and special role of Israel within the Faith. I learned of the history of the Bahá'ís in Palestine before the founding of the State of Israel. I saw the special affection and respect for the presence of the Bahá'ís on Mount Carmel in Haifa.

I knew from my visit at the Bahá'í youth conference and from Eloy that the Peruvian Bahá'í community was a large and active one. Depending on the time available, I could find much to occupy myself from that. That cheered me and helped me believe that the decision to go to Peru was right.

My professional vocation had gelled substantially as well. I was now over 30 and thus overdue to confirm I was on a righteous and useful life path. I would have the opportunity to spend the next two years working within a USAID mission in Lima. I hoped I would gain an understanding and experience of how it was in the bowels of an international donor.

As Paul Hartenberger had intimated, it would be a good way to learn the folkways of the enemy. Working with Ed from the Peace Corps training days would also be great, as he was working at the USAID Peru Mission.

I had deep doubts about what USAID and other big donors were achieving. I doubted they could fundamentally contribute to community development and well-being among the poor. There did not seem to be much of a good track record on human-centered development.

I also knew that I had gained practical community-level experience and a practical understanding of what it took to put together and successfully manage a development project. I hoped that working in USAID would give me a broader and more complete view of the governmental and political factors behind development.

I had wanted to join the Peace Corps since an early age, not because it was easy but because it was there, to paraphrase JFK. I suppose I had also started out with the idea of Peace Corps service as once and done. But as I propelled myself through the experiences in rural Ecuador and later on in Bolivia, I knew it wasn't so simple.

I had found what people far better than me have always known: that once you are living a life of service, you gain so much more than what you give. There is a profound satisfaction of sitting down with those who are marginalized and listening to their problems. And then together helping to find ways to overcome them.

These experiences had given me, unexpectedly, a compass for my life. It gave me a meaning and a purpose. This was brought into higher definition and clarity with my encounter with the Bahá'í principles, Bahá'í teaching and community.

I have intentionally not gone into too detailed specifics of particular books or quotations. I have not wanted to give the impression that this book is intended to primarily proclaim to the unaware the teachings of the Bahá'í Faith. It is not and I am not an appropriate channel for that. But one example, originally raised to me by Eloy Anello and Farzam Arbab, was particularly relevant to my search for purpose and meaning.

The Secret of Divine Civilization was written in 1875 in what was then Ottoman Palestine. It offered an extraordinary treatise on what was required for modernization in Persia, modern-day Iran. It was 'Abdu'l-Bahá's elaboration of the principles enunciated by Bahá'u'lláh in His Tablets to the rulers of the earth. But it could easily be read in the context of the very real and existing constraints of so many developing countries in the late twentieth century. And even today. Compared with current studies and works on community and national development and the poverty of nations, it almost stands alone.

'Abdu'l-Bahá's integrated and insightful program called for universal education. It called for the eradication of ignorance, extremism and fanaticism. Individual responsibility and community participation of the people governed through representative assembly. It articulated concepts that would not appear in the writings of other reformers for decades in the future.

As I read it just over a century from its publication, *The Secret of Divine Civilization* offered so much. A comprehensive guide for overcoming the economic and spiritual impoverishment of the developing world. As well as the so-called modern developed one. This book, and so many other writings from the Central

Figures of the Bahá'í Faith, spoke to me with a clarity and focus. It left me little choice on how I should steer my life.

As I prepared to move to Lima Peru, I was still amazed by the lack of understanding by so many people about a vocation for international development. I saw and heard so many misunderstandings about the scale, purpose and meaning of foreign aid. I think most Americans have a visceral desire to do what they could in the face of natural disasters and the need for humanitarian assistance.

I've seen that Americans were often generous and compassionate with contributions to their churches, for projects overseas to help the poor. But all too often, compared to Europeans and others, Americans seemed to be completely oblivious to the need for true longer-term community development efforts.

Americans viewed corruption cynically and as hopelessly endemic in all the poorest countries. They were sure that the U.S. government's help was pouring good money after bad, just dumping it into a rathole. They believed that 'foreign aid' was too large a share of the U.S. government budget and their taxes, and they wanted to see less of it if at all possible.

In this confusion, Americans were abetted by the most reactionary politicians. Heartless right-wingers who fed that narrative, lying and misrepresenting the facts of the matter.

This blindness, this blitheness about the underlying injustices in societies around the world, seemed short-sighted. Particularly from those espousing a Judeo-Christian faith, did people not see themselves on some level as "their brother's keeper"?

I felt I had to continue the journey I was on and find new and more effective ways that I could do more. I felt I had learned a great deal about projects and programs that worked in Ecuador and Bolivia. I enjoyed working with teams sharing common aspirations and objectives. I wanted to learn how to best draw on the U.S. government bureaucracy in my work overseas. I also wanted to learn how to better educate people back at home in the USA about Latin America and the Third World.

I wanted to counter the futility of those international development projects which were just Band-Aids. There was an unstated hypocrisy there. Some organizations seemed bent on trying to help people feel a bit better but were never capable of addressing contradictions and forces that marginalize and hold people back and their communities.

The social forces on behalf of the elites of different countries that are in bed with the elites here were sobering and daunting. How could I as an individual achieve much against them? I wanted to try to find more ways to use Bahá'í principles as an important part of the toolbox for social justice and human development.

Finally, I got word that my security clearance and medical clearance had been approved, and I was to prepare for departure for Lima. I searched for a car I could take to Lima since my State Department freight allowance covered that easily. Finding a modest non-assuming car in the States would be much cheaper. This was the prudent course given the rise of terrorist attacks in Lima and the concern about carjacking.

With great luck, I found the perfect car through newspaper ads in a Connecticut suburb near Westport: a ten-year-old Toyota Tercel hatchback in perfect condition, low mileage, and one owner for only $1000. It was an unbelievable steal of a price and was to be perfect for my needs. It seemed the perfect car for a place where car thieves were running wild. Who would want to bother to steal a ten-year-old light blue Toyota hatchback?

I bought a decent stereo sound system, had plenty of books and CD music to ship, but with all I was still well below my weight allowance for household effects. The movers came and packed both my belongings and the modest Toyota in the same shipping container, which would arrive a month later in Lima.

I hoped service opportunities would continue even with my new job in Peru. I hoped it would all play as significant a role in my future life choices as my time in Bolivia and Ecuador had. I had no idea how much that would prove to be true given what was coming!

CHAPTER 8

PERU BAPTISM BY FIRE, FOG AND FALLACIES

I arrived at a Lima still wrapped in a rainy chilly gloom of the austral winter. The foggy and drizzly dampness of the Lima winter in late August was admittedly nothing like a New York winter nor even as bad as a 'surazo' chill wind in the Bolivian Chaco, but it was still a big change from the hot late August I was coming from. While normally spring starts in the southern hemisphere with the September 21 equinox, the seasons were slow to change that year.

Still I was met with summer warmth from the re-kindled friendship of Ed and his wife Romana. They had been married about 6 years and had two sons at that point and had been in Lima for over eighteen months. They were my official Embassy and USAID social sponsors and helped to get me settled. They were diligent at both.

Sponsors fit an important voluntary function in Embassies and USAID Missions for new arriving staff. Your office sponsor takes you around and introduces you throughout the key offices of the workplace. USAID Peru was pretty big, with seven floors and several hundred people working there. Your social sponsor helps you find what you will need for your new home, pending the arrival of your vehicle from the States, and usually holds one or more parties or receptions to introduce you socially to both American and Peruvian colleagues.

Ed and Romana quickly introduced me to the Peruvian realtor they had used. There were different options for different neighborhoods, some with more apartment living, some with houses in residential areas. They encouraged me, as a single person who enjoyed nightlife, to stay in Miraflores, near the sea.

I thought that made perfect sense, and with the help of the realtor, I quickly found a furnished three-bedroom apartment available on the fifteenth floor of a modern high-security apartment building on Malecon de la Reserva, just below the penthouse floor and overlooking the cliffs and Pacific Ocean. It was just a couple blocks up from where Ed and Romana lived as well.

The apartment was huge, big living room/dining room combination, an interior sitting room with shelves for books. Decent size kitchen opening to a back patio with space for a BBQ. The biggest selling point in my mind was the view. I would never tire of it from the huge windows overlooking the western exposure and ocean.

During much of the year there would be overcast and clouds, and sometimes the fog would roll in from the Pacific and would completely blanket the city below in the view. During the summer, the humidity eases a bit, and we see the sun for a while. But I didn't mind the clouds with the ocean. If I couldn't have snowcapped mountains to gaze at, I definitely loved being right on the ocean.

There seemed always to be one hang glider visible in the sky not far from the building. Over the next two years that I lived there, hang gliders and parasails would frequently be seen darting around and between some of the different high-rise apartment buildings in the area. The cliffs down to the beach and what the locals called the 'Costa Verde' created ideal updrafts to help them remain afloat, and a launching area was not far away.

The rent was about $1700 per month. Lima was a 'Living Quarters Allowance' post, which meant that as an offshore hire from outside Peru, as I was classified, USAID would reimburse me for the rent monthly. I would have to pay the realtor myself and pay the security deposit. The building was quite secure in terms of entry, as was a semi-underground garage.

Security was important and a top priority of the U.S. Embassy and USAID Mission. With the Shining Path\Sendero Luminoso getting bolder by the week, there was a big concern over the risk of kidnapping or car bombs. Expat staff at that time were transported most of the time between work and home by a scheduled armored car shuttle.

I went in with Ed the first day. He and I were both Child Survival Coordinators with the Office of Health and Education at USAID/Peru. We shared the roles with a long-time Bolivian employee, Gerardo. Gerardo had worked many years as a local hire employee at USAID in La Paz but had then gone on to far better-paying expatriate personal service contractor jobs, first in Colombia and then in Peru.

Our Population, Health and Nutrition (PHN) division included several other local hire professional staff and was led by a Peruvian public health physician, Edgar. Edgar reported to an American Foreign Service Officer who served as the overall Office Director. We also had a four-person secretarial pool that supported all the professional and senior staff, made up of Libertad, Myriam, Lissie, and Carla.

I quickly learned that much of the professional and technical work of the different USAID offices in the Peru Mission relied heavily on the bedrock foundation of the Peruvian staff, known as Foreign Service Nationals. This is because they were local-hire staff from the country where the USAID mission was located. This aspect of USAID contrasted substantially with the State Department sections of the U.S. Embassy.

Whereas the State Department filled many positions with far more expensive American staff, either career Foreign Service Officers or shorter-term non-career hires, USAID relied substantially on local citizens competitively hired to fill many positions, usually with American mid-level and senior supervisors.

Hiring Peruvians for jobs instead of Americans was far cheaper in terms of salaries. It was also usually far more effective and capable in many ways. Local staff always understood the country better than any outside American. They had the key contacts and networks of associates in key government offices and ministries.

Offshore PSCs, such as Ed, Gerardo, and I in the PHN division, were neither fish nor fowl. We received decent salaries in dollars at what were considered low-mid level pay grades and some of the benefits and privileges of the American staff. We received reimbursement for some of our health and life insurance costs. We could use the government army post office (APO) arrangements which allowed mail to go to an address at Homestead Air Force Base outside Miami for expedited customs-free delivery to Lima. There were some limitations compared to those enjoyed by Foreign Service direct hire staff, but they were still useful otherwise.

We were technically contractors and not direct employees, so there were formal limits to our authorities and responsibilities in the office. In theory, we were limited to working on specific projects rather than the wider portfolio or program and not taking on "inherently governmental functions." This was a grey area, but it mostly referred to formal final signature authority on some of the administrative paperwork.

However, although the government claimed we were not employees, for tax purposes, we were certainly classified as such. We were unable to take advantage of income tax arrangements that people working overseas in the private sector or in NGOs and PVOs enjoyed. To Uncle Sam, we were all still liable like anyone else. This was partially mitigated by the danger pay and hazard pay we earned in Lima, which would mysteriously go up and down based on some bureaucratic calculation back in Washington.

It was all a bit confusing and contradictory. However, the whole idea for PSCs was basically a USAID invention as a workaround to the sad legacy of its funding. USAID was an independent statutory agency, but the funding it received from Congress was unlike almost any other. USAID received a regular and ample program budget, based on the Congressional appropriations for foreign aid. In theory, it was under the oversight of the Secretary of State, but at that time, USAID still had a lot of autonomy from the State Department.

However, none of the career direct hire staff at USAID could be paid from that program budget. USAID received a second funding line called the Operational Expenses (OE) Budget. All staff and related operational expenses for the staff and offices had to come out of that separate budget. For many years, Congress had perversely kept the OE budget artificially low even while the foreign aid, disaster relief, and humanitarian assistance budgets might rise. This had started in Congresses under Democratic party control, but it would worsen even more when the Republicans took over Congress in the mid-1990s and would not be alleviated for many years.

The logic of this was hard to decipher. The practical result was that USAID never had enough money for staff or travel expenses to provide adequate oversight of programs from the direct hire staff subject to the OE budget.

USAID's workaround was to hire staff with a certain percentage of program funds in each country. These would be the technical advisors and specialists it needed to oversee the programs, such as we PSCs. The convenient fiction was that these staff were hired as non-career under two-year contracts and supposedly temporary recruitments. But quite a few would work under these arrangements for one or even two decades.

Still, it meant PSCs could easily travel as needed since travel money was included in our base contracts and not subject to any Congressional OE restrictions. I marveled at these arrangements and thought back to Paul Hartenberger's invocations of the "folkways of the enemy."

THE WOLF PACK

The three of us, plus Edgar as well, became quite a gang together. We mixed with much of the staff from other offices, but the HPN group probably had the highest morale and fun of any. We'd take advantage of a modest gym facility in the basement of the Mission a few times a week, thanks to equipment procured from the Marines detachment.

We'd lunch together frequently. There was a fantastic hole-in-the-wall fresh ceviche place a few blocks from the office that we would visit at least once a week. It had no sign, but we called it "La Pared Azul" because of a bright sky-blue painted exterior wall.

It looked dodgy, but Edgar and Gerardo assured me they were hygienic behind the counter while preparing the fish for the ceviche. The ceviche, tiradito and 'leche de tigre' were always delicious. I don't think any of us ever got sick there; we continued eating there even during the height of what would become the notorious Peruvian Cholera Epidemic in early 1991, albeit surreptitiously.

There were a few other favorites a little further afield for special occasions. One was the Arequipa Social Club, which required ties and jackets and had spicy and delectable dishes from that part of Peru. There was another dodgier, more informal Arequipan restaurant. We referred to the first as the Embassy of Arequipa and the second one as the Consulate of Arequipa to play on the well-known pride and separatist-minded people of Arequipa to the south.

Ed would move on eventually; he and his family left Lima to take a job in Central America some months after I arrived. In the meantime, in our HPN wolf pack, Edgar somehow picked up the nickname of 'Wolfie,', and Gerardo was 'Hermano Lobo.' I was 'Lobito'.

I think this was in part due to the Peruvian penchant for nicknames. The new Foreign Service Health Officer who arrived was a bit frenetic and at times agitated with different office issues. That sounds perhaps a little sexist to the 21st century ear, but that's the way she seemed to behave with us in different circumstances. She was baptized by the Wolf Pack with the name 'La Nerviosa'.

In the USAID Peru Mission management ladder, the FSOs in each office reported to the Deputy Mission Director, who reported to the Mission Director. The Deputy was Barbara Kennedy, who had initially served as the Office Director for Health and Education. She was fiercely effective in her work in the office, protective of her staff, and fully committed to a better and stronger relationship with our Peruvian government counterparts. It was perhaps inevitable that we recognized her as 'La Tigresa'.

Barbara moved up to be the Deputy Mission Director and remained a mentor not just for some American staff, but for many of the Peruvians working there. I, too, saw her as a mentor and would always respect her over the course of our mutual career paths.

The Mission Director for my first year was the serious, demanding, and intimidating Craig Buck. He was feared by many in the Mission. Craig was the sort of person who would not suffer fools. He was smart, a bit of a chain smoker and inclined to be skeptical of many HPN or social sector activities. He was a conservative guy, with some ideas that could seem old-fashioned. He would sometimes make comments deriding different actors and musicians as 'left-wing' and 'talentless'. One in particular that seemed to bug him was Madonna.

He was strongly inclined to favor the anti-narcotic 'alternative development' and economic growth portfolios, followed by the democracy and governance programs. He viewed HPN as too social sector\social welfare-oriented. But he recognized and understood practical results and impact from wherever they would come. He wanted a more balanced program for USAID; I saw he was frustrated by the fact that his Mission budgets tended to be lop-sided in favor of health. There wasn't much leeway to change that, even then.

I personally was not that intimidated by Craig. Perhaps I was naïve, but since I wasn't career in USAID I thought I could just focus on my job and not worry about other things. I saw in him somebody who needed to be logically convinced of the merits, effectiveness, and efficacy of programs and not someone to be written off as an ideologue. Nor someone who could just be smooth-talked.

I also watched how Barbara Kennedy handled Craig as she moved up to be Deputy Mission Director. Barbara was a health officer when she entered USAID and not inclined to just accept Craig's first opinions. I was relatively low on the food chain, but I thought I should follow a similar approach.

I adapted quickly to the office work, and the opportunities to travel around Peru and provide oversight to the U.S. development assistance with the Ministry of Health of Peru. We were funded through the Ministry of Child Survival and Maternal Child Health Activities to reduce infant and maternal mortality rates.

This included a major push for universal infant immunizations, especially polio eradication. In January 1991, cholera became a major public health, social, and political concern after shipping vessels from Asia dumped contaminated waters off Lima's ports.

The Peruvian government presented some interesting opportunities and challenges. The newly elected President of Peru, Alberto Fujimori, was a second-generation Japanese Peruvian. He had launched a populist and reformist political movement, CAMBIO-90. It had come out of nowhere and brought Fujimori to the presidency in July the previous year. His support, however, did not translate into a majority for his party in Congress, which created political instability for Peru.

Victor Yamamoto, a Japanese Peruvian surgeon, was named Minister of Health in February by President Fujimori. As I was taking the lead on polio and other infant immunizations, I joined other international donor representatives to welcome him for the kickoff of the latest eradication campaigns. He motioned me to come to the front of the table within sight of the television cameras and press photographers.

"Thank you for your support, Minister." I intoned. "This is an important opportunity for Peru. Good luck."

He nodded and smiled broadly. He spoke in an accented Spanish with Japanese tones.

"We are always grateful for our American friends as well as our friends from the Pan-American Health Organization. But we need more than luck. We need the help of Buddha as well."

Dr. Yamamoto reached over and rubbed my ample belly under my suit jacket for the cameras.

"We don't have a Buddha here so our American friend will have to do. May he bring us all the fortune for us Peruvians to come together to wipe out polio in Peru once and for all."

We both laughed, and it brought lots of other ribbing and kidding from others present. The press ate it up.

I confessed to the Health Minister that my colleagues and I were still going to our favorite ceviche haunt despite the cholera epidemic.

"Ah excellent, you like ceviche?" he asked.

"Of course." I said. I winked at him. "But I think my ceviche may be more trustworthy than that of His Excellency the President."

The Minister gave his own version of a Buddha belly laugh and crinkled up his eyes in appreciation of the joke, but then looked around in faux alarm to make sure no one was listening directly.

"Between you and me, me too!" he said with great mirth. We recognized that President Fujimori had staged a couple of weeks before a big show for TV where he had prepared and eaten some half-raw 'tiradito,' thin slices of flounder or other fish. And then had disappeared for a week or so with a gastro-intestinal complaint which was widely rumored to be cholera.

Craig Buck congratulated me the next day when I returned to USAID, saying he liked to see my good relationship with the Minister.

It was a critical campaign. We got off on the right foot. Gerardo's management of USAID's Field Epidemiology Training Program with CDC also proved invaluable for building up the core public health expertise for tracing polio cases and helping Peru move toward complete polio eradication.

While my position was nominally in charge of public sector child survival activity, I was also assigned broader responsibilities with Peruvian NGOs. I provided oversight and technical and management assistance on several grants and cooperative assistance instruments. This included developing and reviewing scopes of work, work plans, operational research proposals, and the recruitment and supervision of outside consultants.

When the USAID Mission's Population Officer prepared to leave post, I was also asked to take over responsibilities for the family planning and population portfolio. I could handle the reading, document review, and comment drafting where needed. But I particularly enjoyed visiting different NGO offices and program locations and getting the chance to view in person what they were doing, with whom, and why.

Someone needed to take over the early HIV-AIDS work that USAID\Peru supported at the time, and I volunteered. This included condom distribution and public health education with various public and nonprofit organizations, including some of the most prestigious in South America, like PRISMA, which also supported a social marketing program in family planning.

PRISMA took me out on more than one occasion to observe their work with commercial sex workers. They would go to points where those who we used to call "prostitutes" or "streetwalkers" would gather and hand out condoms and other materials promoting safe sex. I realized in staff meetings that this was not Craig's cup of tea, but Barbara was professionally a big supporter of this necessary work. Others clearly found it a bit titillating.

Far more controversial was our work with MOHL – the Lima Homosexual Movement. I was tasked with managing a small grant we had with the group. It was an advocacy group for homosexual rights in Peru that was, at that point, still being shunned by the Ministry of Health.

Homosexuality remained illegal in Peru at that time; needless to say, conservative political forces in the U.S. also looked down on our using any U.S. government money to work with groups like MOHL. To disguise it a little, we ran much of the support through a more conventional group like PRISMA and guided them to do sub-grants with MOHL.

This was new to me, but I also understood the importance of working with all stakeholders on addressing HIV-AIDS. At that point in Peru, AIDS was still primarily being transmitted through gay men and their sexual encounters, but we understood the risk and likelihood of wider transmission in the future. I believe the work with MOHL in Peru was one of the earliest interventions of this kind within USAID.

Craig decided to throw more challenges my way when he delegated to me the responsibilities of developing the new USAID\Peru private sector Strengthening Health Institutions Project after I had previously prepared the New Project Descriptions for the Mission Action Plan and the five-year strategy within a few months of my arrival. He had respected my spunk in pushing him and advocating support for the new type of health program.

In March 1991, I recruited a team of outside consultants to work with me in developing the USAID Project Identification Document and later recruited a larger team to work with me as Chief of Party to develop the project design and Project Paper. In each case, I led the teams through a bifurcated design, in which the project proposed a southern and northern component for Peru.

I envisioned the northern component, MAXSALUD, as an adaptation of the Bolivian PROSALUD experience for the city of Chiclayo in northern Peru. The southern component, for the departments of Arequipa and Puno, was to be called MAXSERV and was designed to be an umbrella program, grouping local NGOs in a network providing health and educational services in southern Peru, with mechanisms for sub-grants and the provision of training, technical assistance, and logistics support.

Craig and Barbara, the mission director and deputy mission director, invited me to travel with Craig to Washington for the official project paper defense before all the stakeholder bureaus in USAID\Washington, and with the helpful desk officer Carol Dabbs, and a supportive Washington new hire, Carrie Thompson.

This was a big opportunity for me and unusual for a PSC. There was no one else traveling to Washington from the Lima Mission other than Craig and me. It was an excellent opportunity for me to see Craig in action and to meet a number of people from USAID\Washington who were advocates for the Peru health program for the first time.

The overall SHIP project was approved and authorized in Washington in September 1991. The MAXSERV NGO component was ultimately implemented through a cooperative agreement between USAID and CARE\Peru, which I drafted and negotiated. MAXSALUD's contract would be competed and awarded to the University Research Corporation for implementation.

That was not the best scenario, but it was the way things had been carried out in the full and open competition for the contract. I had quietly hoped Management Sciences for Health would succeed in the contract bidding process and build on their successful effort in Bolivia. I believed this would help synergize efforts between the two countries. In another valuable lesson about U.S. governmental contractual processes, I learned that what objectively might seem the most desirable outcome depended greatly on bidding companies' actual technical and cost proposals.

SOCIAL MEDIA IN PERU

Meanwhile, I found the most active social and personal life in Peru. The urban Lima lifestyle was far more sophisticated than rural Ecuador and Bolivia. It wasn't a level playing field at all. Lima was a huge metropolis of over six million people, just under a third of the country's population then. The city had a huge variety of restaurants, music halls, theatres, and so much more, apart from the charms of different neighborhoods around town.

Within the USAID mission, I became good friends with many colleagues, some of whom didn't wait for me to ask them out but boldly took the first step for me. I rarely cooked or relied on meals prepared by my part-time housekeeper.

Peruvian cuisine was full of delights that Peruvian friends were determined to share with me. There were also plenty of top-notch international choices, including truly world class Chinese food on a par with San Francisco and Hong Kong.

Quite a few of the Peruvian friends and colleagues I made then remain close friends, nearly three decades later.

There was also the dynamic Peruvian Bahá'í community. The Lima community was so large and decentralized into different municipalities and neighborhoods that there were over a dozen local community assemblies in the central Lima neighborhoods, even more when the outlying suburban communities and settlements of the Cono Sur and Cono Norte were included.

I decided to host some parties to inaugurate my apartment. I invited some younger adults from USAID, as well as from among Bahá'í friends, to encourage some mixing and cross-fertilization. I had a BBQ, and with the help of my housekeeper, we cooked several trays of "*anticuchos*" for the party. These are small skewered beefhearts cooked in a special sauce and a Peruvian favorite. I also had small ceviche plates and some good sweets.

I had brought a lot of CDs with the stereo music system I'd purchased before departure. We had a great mix of American and Peruvian music, some for listening and some for dancing, as things got more active and exciting. Several dozen friends came. I also invited my neighbors on the other side of the 15th floor to be polite.

Wolfie and Hermano Lobo came, and about a dozen friends from USAID including three of the secretaries from HPN. There were another one or two dozen Bahá'í friends.

To my great surprise, Craig came, still in his jacket and tie. While I had made a friendly invitation at the encouragement of colleagues in the USAID Mission, I was told that he would not come. He usually didn't do that. He also lived in a distant part of Lima.

Yet here he was. I encouraged him to shed the jacket and remove the tie if he liked. A couple of the secretaries began to surround and fuss over him, which I took as the cue to increase the music volume and get the party rocking. I put on some dance music and went out to the kitchen and service area of the apartment.

My housekeeper was doing extra duty on the anticuchos. The charcoals were at a good temperature and had stopped smoking, just getting a good ash. We put the anticuchos on. We flipped them over, and they were almost ready on the grill.

I noticed some flashing lights on the streets below. It looked like a fire truck, but it wasn't clear which building they would go to.

I went back to the party, where people seemed to be having a good time. I put on a CD of Madonna, and that drew a lot of people to the improvised dance floor in the living room. Wolfie and Hermano Lobo required little encouragement to get others to join them. Craig got pulled to the floor and was soon dancing up a storm. His arms were all akimbo—not my preferred dance moves, but he was clearly enthusiastic about it.

He turned to me and shouted, "This is great dance music!"

I smiled and gave him a thumbs up. "Glad you like it!"

"Who is this?" he asked. "Really great music." Priceless question.

I paused for a moment and smiled. "Madonna!"

His look of surprise was rewarding.

I then heard some heavy banging. I looked to see where it was coming from—not the front door of the apartment, but the rear service entrance near where my housekeeper was helping with the food.

I went out and saw she had a worried look about her. I thought maybe someone was complaining that the music was too loud. This wasn't *Gringolandia*. People were usually more tolerant in places like Lima on a Friday night.

I opened the iron security gate and looked through the peephole. A bunch of uniformed men outside. I threw open the door just as a fireman seemed ready to position an axe for the door.

"Where's the fire?" they asked.

"No fire, no fire," I reassured them, pointing at the BBQ grill where the anticuchos were done.

Someone had seen smoke coming from the semi-covered terrace and called the fire department.

They were annoyed but relieved at the same time. I gave them a bunch of anticuchos and beer someone had brought to assuage the false alarm.

Some months after joining USAID/Peru, I learned that a regional USAID Project Implementation Course had been scheduled to take place in Quito, Ecuador. Encouraged by colleagues in the Health office, I heard that this increasingly rare opportunity was not something to miss.

In years past, the training calendar in USAID had been much more robust. Operating Expense budget restrictions and other constraints had meant an unfortunate paring down of things like training for direct hire staff. This included the gutting of a lot of language training, which seemed incredibly short-sighted. It almost meant the near disappearance of basic foundational training such as the Project Implementation Course, one of the fundamental courses focused on project design, management, procurement, resource management, and evaluation.

This was one of the first signs I would see of internal inequities and unfairness within the U.S. Government, although not the last. There were virtually no such training limitations for the personnel at the U.S. State Department. But the limitations imposed on the U.S. Agency for International Development seemed needlessly crippling and mean-spirited, in fact. The reduced availability, if not lack of language training, meant that USAID Foreign Service Officers were often not as well prepared in local languages and culture, even though by the nature of their job, they often required those skills more than that of the State Department Foreign Service Officers, who might spend the entire workday with English.

In any case, I was lucky. As a project-funded PSC, I had more flexibility to take advantage of this training. Both Ed and Gerardo had previously been able to do so in trainings held in Washington, D.C.

The location of this week-long iteration of the course in Quito was providential. It was a bit of a homecoming for me, of course. I had lived in Ecuador six years earlier, and USAID Ecuador had been an important point of contact for me in my latter years there, almost a touchstone.

Of course, the USAID health Foreign Service career staff I had known were no longer there. They had moved on. Herb Caudill, though, was still there as a local hire resource.

I received a special surprise that week when I was contacted by email by Jeremy Martin at Nur University, back in Santa Cruz,

Bolivia. Regis Viveros would be passing through Quito, traveling overland from Bolivia. He was headed to Colombia to study there.

I was so impressed with how far Regis had gone from his earliest days with us in the Chaco. I thought he would spend the night in Quito, but his stopover was just a few hours. Still, I had the chance to invite him for a meal and reminisce.

Following the course, I asked to take five days of vacation leave from the office back in Lima. I couldn't resist the chance to see more of Ecuador while I was there, so I rented a jeep and drove down through the valleys to Santo Domingo, Buena Fe, and Quevedo to see the changes since I had left.

I had an affectionate homecoming with the Montes family in Buena Fe. Everyone was well, which was reassuring. They knew I had gone to Bolivia but had not heard I had since moved to Peru.

The town had grown remarkably since I left and was now on its way to becoming a cantonal center. It was lovely to be reminded again of the journey of discovery I had been on since my first days there.

Back in Lima, there was plenty to catch up with at work. Still, the weekends were always a great time to enjoy the beaches. While there were beaches just below the cliffs that ran along the coast of Miraflores and, further north, the famous Costa Verde, these were dirty and too close to the city to inspire much confidence in the water quality. This was a particular concern during the time of cholera. My little blue Toyota Tercel hatchback was a big help in this regard.

South of Lima, there were great beaches that were an hour's drive or so. Quite a few of us would use the summer weekends as a chance to drive down to enjoy the sun that was easier to find south of Lima, going to beaches such as El Silencio, or further south towards Asia. Many of us would head out with picnic baskets or rely on local vendors who could usually be found near the beach with fresh fish.

The only challenge was that the water was not at all like the beaches I remembered in Ecuador to the north. Here off the Peruvian coast, the Humboldt current reigned. It flowed north from Antarctica along the Chilean and then the Peruvian coast, only moving away from the shore as it encountered tropical waters coming from the equator somewhere in northern Peru.

I went in lots of times, but it was bone-chilling cold. You could get used to it a bit, but you could not usually stay for more than fifteen minutes at a time. Still, the beach was another thing. It was a great place to relax and enjoy oneself with friends.

One time I found myself drafted for an excursion further south. I had hit it off with Charo, one of the project assistants in USAID's Office of Agriculture.

"Alonzo, we have to go to Paracas!" she exclaimed.

I remembered hearing of Pisco and Paracas on my previous trips to Peru, but I had never been there.

"You'll see, you'll see. What are you doing this weekend? It's only a couple of hours away. We could go on Saturday and come back Sunday."

I was game. I promised to pick her up early Saturday morning from her house in my Toyota hatchback. When I arrived, I realized that this was not just a little jaunt for Charo and me. Her two cousins, Mila and Maritza, were joining us.

OK, the more the merrier. The Toyota was up for it, and Charo loaded us down with provisions and extra towels. The trip was more than two hours. It was more like three hours south down the *Carretera Panamericana*, well past the furthest beaches south of Lima.

In truth, I wasn't that surprised. I had read up a bit about it the evening before. Paracas was a town bordering a beautiful peninsula jutting out into the Pacific. There were huge seal and walrus colonies on islands and beaches scattered about the peninsula.

We took a boat tour and saw what must have been thousands of them. Small islands dotting the ocean off the peninsula also hosted seabirds dropping guano excavated for fertilizer. It was a memorable smell, but the weather was gorgeous, and it was great being out in the ocean.

There were also huge petroglyphs and geoglyphs carved into the cliffs and sand on the hillsides of the peninsula, notably one resembling a huge candelabra. According to the archeologists, these were from well before the Incan and immediate pre-Incan days and were estimated to be nearly 2000 years old. It was a memorable weekend jaunt.

I was elected to the local assembly in Miraflores six months after my arrival. Each assembly had nine members elected democratically from the Bahá'ís of that community. The following month, April, I found myself elected to the National Assembly of the Bahá'ís and then selected to be the National Treasurer. This demanded between five and eight hours a week of my spare time.

The Bahá'í National Centre was in the Jesus Maria neighborhood of Lima, not far from the USAID office. I became close friends with many of the Bahá'ís, including some whom I had met when I attended the International Youth Conference in Lima almost six years before.

There was a wide range of activities supported by different Bahá'ís. There was a regular fireside in Miraflores, near my house, supported by Farid and Roya. They were Persians and a young married couple. Roya was a relatively new arrival from California, but Farid had lived and studied in Lima for many years. Firesides were informal get-togethers where people who wanted to know more about Bahá'ís and the Bahá'í faith were encouraged to join. It was a great way to show hospitality.

Farid was a recent graduate of dental school and was opening his clinic. Farid was also originally from a part of Iran where comics and jokers were overabundant. This was all too evident with Farid, but his timing was usually atrocious. I made the mistake of going to get a dental check-up with him. While his hands were in my mouth, he would tell one or another joke.

"No, wait, don't laugh, I have more to do here," He would usually say.

Then, he would continue with another set of jokes while working. It was punishment for me of sorts, even though he was a talented dentist.

I learned that a popular annual get-together for the Peruvian Bahá'ís was the 'Bahá'í Summer School'. It was a sort of mini university with a wide range of workshops and classes on different topics. It was held ten days during the local summer vacation time, usually in a beach town to the south or north of Lima. The summer school was scheduled for Punta Hermosa, which had a nice stretch of beach that was only a little over an hour south. There would be about 100 people participating, mostly youth and young adults.

I was invited by the Summer School organizing committee to give a talk about international development, interwoven with relevant Bahá'í teachings. I didn't have the time during the week to go down, so it was scheduled for a Saturday. I would have about two hours, and I planned to include some small group activities to help reinforce my own prepared remarks.

The invitation to speak to the youth at Punta Hermosa about development gave me a chance to reflect again on my work. What could I say that would be meaningful? Eight years before, the Universal House of Justice, the supreme body of the Faith, had released an encyclical letter about socio-economic development. I also drew on it for ideas.

There was a lot of interest in different approaches to international development by government, donors, and nongovernmental organizations. I didn't claim to be an expert but shared insights from my experiences in several countries.

Persistent underdevelopment in Latin America and other parts of the world was not an accident. It was not caused by a run of bad luck or just because of government fecklessness and corruption, although the latter did play a role.

I mused about the gross inequities in society. A country like Peru had tremendous wealth and abject poverty. There were gross inequities in the society. If anything, the gap had probably broadened since colonial days and over Peru's 160-year history.

The level and health of democracy and popular participation must also be part of the explanation. Peru was facing anti-democratic uprisings and a rash of terrorist acts that were surely instigated in part by the inadequacies of political openness and the lack of a voice of marginalized communities, as well as by the gross extremes of wealth and poverty.

I doubted in part the role of big international donor agencies like USAID, my employer. Some of the work was valuable and important, particularly when in concert with the plans and resources of the host government. I noted the need for public health interventions and the value of initiatives like eradicating polio and other diseases and addressing the accessibility of healthcare services for marginalized populations. However, I noted that so much of the work of different international donors was easily divorced from national and local governments' resources, strategies, and commitments. And there was little action taken in practical terms to change that.

Was there a role for faith and faith-based organizations? I recognized that many Bahá'í writings and teachings very directly addressed the needs of human and community development. This did not mean that the Bahá'ís had a monopoly of understanding. Many faiths shared a common foundation of understanding about what was needed.

To promote change, growth, and development in our families and communities, we needed to look to initiatives that would help enable and ennoble all people within the community. We needed to build the structures within our communities that would ensure the broadest possible access, outreach, and voice for people.

We needed to view the mass of people within society as largely disenfranchised and kept apart from power and decision-making. It wasn't a matter of simply embracing a "Power to the People" ideology; we needed to provide communities with tools to truly be empowered and supported to make rational choices about their self-improvement and upliftment. There were clear connections in the Bahá'í writings that could guide us in that journey.

In the small group session that followed, I challenged the participants to develop specific Bahá'í teachings and link them to practical and meaningful community-building activities that could improve community participation, education, and health. It went well, and there was a lot of constructive engagement.

However, I was unprepared for another dimension of summer school. While Persians were not the majority of Bahá'ís in Peru, they were an important and influential minority. While the formal program and curriculum of the summer school were certainly important, the social aspects were also prized.

Within the social aspects were the informal efforts of what I can only describe as the Iranian *yentas*. The matchmakers. The rack and stack of eligible bachelors and bachelorettes within the Bahá'í community and the little nudges here and there to see what might come from it. Diversity and contrasts were always to be encouraged.

Farid and Roya were doing their share to support this cultural tradition. They were helped along by Fariba, a Persian Bahá'í who had lived many years in Peru but had married and moved to

Amsterdam. She was visiting that month from Europe and had ample relatives in different parts of Peru who were part of the Persian Bahá'í diaspora that had arrived in force in Peru after the 1979 Iranian Revolution, many as refugees with UN documents and safe conduct passes.

Fariba looked me up and down surreptitiously and decided to instigate introductions. She introduced me to her close Peruvian friend Mabel, who wasn't Bahá'í but had joined Fariba at the summer school. She encouraged us to get to know each other in a not particularly discrete way. Her lack of discretion was not an issue, as I was a bit oblivious to the machinations involved.

Mabel was wearing a brightly colored blouse with tan culottes that I liked a lot. She was tanned from the sun and her own mellow complexion. She had two birthmarks on her upper lip, which caught my attention, as did her large almond eyes. We chatted a bit, but I could not stay too long nor bunk with most of those staying overnight at the summer school. I had to return to Lima.

Fariba stayed with Mabel during her visit in Lima and organized several other trips to the beach in the coming weeks. I agreed to join them and offered to drive. I was getting interested in Mabel; she, not so much. I learned afterward that a few times I came calling, she told her sister to tell me she wasn't there. She was not interested. Still, Fariba together with her allies Roya and Farid were nothing if not persistent. They were openly matchmaking.

We began to date, going to different restaurants in Lima. I found that she lived with her parents in Miraflores, not far from where I lived. When we made that subsequent beach trip with some friends from my office, I faced her and her beach towel so much that I got sunburned completely on one side of my face and body. That was a little embarrassing.

Over time, against all odds, it became increasingly serious. I met her parents and family. They were a family of lawyers for the most part. Mabel's father had been a successful lawyer, district attorney, and then Mayor of Ayacucho during the height of the terrorism there. I managed not to make a fool of myself. Her brother, also a lawyer, initially teased me with some commentary that reflected some classic Latin American left-wing anti-American tropes, but I gave as good as I got in a good-natured way. Her sister married an executive from Occidental Petroleum and lived around the corner with her three children.

I met the brother and sister of her best friend from university, Edgar and Colette Lau, in Lima. They and their older sister Coleen were Chinese Peruvians. Mabel's friend Coleen was married to an Israeli Jew and lived in Jerusalem. The Laus were all such good friends with Mabel that they were like an extended family.

I was invited to a famous Chinese restaurant in Miraflores, where Mabel and I were escorted into one of the back rooms. There, Colette's parents presided along with their brother Edgar, and we all sat around a large round table with revolving dishes in the center. I felt myself under inspection again.

The meal's highlight was something called *"Sopa de Remedios"* which included all sorts of special ingredients, many better not to ask. I felt like I was being interviewed for an executive position. The interrogation covered a range of topics. The family patriarch looked me over closely. The Laus were always very protective of Mabel; she was almost an adopted daughter within the family. Luckily, I passed muster. By evening end, Colette and their brother Edgar were treating me as an adopted extended family member and teasing me about my accent.

Friends at USAID organized a boat trip off Callao, a northern port of Lima. Mabel and I went. The water was a little chilly and choppy. Mabel was not the most enthusiastic on the water but proved to be a good sport. It was a good way to introduce her to my colleagues, too. We joined another Embassy-organized trip driving to Huaraz in the mountains, which was a similar opportunity.

After a short courtship, I proposed marriage. I wasn't rejected but deflected at first and then again. After a bit of misunderstanding and intercultural clarification, I learned that I would first have to formally ask for her hand at a dinner with her parents and family. I hadn't realized this. I also hadn't realized that a proposal was just an empty proposition without a ring.

With the help of a Peruvian Bahá'í jeweler friend, I quickly went out to get a diamond engagement ring. I had been a bit clueless. We scheduled the dinner, known as "La Pedida de Mano", the request for the hand. There was a whole choreography to it, which Mabel and her sister briefed me on.

With our engagement now formalized, we traveled to the States to share the news and introductions with my family. We flew to Florida and stopped to visit NASA. I had the bright idea that it might interest Mabel to see a bit of the United States while there. This was probably not my brightest idea since you can see only so much going up that long I-95 drive.

We drove to New York without mishap. Going through Washington, I remember Mabel being surprised when we didn't see almost any Caucasians, only African Americans on the streets. This was new for her, although Peru had some small Afro-Peruvian communities around and outside Lima. And more than a little startling for her expectations, given what was a capital city. In Washington, we stopped to visit with Carol Dabbs, my erstwhile USAID colleague and friend.

My mother was charmed by Mabel and fussed over her petite size. My sister and mother were incredibly happy with the engagement, and my sister offered to fly down for the wedding, which we planned to have in Lima. Still, there were other intercultural hiccups.

Mabel turned to me, puzzled and worried.

"Your mother must hate me. Why is she mad at me?" she asked.

"She loves you; she is delighted to meet you. Why would you think that?" I responded.

"Because she is always yelling at me. I don't know why."

This required explaining how New York, or perhaps especially Brooklyn Jews, tend to talk. Everyone is loud and raucous, particularly compared to most Peruvians.

The concern was repeated again when we went to a New York deli to eat with Tim, a former friend from the Peace Corps. Mabel stumbled over the menu, which could have been written in Chinese for all the use it provided her. I translated not just the English but the ethnic coloring of the dishes.

Mabel picked something more recognizable and trustworthy to the impatient and loud waiter. She was startled when the waiter returned to the table and slammed a plate on the table loudly with an insistent, "Here, eat this. You are too skinny, and you must put some meat on those bones!"

I shrugged and raised my eyes, explaining that this was the "shtick" of many old delis and their eternal waiters. They sometimes bring you what they think you should eat, but they do not always bring you what you ask for.

WEDDING BELLE MABEL

We returned from New York; there wasn't much time for the wedding preparations. Many friends at USAID and from among the Bahá'ís pitched in to help.

We wondered about a locale for it. We looked over different options, none of which really inspired us. While there would have to be a small and intimate civil ceremony at the Miraflores mayor's office the night before, just with Mabel's immediate family and with a few official witnesses, the Bahá'í religious ceremony was something we wanted to make special. Since Bahá'ís don't have churches or temples, and the National Center building didn't seem to be the best space for a ceremony, we favored the idea of a garden.

A guardian angel intervened from USAID. Dayna and Rudi Griego, from USAID's Office of Food and Agriculture, were getting ready to leave Lima soon. They lived in a house with a spacious garden in Camacho, a leafy residential suburb of Lima. They offered the garden for the ceremony, which could easily manage a group of fifty or more. I was assured I could rent chairs, tables, and tents from the USAID warehouse for the event.

We developed a list of invitees, and though we thought to keep it to a reasonable size, it kept growing. Mabel had plenty of friends from her hometown and university that she wanted to invite. I had many friends and co-workers who wanted to join us. My sister would come from the USA; my mother was a difficult traveler by plane and felt she could not face a six-hour flight from New York.

I soon got a call from the U.S. Ambassador's office. I learned that Ambassador Anthony Quainton and his wife certainly hoped and expected to attend. He couldn't miss a Bahá'í wedding ceremony. He had never been to one. I had briefed the genteel, genial, and effective Ambassador multiple times. Night and day from Gelbard in Bolivia. The Quaintons, of course, got added to the list. We also had to make sure we were aware of any security requirements.

The wedding came off without a hitch. We ended up with about 65 couples at it or about 130 people. We had Jewish, Christian, and Bahá'í prayers as part of the program. One of my USAID secretaries, Carla, was a cousin to the famed soprano Piero Solari. As a lovely gift from Carla, he graciously performed 'Ave Maria' as part of the program. Mabel's youngest niece, Alexandra, served as the ring bearer, but had to be watched like a hawk by Mabel's sister and mother that she didn't do anything naughty and lose the rings off the pillow they were tied to. Her other nieces were flower girls. Roya spoke on behalf of the local Bahá'í community, presiding as we exchanged our vows and the Bahá'í wedding prayers.

The wedding was catered with the help of one of the Bahá'í friends who had a catering business. There were some delectable Peruvian recipes and dishes out there for the guests. We barely had a chance to eat anything at all, as we circulated around to each table, making sure to thank the guests for coming.

By the time we managed to eat a little, the cake was already being brought out, and we had to look at that and all the pictures. Mabel still blamed me for years afterward for rushing her and not letting her eat some of the delicious dishes, most of which we would never touch today!

We had a sendoff from the wedding party in a hired classic antique car, which was a nice photogenic touch. After a night in one of the new hotels in downtown Miraflores, we flew up to northern Peru to have our honeymoon at the Punta Sal resort on the beach in Tumbes. The beaches had wide white sand and tropical water flowing from the Ecuadorian coast further north.

Getting married to Mabel meant marrying into her extended family network, which included the Laus, who endorsed my marital intentions a couple of months before. We frequently joined them on the weekend for Dim Sum in Capon, the Chinatown of Lima. If Lima had world-class Chinese food generally, this was even more true at select locations in Capon, where you had to really go with the cognoscenti to be able to best appreciate it.

Mabel and I loved the variety and richness of the dumplings and other dishes offered in traditional Dim Sum, where the waiters come around with steaming carts, and you select what you want and don't want. I became a real aficionado.

Going out for Dim Sum with the Laus meant almost a full day slow food proposition with lots of conversation and exchange, what the Peruvians call in traditional Spanish "*sobremesa*." In Spanish, which I learned in high school, and Ecuador, that word usually meant dessert. But in Spain, as in Peru, "sobremesa" refers to the relaxing chit-chat, card-playing, coffee, and usually leisurely end to the main meal of the day, between two and three in the afternoon.

In April, I had to attend on behalf of USAID, a regional Pan American Health Organization meeting for several days in Recife, Brazil, regarding the expanded program of immunizations. On my return, President Fujimori upturned the political dynamic in the country by closing the combative Peruvian Congress and declaring an *"autogolpe"* or "self-coup." He argued that he had tried to push through economic reform and anti-terrorist legislation through the Peruvian Congress to no avail. It proved to be a hugely popular measure which many Peruvians, perhaps even most widely supported.

The *autogolpe* left the USAID mission and the Embassy in a quandary. There was much discussion over the stance and direction of U.S. policy. After a brief pause, the Bush 41 Administration in Washington condemned the interruption of the democratic process in Peru. Sanctions were imposed on the Peruvian government. USAID was no longer able to work officially with the government and had to find ways to work with only the private or nonprofit sectors.

I was getting an earful from in-laws as well as other Peruvians I knew inside and outside the Mission. It was a complicated dance. Luckily, the SHIP project I had designed the year before was coming online, enabling our health program to continue in some fashion.

It was hard not to initially sympathize with the stance many Peruvians took. Fujimori made major strides that year in aggressively pursuing the Shining Path and MRTA terrorists who had begun heavier attacks. His economic measures proved to be increasingly successful, or at least appeared to be. Was this a case of America following a stereotypical role of trying to impose its will on the region? Other Latin American countries were taking a much more nuanced view of Fujimori's actions, at least initially.

Fujimori would easily win re-election in 1995, defeat Shining Path definitively, and create macroeconomic stability. But in his second term, he would also prove to be increasingly authoritarian, corrupt, and anti-democratic. That would lead to his eventual downfall and overthrow in November 2000.

Meanwhile, the Bahá'í world was all astir for what was being called a Bahá'í Holy Year. The Centenary of the Passing of Bahá'u'lláh will be recognized in Haifa, Israel, in May. Mabel, who was pregnant, and I were invited to join the Peruvian delegation for the ceremonial events. The ceremonies would involve over 3,800 Bahá'ís from around the world visiting the Bahá'í World Centre on the slopes of Mount Carmel and Bahá'í holy sites in Haifa and Akko.

We decided to break up the long trip by stopping for a few days in England. Mabel and I were met by my friend Judy, who took us to her house in Cambridge and offered generous and affectionate hospitality. I remember both of us being surprised during that trip how bright the sky remained in Cambridge that time of year well into the evening, 9 or 10 PM.

The trip was the start of a joint love affair Mabel and I would have with England and Israel. We would return to visit both countries many times in subsequent years.

The Bahá'í ceremonies were moving and impressive. There was a lot of walking, often on paths paved by broken red brick fragments through the Bahá'í gardens. It was stunning to see the thousands of Bahá'ís from around the world, often in their native dress or costume.

The Haifa shops and taxi drivers were clearly well prepared for the Bahá'í invasion. Everywhere you could see signs in English 'Special Discount for Bahá'ís – 15% Off'. And taxi drivers around Haifa were remarkably, if not unusually, patient and helpful. I thought the Mayor must have sent them all off to charm school in the previous weeks.

The trip for my wife was even more remarkable when she reunited after years with her best friend, Coleen Lau, whom I finally met. We visited her and her husband Alon and son in Jerusalem. I had a chance to marvel at Mabel's negotiating skills in the souk there. No known common language with the Palestinian traders did not stand in the way of her ability to bargain.

We returned to Peru on edge with different terrorist attacks. Then, on July 16, there was a huge car bomb attack at a bank on Tarata Street in Miraflores, around the corner and two blocks from the apartment of Farid and Roya. The windows shook violently with the blast pressure in our apartment, which was less than a half mile away, but the windows in their apartment and other floors were blown out.

The Tarata attack would prove to be the biggest and most deadly explosion by Shining Path, about the equivalent of one ton of explosives, with two dozen killed and over 150 wounded. It would kick off a reign of terror and an anti-government strike that week in Lima that would leave another few dozen dead. The public outcry helped President Fujimori have a free hand in attacking far more aggressively against the Maoist terrorist group.

Mabel and I had to deal with further security lockdown procedures from the U.S. Embassy. Craig Buck had already moved on from Peru, recalled by Washington to meet needs in Central Asia released from the Soviet grip. Barbara Kennedy took over for a time as Acting Mission Director. My PSC contract was coming up for renewal, and I still hadn't heard if it would be renewed. There was a lot of uncertainty in the Mission.

Mabel was getting prenatal care from Wolfie's ex-wife, a great gynecologist. She recommended that a close colleague serve as the attending obstetrician when she came due.

I followed up with Edgar and La Nerviosa regarding my contract in early August. La Nerviosa had been acting strangely with me ever since a birthday party the month before where, at a critical moment, we had dunked her into the house swimming pool. (I don't remember all the details, but I don't doubt she deserved it. Although it had also been part of the general merriment of the party.)

Then, one day, I was called into her office together with the Executive Officer of the Mission. My past was, in fact, coming back to haunt me.

"We can't renew your contract, Alonzo. I am so sorry," she said. She didn't look very sorry.

I blinked twice. "Why is that?" I asked. "What happened?"

The Executive Officer hemmed a bit and said, "We were doing a credential check, and we called the University of Chicago. We discovered you don't actually have your B.A. degree."

I turned red. "Well, it's true, I had some incompletes at the end. I still have plans to finish them when I return to the States."

"Well, that's not good enough. It's a condition of employment that you have your actual degree. And despite your experience, you don't have that. At least not yet."

I couldn't believe it. I had gone through two security checks. One for Limited Official Use when I joined, and another for actual Secret-level clearance that the Mission had pursued a few months after I arrived so I could be flexible with additional duties. And this had never come up.

The Executive Officer said, "You put down that you had studied at the university from 1976 to 1980 in a political science and biology degree program."

"Well that's true," I said.

He looked pained. "But you don't have your actual degree...." His voice trailed off.

La Nerviosa had one of those faces like the smile of a Cheshire Cat, while trying to make believe she was deeply regretting the sorrowful situation.

"Is this because of the swimming pool last month?" I asked.

"Of course not, of course not." But her eyes said something different.

I went to talk with La Tigresa. She was sympathetic, but she explained that she could do nothing. This was in the bailiwick of the Executive Office. She couldn't get involved. Why didn't I plan to go back and finish the degree and be done with it?

There's no denying that this was a major life screw-up—an unforced error. The circumstances of my original mistakes in 1980 were, even if defensible, hard to justify as not having been corrected somehow in the ensuing twelve years. I had procrastinated and allowed myself to be paralyzed, putting it off. And now, I had slammed into a wall as a result.

I found myself without a renewed contract, and in a couple of weeks, I would be without a job in Peru. I was humiliated. I had been brought low.

I refused to plan a return to the States at that point. Mabel was about ready to give birth, and there was no way we wanted that to happen in the United States, even had she been in a position to travel. She wouldn't have the help and network she was used to.

With all the safety net and accommodations possible, Peru was a much more appropriate place for Mabel and us. We had already reserved and paid for a birthing center location for her in Camacho, which would be comfortable with an obstetrician she trusted.

I was confused about the next steps and the chaos and uncertainty now ahead of us. But there was no time to overthink about that then.

Mabel's parents had an apartment about a mile away from my U.S. government-supplied apartment. They immediately set about accommodating it to meet our needs and the arrival of the baby. We rushed about making different arrangements, picking up furniture and other things we would need, including electrical converters for Lima's 220-volt current for my 110-volt appliances.

While we started out thinking our baby would be born by natural childbirth, she proved to be stubborn in that regard and we had to schedule a caesarian. I was there gowned and gloved with Mabel for the procedure.

I remember when the obstetrician and her assistant carefully made the incision and scooped Katrina Rose out from her mother. She came out with a look of annoyance and irritation. It looked like she was ready to slap the obstetrician and say to her, "Put me back! You interrupted my nap, and I'm not ready yet." It was not her choice.

The assistant announced to both me and Mabel, "Sex, Feminine." And made a quick pass of waving our baby's nether region in our direction. It was an oddly clinical way to let us know that we had a girl, as expected. Mabel laughed in amazement at her face. She was small but healthy at 6 lbs. This was not a surprise to us, as Mabel had hardly gained a pound for much of her pregnancy and almost didn't begin to show until the eighth month.

A few weeks after Katrina Rose's birth, we had settled into a reasonable routine, helped so much by Mabel's mother and her sister. I began to look around for consultancies and short-term assignments.

Mabel was able to persuasively get a phone line installed in her parents' apartment in Miraflores. This was a great achievement. Getting phones in Lima was often so difficult that people gave up trying after being on a waiting list for years. Somehow, the Peruvian telephone company had modernized very recently and been able to expand the number of phone lines available in the neighborhood of her apartment.

The phone line was great for staying in contact. I was also able to put in a modem connection for email and internet access for my computer in an office we were able to set up in a room upstairs. This gave me greater flexibility for pursuing potential consultant assignments as well.

Following my departure from USAID, I was soon recruited by PACT to assist them in developing a proposal for an NGO umbrella group mechanism. This was envisioned to channel technical assistance and sub-grant funding under PL 480 food aid monetization assistance to a multisectoral group of Peruvian NGOs.

It played to my strengths and background, both my familiarity with USAID and my prior work in Bolivia with NGO networks. I did not have much experience with PL 480 food aid at that point, although I had helped FUNDESIB with a proposal for similar resources a few years before. PL 480 monetization resources were local currency funds available from the sale of donated food assistance.

I researched the NGO requirements, conducted an initial inventory and needs assessment, obtained letters of intent from participating agencies, and provided 15-20 pages of text to use in the technical project design.

At the same time, Technoserve, a respected PVO with broad expertise in agriculture, food security, water, and sanitation, reached out to me to join their team for this competitive bid and wanted to include my resume in their proposal.

I came to believe Technoserve had a better chance at winning than PACT, since Technoserve had actual programs on the ground. So, in the end, I turned down an offer from PACT for a position on the Technical Assistance team. This proved to be a mistake and a rueful lesson as well. The PACT bid ultimately proved successful against other competitors with programs on the ground, such as Technoserve.

We decided I should travel back to New York in November to look into consultancies and job prospects there and in Washington. Mabel and Katrina Rose were not yet comfortable traveling, and they had a far better support network in Lima.

I flew back to New York and reunited with my mom. The trip in late November coincided with the Bahá'í World Congress in New York. This was the second global event commemorating the centenary of the passing of the Faith's founder. It was held at the Jacob Javits Center in New York, with 30,000 Bahá'ís attending.

I went each day for the four-day event. I was able to connect up with old friends from Bolivia, including John Kepner.

John had worked for PROCOSI as their Executive Director for a bit over a year and a half while I was at USAID\Peru. He had recently been recruited by Project Concern International to serve as their Country Director in Guatemala. I shared my resume and let him know I was looking for short and long-term consultancies.

I knew that the sad reality of this work among the international NGOs often came down to who you knew. Many capable people were out there, and even more who marketed themselves as such. When push came to shove, and you needed to hire a consultant to undertake some work, it was usually better to look to people you knew had done the job and could do so again. I hoped to plumb those contacts.

I also met Bonnie at the World Congress in New York. She was a wealthy New Yorker who had set up a modest family foundation called the World Community Foundation to support charitable work overseas. She needed help steering it toward a more systematic approach to assessing viable development projects. I offered to help after the New Year, in the following spring.

The International Eye Foundation (IEF) hired me as a consultant to support their programs in Honduras and Guatemala. They needed someone experienced with USAID-funded Child Survival projects to help them complete a project evaluation, and then the development of a USAID-required Detailed Implementation Plan for the new project.

I got to know the team at IEF well, which had headquarters in Silver Spring, Maryland, in the suburbs of Washington, DC. I then traveled to Central America to work with their project teams.

IEF initially worked on child blindness issues in developing countries, and as part of that, they had been active in addressing micronutrient deficiencies that impacted that area as well as broader child survival concerns such as acute respiratory illness and diarrheal disease. I helped the project teams complete the assignments and won plaudits for some creative solutions to problems that had been found.

I got a warm surprise when I learned from IEF's team that my old mentor and friend from USAID Bolivia, Paul Hartenberger, was the current health office chief at the USAID Mission in Tegucigalpa. I called Paul's office, and we were able to get together for lunch. Paul was always a kick. Full of plans, ideas, and ambitions to take some of the successes from the USAID Bolivia health program to Honduras. I shared with him my own efforts in Lima, and the ups and downs I had faced. He wished me well on the consultancy assignment and offered to keep me in mind as a resource if anything might pop up.

During this time, Mabel's father progressively worsened in a chronic illness. He passed away peacefully. This saddened me; he was a kind, patient, supportive father-in-law. It was tough for the entire family. Mabel and her mother had been consoled partly by the fact that he had at least some months getting to know baby Katrina Rose. He had so enjoyed the time with his youngest grandchild, and perhaps this had also helped prolong his time on earth a bit longer.

After completing the work with IEF, I thought it might make sense if my new family looked to re-settle for a time in New York particularly if I was going to help the World Community Foundation for a stint. I knew it would be a big change for us, particularly Mabel, but she was up for the adventure. We also talked about inviting Mabel's mother to join us in New York once we had settled.

My mom was thrilled to see and play with her first granddaughter. She was more than happy to have Mabel, Katrina, and I stay for a bit, but I wanted to look for a place in Manhattan.

In this, I was incredibly lucky. I found an apartment in midtown Manhattan, just south of Central Park. It was occupied under rent control laws by an English Jewish family who spent half the year in New York and half the year abroad in London. It was an unofficial sublet as is wont to happen in New York City. But that meant it could be available to us at a very reasonable price, furnished and in an ideal location in midtown Manhattan for up to six months. This seemed ideal for our changeable and unpredictable circumstances. We grabbed the place.

We spent the next six months in Manhattan. It was, in many ways, an idyllic experience for us. The apartment had some drawbacks. We had to be careful not to allow neighbors or building management to know that we were sub-letting. The apartment was furnished in a New York fashion, which meant it was already stuffed to the gills before we moved in. We could barely fit our suitcases into the mix. But it was relatively big, as apartments in New York go, and even had a baby grand piano for Mabel to practice on.

Every other night it seemed there would be some terrible bashing noise coming from the street seven floors below, which initially would wake up a fussy Katrina Rose. It was the cacophony of the garbage trucks coming through, but we called the noise "the building destroyers" as they banged and clanged down the street around 8 or 9 PM.

Still, there were many positives. It was a scant block and half away from the Plaza Hotel on Central Park South and the entrance to Central Park, close to the Zoo. It was near Fifth Avenue's famed FAO Schwartz toy store. It was a great location for Katrina Rose and her stroller.

After a couple of months, Mabel's mother was able to make the trip to New York—her first visit to the United States. She was a great traveler and very open to adventure and new experiences. She was truly the best mother-in-law one could imagine, always cheerful, generous, and uncomplaining.

My mom and Mabel's mom had lovely experiences together in New York that transcended language. Mabel's mom never learned English, and my mom never learned Spanish. But somehow, they were able to easily overcome that linguistic barrier through their shared love and adoration of Katrina Rose.

I was sorry that Mabel's father had only months to live when Katrina Rose was born, and he could not share fully the range of experiences that my mother-in-law would. I had enjoyed speaking with him in Peru and learning about his wide-ranging experiences.

From time to time, Mabel and her family saw echoes of him in our daughter. Certain hand gestures and movements made by Katrina Rose evoked her maternal grandfather. I couldn't say the same from my side of the family, although I thought Katrina Rose was lucky to have received so much of her genetic inheritance from her Peruvian family.

Mabel and her mom would take Katrina Rose out on temperate days to stroll toward Central Park and the Zoo. Our baby had large, striking olive-shaped eyes, which seemed to attract the attention of a host of Japanese tourists who would see her in a hat and jumper and want to take pictures of her in the stroller.

It was hard to know what to make of this reaction by tourists, but it was exceedingly amusing. Katrina Rose herself contributed a great deal of charisma to the outings. She would often begin to speak out to people who stopped to see her with expressions of great emphasis and personality. Her hands would sometimes go back and forth as if she were making some important points. People would nod in encouragement.

Of course, it was entirely unintelligible. Perhaps she had a clear idea of what she was saying but for the rest of us it was gobbledygook. She seemed so self-assured.

People would ask, startled, "What language is she speaking?" It got to the point that we would add any language that came to mind.

Businessmen and women would stop and stare at times for a moment. Both Mabel and her mother found that New York pedestrians would immediately rush to help if they were trying to go down the stairs to a subway platform with the stroller. It left them both with the impression that New Yorkers must surely be among the most polite and helpful people they could encounter.

Katrina Rose took her first careful and unsupported steps in that Manhattan apartment, together with Mabel and I, her mother, and my mom and sister visiting for her first birthday. Her first steps were a symbolic milestone moment for all of us, even the Lau family. Our dear friends were in transit from Peru to visit Coleen in Israel and stayed with us for Katrina Rose's birthday.

Our daughter had done plenty of crawling and would move around the living room, holding herself up on some oversized cushions along the wall. We'd wondered when she would take that first unsupported step. When she stood up to walk to my sister, she did so decisively, surprisingly, and without any hesitation. I was sure it augured well for her. I hoped it would be for all of us as well.

Most days, I would walk up to Columbus Circle and Broadway to Bonnie's outpost for the Foundation. There, we worked together as I reviewed funding requests and proposed ways to systematize and formalize some approaches for the Foundation.

Bonnie kept things relaxed and flexible. She had provided support to a number of different educational and development initiatives largely on faith. She was generous and wanted to remain responsive to needy efforts around the world. But she was also increasingly aware that it would not take much for requests and proposals to outstrip the resources that she had available to donate charitably each year.

My old Bolivian partners, FUNDESIB, applied for funding to support the Dr. William K. Baker Center for Appropriate Technology. I had visited the center outside of Cochabamba while living in Bolivia. FUNDESIB and Universidad Nur had made prior invitations to Bonnie to visit. Bonnie suggested that we both go, given my familiarity with Bolivia and with the partners involved.

I was thrilled with the idea of returning to Bolivia to see what had changed over the ensuing three years since I had left. I promised Bonnie that I would still remain neutral and impartial regarding any grant they sought, and I encouraged her to be noncommittal as well. She was reluctant to say no. I understood that she wanted to help everyone possible, but it seemed essential that we set objective standards and expectations.

Bonnie's generosity was admirable and thoughtful, not only in money and time but particularly in spirit. I tried to reach out to other Bahá'í inspired or centered charities to gauge their experiences and compare what had worked best for them.

The trip to Bolivia was a quick one, but it did allow me to see that Nur had kept up the trajectory of progress and growth. Despite some inevitable challenges in Bolivia's political economy, the university seemed to be thriving.

Shortly after we returned, I had a chance to do another outside consultancy with Bonnie's blessing. I arranged a meeting in Washington with representatives of Hernando de Soto, a highly respected Peruvian free market economist whom I had known while in USAID.

De Soto had formed a think tank called the Institute for Freedom and Democracy, known by its initials in Spanish as ILD. ILD had been pretty successful in getting a number of USAID grants, but Hernando wisely sought ways to diversify his potential funding. He was looking for someone with development and USAID expertise to help them fundraise. He took me out to a World Bank-sponsored Peruvian musical event. There, by a remarkable coincidence, a famous guitarist who performed knew and remembered with fondness Mabel's father.

De Soto was intrigued by my background and invited me to travel back to Peru for a couple of weeks to work with him and his team in Lima. As it turned out, de Soto's chief operating officer at ILD, Manuel Mayorga, had also known Mabel's father many years earlier. I let him know of the recent passing and invited him to stop in New York when he had a chance to meet Mabel and our daughter.

In the early autumn, John contacted me from Guatemala. Project Concern International needed a consultant for about six weeks to evaluate their child survival project centered around Lago Atitlan and the towns of Santiago and San Pablo. John felt no one else could combine my experience from USAID and leading child survival projects in Bolivia.

"Are you up for it, brother?" John asked. "I really need your help."

He hoped I could take on and support the extended consultancy in Guatemala, helping PCI.

He added, "Why not bring Mabel and Katrina Rose as well? They could come and stay in the house with Pati and me in Guatemala City with our two youngest kids while you are in the field with the project. And afterwards you could travel a bit around the country with them."

What serendipity and what a timely opportunity! Between the friends, the climate, and the magnificent indigenous cultures there, I thought both Mabel and Katrina Rose would love Guatemala. I wrapped up my work with Bonnie. We grabbed the opportunity to see what sort of adventure might come next.

EPILOGUE

Our trip to Guatemala opened even more experiences that would take our new family to a host of other countries. The search for meaning, purpose, and discovery would continue, at times with pain and anguish but with an important share of growth and progress as well. Such is the course and rhythm of struggle over a life of service.

I would eventually overcome my failure over the university course incompletes, albeit not without some additional procrastination. I was finally contacted out of the blue three or four years later by the Dean of Students at the University of Chicago, Lorna P. Straus, remarkably still in the same role as fifteen years earlier.

She asked, "Allan, wouldn't you like to tie up loose ends and finish your degree? It won't be hard to do."

Indeed, all my credits had remained valid, and all I needed to do was take three elective courses of my choice online from any school, have the grades sent back to the U of C registrar, and they would issue my degree. I ruefully wished I had made the effort sooner, but I finally got it done.

A dear friend noted that my life has had a constant chain of obstacles and failures to overcome. It was as if I charted a course with a grand design which might have been the easy path to success had I stayed with it. I knew I was also guilty of too many self-inflicted injuries. Looking back, I realized I had repeatedly sabotaged myself and then fought back to overcome the consequences of that sabotage. It would take time to stop myself from doing that.

I hope I have communicated a sense of the draw and fascination with service to higher ideals that were my guardrails on this journey. I certainly don't recommend that anyone follow the exact sort of life choices I ended up facing. But I would hope that there may be extracts here that can power and resonate your own search for meaning, purpose and discovery.

Words have power. This truism took shape in the perverted upside-down world of 2020, considering the protests that took shape in different cities around the nation over the treatment of the marginalized, the undocumented refugees and those who fruitlessly sought asylum, people of color broadly, and specifically our Black citizens. And perhaps even more so in 2024, with the horrors we now find in the Middle East and as we listen to the cacophony from an openly criminal past regime in Washington with its defenders, abettors, and sycophants that actively seek to destroy our democracy. A network of unindicted co-conspirators that have savaged this country and much of the world.

Words have power. I was much taken by a recent article by Ann Hendrix-Jenkins on the Opendemocracy.net website that raised the demand once again, which has echoed from time to time in recent decades in international development circles, "It's Time to Put an End to Supremacy in International Development." Ann is the most recent to raise questions so many of us in the field must eventually confront: "Don't the words we use in aid agencies and NGOs draw imaginary lines between 'us' and 'them'?

"Why do those of us in or adjacent to the foreign aid industry continue to rely on a discourse that reeks of colonialism, militarism, and capitalism?"

Hendrix-Jenkins suggests that "…a good starting point for transformation is to drop the language of supremacy and the mental models that accompany it so that we can reimagine new ways to come together and act."

I have many regrets about mistakes I made in life, including my adhesion to some of those mental models for far too long. However, I don't regret trying to pursue meaning, purpose, discovery, and transformation where I could find it.

There is a quotation attributed to Winston Churchill that always bemused me. "Americans will always do the right thing, only after they have tried everything else." Apparently, he never actually said it. It's been quoted innumerable times by politicians, TV talking heads, and plenty of other personalities. But as one politician once said, "If he never did say it, he should have."

I struggled to do the right thing, to find deeper spiritual meaning in the work I did, and to reconcile my family to the responsibilities of a life of service. I know I frequently fell short. But I tried to keep plugging onward. My wife and daughter patiently, or sometimes not so patiently, accepted this.

For some readers, it may be worth remembering how young I was through all of these adventures in absolute and relative terms. I sometimes forget that.

I was just 21 when I left to join Peace Corps training to prepare for Ecuador. I was still only 25 when I took the job of Bolivia Country Director for Esperança. During my time on the PROCOSI Board of Directors, together with the other PVO and NGO country directors, I was always 10 to 25 years younger than my peers. I had just turned 31 when I joined USAID\Peru as a PSC Child Survival Coordinator.

I would finally join USAID as a career Foreign Service Officer just after I turned 40, something that I never thought I would do but which happened some years after the events of this book.

I'd like to think that the anecdotes here remind us of the power and potential of youth in humanitarian and international service.

The Andean countries and Latin America as a whole left a profound mark on me as a young volunteer and adventurer. I found myself returning over and over. Peru, of course, changed my life forever as I found my wife, and we were blessed with a child.

All three Andean countries repeatedly challenged me to focus and clarify what should be the next steps in my life. All three countries, and others later, provided enduring friendships, raised profound questions, and, at times, painful lessons that have kept me always asking and thinking about my role, my duty, and my responsibilities to help others.

MAP OF ECUADOR

MAP OF SOUTH AMERICA

MAP OF BOLIVIA

MAP OF PERU

DEAR READER

Thank you for taking the time to read ANDEAN ADVENTURES. If you enjoyed this book, please consider telling your friends about it, and also consider posting a short review on Amazon or where you obtained the book.

Word of mouth and reviews are an author's best friends, and we deeply appreciate every review and referral you give.

I hope to share more of my search for meaning, purpose and discovery in subsequent books. There are still many adventures to share, with your help. Feel free also to join my mailing list and visit my website: https://enableennoble.net

You might also be interested in my latest book about my two years in Gaza, the occupied Palestinian territories and Israel. It is available from different booksellers here:

https://books2read.com/u/mg8LBx

Thank you again-

Alonzo

AUTHOR'S BIO

Allan J. "Alonzo" Wind served from February 2022 – December 2023 as the International Medical Corps Mission Director in Gaza and the occupied Palestinian territories (oPt), supervising a staff of seven expats of different nationalities and over 75 local Palestinian staff, in Gaza and Bethlehem. He was elected in 2022 to the Executive Committee of the Association for International Development Agencies (AIDA) and asked to serve on the UN OCHA Humanitarian Fund Advisory Board. Mr. Wind was resident in both Gaza and East Jerusalem for nearly two years, and in a unique position in Gaza as a senior Jewish American INGO leader, also connected with the Baha'i Community. Mr. Wind is a retired Senior Foreign Service Officer from the U.S. Agency for International Development (USAID), having worked for 22 years on diplomatic assignments with USAID primarily overseas in Peru, Nicaragua, Angola, Nigeria, Iraq, Afghanistan and South Africa. He is a Senior Advisor and Scholar for the Foundation for Law and International Affairs (FLIA).

Mr. Wind previously worked for fifteen years for different nonprofit private voluntary organizations in Ecuador, Bolivia, Dominican Republic and the UK among others, also serving as the Global Programme Coordinator of the International Save the Children Alliance Secretariat. He began his career as a Public Health Peace Corps Volunteer in Ecuador, and his experiences described here led to his lifelong vocation for global service and international development, living in over a dozen countries and familiar with at least fifty more in Latin America and the Caribbean, Africa, Europe and Asia.

He and his wife reside in Fairfax County Virginia, and their daughter lives and works in Berlin. Mr. Wind also serves on the Boards of Directors of different NGOs, including Hunger Relief International, supporting their efforts with the neediest in Guatemala and Haiti.